CONTENTS

PREFACE

The books in this series present leading-edge research in the field of computer research, technology and applications. Each contribution has been carefully selected for inclusion based on the significance of the research to the field. Summaries of all chapters are gathered at the beginning of the book and an in-depth index is presented to facilitate access.

Digital electrical engineering is a non-formalized theory and one of the major causes of this situation consists in the complexity of Mother Nature, things cannot be completely different from those in medicine, for example. We are too restricted to finding quick solutions to the problems that arise in order to take the time to strengthen a sound theoretical foundation of the reasoning that we do. Obviously, the political, military, economical and technological importance of digital electrical engineering is itself an obstacle in the spreading of consolidated theories. In fact, the reader of such literature can remark the existing distance from the deductive theories, the way that the mathematicians use them. Chapter 1 reproduces a point of view that is considered to be representative in this direction belonging to L. Rougier: '*Reasoning is deductive or is not at all*'.

One of the most important problems of hybrid systems is the *reachability problem*. As this problem has been shown to be undecidable even for certain classes of linear hybrid systems, the main focus of the hybrid systems literature appears to be to find *effective* semi-decision procedures for this problem. Such an algorithmic approach involves finding methods of computation and representation of reach sets of the continuous variables within a discrete state of a hybrid system. In chapter 2, after presenting a brief introduction to hybrid systems and reachability problem, the authors propose a computational method for obtaining the reach sets of continuous variables in a hybrid system. In addition to this, they also describe a new algorithm to over-approximate with polyhedra the reach sets of the continuous variables with linear dynamics and polyhedral initial set. It also illustrates these algorithms with some simple and interesting examples.

Symbolic computation in algebraic categories enable the automatic modeling of modern algebra theories. On this theoretical background, chapter 3 introduces constructive and algorithmic definitions for the basic concepts (category, domain, etc.) and for a number of algebraic structures. Adopting a parameterized and object oriented approach, the categories defined for the algebraic structures will be particularized in specific domains. Chapter 3 reveals the utility of the parameterized categorical approach by deriving a multivariate polynomial category (over various coefficient domains), which is used by our Mathematica implementation of Buchberger's algorithms for determining the Gröbner basis. These implementations are designed according to domain and category parameterization principles and underline their advantages: operation protection, inheritance, generality, natural extendibility. In particular, such an extension of Mathematica, a widely used symbolic computation system, with a new type system has a certain practical importance.

Chapter 4 directs attentions to the effects of production experiences on the R&D competition and innovations for the next generation product when the R&D knowledge is accumulated by production experiences as well as by R&D expenditure. Based on the numerical analyses of unique Nash strategies in the R&D race, we find that the challenger invests more than the incumbent, and the difference between the challenger's and the incumbent's investment rates increases with the marginal production experience (a rate at which production experiences contribute to the R&D knowledge). However, an increase in this difference is dominated by the increase in the marginal production experience itself, and thus the incumbent has a higher probability to win the R&D race at any time point (conditioned on no occurrence of innovations up to that time point) if the marginal production experience is sufficiently large. Moreover, as the marginal production experience gets higher, the rate of the overall R&D knowledge accumulation increases. The rapid innovations and the persistent leadership in CPUs for personal computers and EPROM chips may be better explained by this effects of production experiences on the R&D competition.

In: New Developments in Computer Science Research
Editor: Susan Shannon, pp. 1-90
ISBN 1-59454-256-2

Chapter 1

Real Time Models of the Asynchronous Circuits: The Delay Theory

Serban E. Vlad
Oradea City Hall, P-ta Unirii, Nr. 1, 410100, Oradea, Romania
www.geocities.com/serban_e_vlad, serban_e_vlad@yahoo.com

List of Abbreviations

SC	Stability condition	6.1.1
DC	Delay condition	6.2.1
CC_{BDC}	Consistency condition (of the bounded delay condition)	7.1.2
BDC	Bounded delay condition	7.2.2
FDC	Fixed delay condition	7.4.2
AIC	Absolute inertial condition	8.1.2
AIDC	Absolute inertial delay condition	8.2.1
CC_{BAIIDC}	Consistency condition (of the bounded absolute inertial delay condition)	8.3.2
BAIDC	Bounded absolute inertial delay condition	8.4.1
RIC	Relative inertial condition	9.1.2
RIDC	Relative inertial delay condition	9.2.1
CC_{BRIDC}	Consistency condition (of the bounded relative inertial delay condition)	9.3.2
BRIDC	Bounded relative inertial delay condition	9.4.1
DBRIDC	Deterministic bounded relative inertial delay condition	9.5.3
BDC', AIC', RIC'	Variants of BDC, AIC, RIC	10.1
DBRIDC', SDBRIDC'	Variants of DBRIDC	10.2.2

1. Introduction

Digital electrical engineering is a non-formalized theory and one of the major causes of this situation consists in the complexity of Mother Nature, things cannot be completely different from those in medicine, for example. We are too restricted to finding quick solutions to the problems that arise in order to take the time to strengthen a sound theoretical foundation of the reasoning that we do. Obviously, the political, military, economical and technological importance of digital electrical engineering is itself an obstacle in the spreading of consolidated theories.

In fact, the reader of such literature can remark the existing distance from the deductive theories, the way that the mathematicians use them. We reproduce a point of view that we consider to be representative in this direction belonging to L. Rougier: '*Reasoning is deductive or is not at all*'.

The consequences of non-formalization are known. Many researchers do not give the right importance to the scientific language and words like *definition*, *theorem*, *proof* are titles of descriptive paragraphs rather than having the meaning that is accepted by the logicians. A fascinating job is, in this context, the translation in a precise mathematical language of what is intuitively, imprecisely explained with natural language by the engineers and this can be done in several ways. Our work has many such examples, let's just mention here the notion of inertia that is important and confusing at the same time. By reading with a ball-point pen in our hand, we infer that the inertia's inertia is not inertia, a paradox that should end the discussion on the validity of a theory. The theoretical construction continues however, without visible implications on the subsequent results, by using the methods of the non-deductive investigations.

The purpose of delay theory is that of writing systems of equations and inequalities with electrical signals, that model the behavior of the asynchronous circuits.

The (*electrical*) *signals* are the functions $f:\boldsymbol{R}\to\{0,1\}$ where $\boldsymbol{R}$, the set of the real numbers, is the time set. We ask that they:

- be constant in the interval $(-\infty,0)$, with the variant that we have used elsewhere: be null in the interval $(-\infty,0)$, in other words 0 is the initial time instant
- be constant on intervals $[t',t'')$ that are left closed and right open
- have a finite number of discontinuity points (i.e. a finite number of switches) in any bounded interval.

The *asynchronous circuits* (also called *asynchronous systems*, or *asynchronous automata* or *timed automata* in literature) are these electrical devices that can be modeled by using signals.

The fundamental (asynchronous) circuit in delay theory is the *delay circuit*, also called *delay buffer*, the circuit that computes the identity $1_{\{0,1\}}$ and the fundamental notion is that of *delay condition*, or shortly *delay*, the real time model of the delay circuit.

We show the way that the 'inertia's paradox' has been solved. First, the definition of the delays is given. Second, the pure delays are defined. Third, all the delays different from the pure delays are considered to be by definition inertial. Fourth, the serial connection of the delays is their composition, as binary relations. The serial connection of the inertial delays results in an inertial delay, but the type of inertia is likely to differ. The bounded delays have the nice property that, under the serial connection, the delays remain bounded and thus the type of inertia remains the same; the absolute inertial delays are in the same situation. The relative inertial delays are not closed under the serial connection, the 'paradox'.

We shall describe now, informally, the work of the delay circuit.

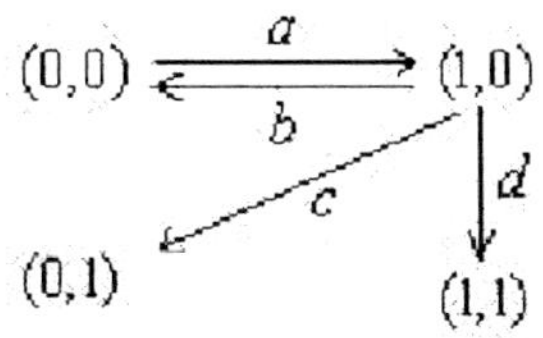

Fig 1

We have noted with $u:\mathbf{R}\to\{0,1\}$ its input and with $x:\mathbf{R}\to\{0,1\}$ its output. Both u,x are signals. In Fig 1, the couples of binary numbers, temporarily called *states*, represent values $(u(t),x(t))$, with $t\in\mathbf{R}$ and a,b,c,d are the *labels* (= the *names*) of the transitions $(u(t'),x(t'))\to(u(t''),x(t''))$. In such transitions, we suppose that $t'<t''$ and that $t''-t'$ is a small infinitesimal. A suitable notation for this is $t'=t''-0$.

The real numbers $0<d_{r,\min}\le d_{r,\max}$ are given, the meaning of the index '*r*' being that of *raise* (switch from 0 to 1) of a signal, event symbolized by the validity of the equation

$$\overline{x(t-0)}\cdot x(t)=1$$

Dually the real numbers $0<d_{f,\min}\le d_{f,\max}$ are given, the meaning of the index '*f*' being that of *fall* (switch from 1 to 0) of a signal and that event is symbolized by the validity of the equation

$$x(t-0)\cdot\overline{x(t)}=1$$

We suppose that at the initial time instant $t_0\ge 0$ the circuit is in the initial state $(0,0)$:

$$\forall\xi\in(-\infty,t_0),u(\xi)=0$$
$$\forall\xi\in(-\infty,t_0],x(\xi)=0$$

This state is *stable*, meaning that the delay circuit could remain indefinitely long there, if the input is 0:

$$\forall h>0,\forall\xi\in[t_0,t_0+h),u(\xi)=0\Rightarrow x(t_0+h)=0$$

A switch of the input takes place at t_0

$$\overline{u(t_0-0)}\cdot u(t_0)=1$$

and the delay circuit follows the trajectory labeled a, i.e. $(0,0)\to(1,0)$. The hypothesis states that both the input and the output remain constant in the interval $[t_0,t_1)$

$$\forall\xi\in[t_0,t_1),u(\xi)=1$$
$$\forall\xi\in[t_0,t_1),x(\xi)=0$$

and the problem is to describe the behavior of the circuit at t_1. Three possibilities exist, those of running one the transitions b,c,d, depending on the values of t_1 and $u(t_1)$.

b: it is necessarily run at t_1 if $t_1 - t_0 < d_{r,\min}$ and if u switches from 1 to 0 at the time instant t_1

$$t_0 < t_1 < t_0 + d_{r,\min} \; and \; u(t_1 - 0) \cdot \overline{u(t_1)} = 1 \; and \; \overline{x(t_1 - 0)} \cdot x(t_1) = 0$$

The interpretation is that the circuit's inertia did not allow a fast switch of x from 0 to 1 happen.

b, c: any of them is possible to be run at t_1 ($x(t_1) = 0$ for *b* and $x(t_1) = 1$ for *c*) if $d_{r,\min} \le t_1 - t_0 < d_{r,\max}$ and if u switches from 1 to 0 at t_1

$$t_0 + d_{r,\min} \le t_1 < t_0 + d_{r,\max} \; and \; u(t_1 - 0) \cdot \overline{u(t_1)} = 1 \; and \; \overline{x(t_1 - 0)} \cdot x(t_1) = 0$$

$$t_0 + d_{r,\min} \le t_1 < t_0 + d_{r,\max} \; and \; u(t_1 - 0) \cdot \overline{u(t_1)} = 1 \; and \; \overline{x(t_1 - 0)} \cdot x(t_1) = 1$$

if $t_1 - t_0 = d_{r,\max}$ and if u switches from 1 to 0 at t_1, then c is necessary

$$t_1 = t_0 + d_{r,\max} \; and \; u(t_1 - 0) \cdot \overline{u(t_1)} = 1 \; and \; \overline{x(t_1 - 0)} \cdot x(t_1) = 1$$

d: if $u(t_1) = 1$, then it is possible at t_1 for $d_{r,\min} \le t_1 - t_0 < d_{r,\max}$ and it is necessary at t_1 for $t_1 - t_0 = d_{r,\max}$:

$$t_0 + d_{r,\min} \le t_1 \le t_0 + d_{r,\max} \; and \; u(t_1 - 0) \cdot \overline{u(t_1)} = 0 \; and \; \overline{x(t_1 - 0)} \cdot x(t_1) = 1$$

The intuitive description of the circuit continues by asking that the dual statements hold also, as resulted by the replacement of '*r*', 0, 1 with '*f*',1,0.

The circuit computes the identity on $\{0,1\}$ because the states (0,0), (1,1) are stable and these are the only stable states of the circuit.

A possible manner of describing the previous facts is given by the system

$$\bigcap_{\xi \in [t - d_{r,\max}, t)} u(\xi) \le x(t) \le \bigcup_{\xi \in [t - d_{f,\max}, t)} u(\xi)$$

$$\overline{x(t-0)} \cdot x(t) \le \bigcap_{\xi \in [t - d_{r,\min}, t)} u(\xi)$$

$$x(t-0) \cdot \overline{x(t)} \le \bigcap_{\xi \in [t - d_{f,\min}, t)} \overline{u(\xi)}$$

and this might seem not quite obvious for the moment.

The chapter is organized in sections, numbered with 1, 2, 3, ... the sections have several paragraphs: 2.1, 3.2, ... and the paragraphs are usually organized in subparagraphs: 2.1.1, 4.5.2, ... The important equations and inequalities have been numbered, as well as all the figures and tables. The notation 3.2 (2) refers to equation or inequality (2) of paragraph 3.2 (that has no subparagraphs, in this case) and the notation 4.1.2 (3) refers to equation or inequality (3) of the subparagraph 2 from the paragraph 4.1.

In Section 2 we give several examples of models for the sake of creating intuition and this is a presentation of our intentions. The theory starting with Section 3 is supposed to be self-contained.

In Section 3 we fix some fundamental concepts and notations on the $\mathbf{R} \to \{0,1\}$ functions.

Section 4 defines the signals and gives some useful properties on them.

In Section 5 we present the informal definitions of the delays, with long quotations from several authors.

The sections that follow represent the core of this chapter. In Section 6 we define the delays, as well as their determinism, order, time invariance, constancy, symmetry and serial connection. Section 7 is dedicated to the bounded delays and in Sections 8, 9 we define and characterize the absolute and the relative inertial conditions and delays. Section 10 shows some variants of the concepts from Sections 7, 8, 9 and introduces a special form of deterministic delays. Section 11 closes the chapter with new examples and a generalization.

We thank in advance to all those that will want to bring corrections and improvements to our results.

2. Motivating Examples

2.1 Example 1: The Delay Circuit

The symbol of the delay circuit is the next one

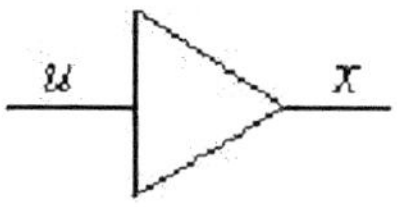

Fig 2

We consider different possibilities of modelation of this circuit, a way to anticipate the facts that will be presented later. u, x are $\boldsymbol{R} \to \{0,1\}$ functions and moreover they are signals, with constant values for any $t < 0$.

SC *Stability*[1] (*unbounded delays*) If u is of the form

$$u(t) = u(t) \cdot \chi_{(-\infty,t_0)}(t) \oplus u(t_0) \cdot \chi_{[t_0,\infty)}(t)$$

then x is of the form

$$x(t) = x(t) \cdot \chi_{(-\infty,t_1)}(t) \oplus u(t_0) \cdot \chi_{[t_1,\infty)}(t)$$

where $t_0 \geq 0, t_1 \geq 0$ and $\chi_{(\ )} : \boldsymbol{R} \to \{0,1\}$ is the *characteristic function*.

BDC' *Upper bounded, lower unbounded delays* $d_r > 0, d_f > 0$ exist so that the next system is satisfied:

$$\bigcap_{\xi \in [t-d_r,t)} u(\xi) \leq x(t) \leq \bigcup_{\xi \in [t-d_f,t)} u(\xi)$$

BDC *Bounded delays* $0 \leq m_r \leq d_r, 0 \leq m_f \leq d_f$ exist and the system is the next one

$$\bigcap_{\xi \in [t-d_r,t-d_r+m_r]} u(\xi) \leq x(t) \leq \bigcup_{\xi \in [t-d_f,t-d_f+m_f]} u(\xi)$$

---

1 In the abbreviations that we use: SC, BDC,... the letter 'C' comes from 'condition': stability (condition), bounded delay (condition),...

FDC *Fixed delays* (*ideal delays*) The relation between u and x is, for $d \geq 0$

$$x(t) = u(t-d)$$

AIC *Absolute inertia* $\delta_r \geq 0, \delta_f \geq 0$ exist so that x satisfies

$$\overline{x(t-0)} \cdot x(t) \leq \bigcap_{\xi \in [t, t+\delta_r]} x(\xi)$$

$$x(t-0) \cdot \overline{x(t)} \leq \bigcap_{\xi \in [t, t+\delta_f]} \overline{x(\xi)}$$

This inertia condition is added to one of SC, BDC', BDC, FDC.

RIC *Relative inertia* $0 \leq \mu_r \leq \delta_r, 0 \leq \mu_f \leq \delta_f$ are given so that

$$\overline{x(t-0)} \cdot x(t) \leq \bigcap_{\xi \in [t-\delta_r, t-\delta_r+\mu_r]} u(\xi)$$

$$x(t-0) \cdot \overline{x(t)} \leq \bigcap_{\xi \in [t-\delta_f, t-\delta_f+\mu_f]} \overline{u(\xi)}$$

are satisfied. Similarly with absolute inertia, relative inertia is a request added to one of SC, BDC', BDC, FDC.

DBRIDC *Deterministic bounded relative inertial delays* If in BDC+RIC $\mu_r, \delta_r, \mu_f, \delta_f$ coincide with m_r, d_r, m_f, d_f the system takes the special deterministic form

$$\overline{x(t-0)} \cdot x(t) = \overline{x(t-0)} \cdot \bigcap_{\xi \in [t-d_r, t-d_r+m_r]} u(\xi)$$

$$x(t-0) \cdot \overline{x(t)} = x(t-0) \cdot \bigcap_{\xi \in [t-d_f, t-d_f+m_f]} \overline{u(\xi)}$$

SDBRIDC' *Symmetrical deterministic upper bounded, lower unbounded relative inertial delays*, version of DBRIDC consisting in the next equation

$$Dx(t) = (x(t-0) \oplus u(t-0)) \cdot \overline{\bigcup_{\xi \in (t-d, t)} Du(\xi)} \cdot \chi_{[d,\infty)}(t)$$

where

$$Dx(t) = \overline{x(t-0)} \cdot x(t) \cup x(t-0) \cdot \overline{x(t)} = x(t-0) \oplus x(t)$$

is the left derivative of x.

All the solutions of BDC', BDC, FDC, DBRIDC, SDBRIDC' satisfy $x(0-0) = u(0-0)$ and some of the previous systems satisfy also supplementary *conditions of consistency* (i.e. the existence of a solution x for any u).

2.2 Example 2 Circuit with Feedback Using a Delay Circuit

In the circuit from 2.1, Fig 2 we suppose that $u = x$ and this corresponds to the next circuit

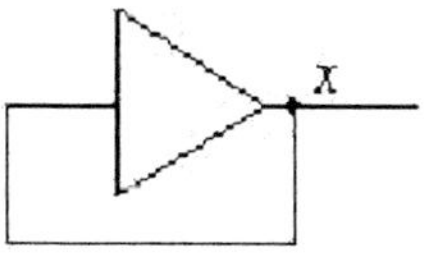

Fig 3

SC The satisfaction of SC does not bring any information on x, as it consists in a tautology of the form $\neg A \vee A$, where the proposition A is the equation

$$\exists t_0 \geq 0, x(t) = x(t) \cdot \chi_{(-\infty,t_0)}(t) \oplus x(t_0) \cdot \chi_{[t_0,\infty)}(t)$$

Interpretation: the circuit can be stable or unstable.

BDC' The system is

$$\bigcap_{\xi \in [t-d_r,t)} x(\xi) \leq x(t) \leq \bigcup_{\xi \in [t-d_f,t)} x(\xi)$$

with $d_r > 0, d_f > 0$. Let $t_0 \geq 0$ so that $\forall t < t_0, x(t) = 0$. Because $\bigcup_{\xi \in [t_0-d_f,t_0)} x(\xi) = 0$, we get $x(t_0) = 0$. Similarly, let $t_0 \geq 0$ so that $\forall t < t_0, x(t) = 1$. Because $\bigcap_{\xi \in [t_0-d_r,t_0)} x(\xi) = 1$, we obtain $x(t_0) = 1$. t_0 was arbitrary previously, so that the only solutions of BDC' are the constant functions.

On the other hand, the constant functions satisfy any supplementary inertial condition AIC, RIC because $\overline{x(t-0)} \cdot x(t) = x(t-0) \cdot \overline{x(t)} = 0$.

BDC We have the system

$$\bigcap_{\xi \in [t-d_r,t-d_r+m_r]} x(\xi) \leq x(t) \leq \bigcup_{\xi \in [t-d_f,t-d_f+m_f]} x(\xi)$$

where $0 \leq m_r \leq d_r, 0 \leq m_f \leq d_f$. Let us suppose in the beginning, when solving it, that $x(0-0) = 0$. The solutions are the next ones.

<u>Case</u> $d_f - m_f > 0$

We can show analogously with BDC' that the only solution is $x(t) = 0$.

<u>Case</u> $d_f - m_f = 0$, $d_r > 0$

As the inequality $x(t) \leq \bigcup_{\xi \in [t-d_f,t]} x(\xi)$ is satisfied by all x, BDC has in this case the same solutions like (in other words: is equivalent with)

$$\bigcap_{\xi \in [t-d_r,t-d_r+m_r]} x(\xi) \leq x(t) \tag{1}$$

and any solution can be written under one of the forms

$$x(t) = 0 \tag{2}$$

$$x(t) = \chi_{[t_0,\infty)}(t) \tag{3}$$

$$x(t) = \chi_{[t_0,t_1)}(t) \oplus \chi_{[t_2,t_3)}(t) \oplus \ldots \oplus \chi_{[t_{2n},t_{2n+1})}(t) \tag{4}$$

$$x(t) = \chi_{[t_0,t_1)}(t) \oplus \chi_{[t_2,t_3)}(t) \oplus \ldots \oplus \chi_{[t_{2n},t_{2n+1})}(t) \oplus \chi_{[t_{2n+2},\infty)}(t) \tag{5}$$

$$x(t)=\chi_{[t_0,t_1)}(t)\oplus\chi_{[t_2,t_3)}(t)\oplus...\oplus\chi_{[t_{2n},t_{2n+1})}(t)\oplus... \quad (6)$$

(2),…,(6) represent all the signals x with $x(0-0)=0$, where $0\le t_0<t_1<t_2<....$ is unbounded, arbitrary. (2), (3) satisfy (1) without supplementary requests. If the term $\chi_{[t_{2k},t_{2k+1})}$ satisfies $t_{2k+1}-t_{2k}>m_r$ we have that

$$\bigcap_{\xi\in[t-d_r,t-d_r+m_r]}\chi_{[t_{2k},t_{2k+1})}(\xi)=\chi_{[t_{2k}+d_r,t_{2k+1}+d_r-m_r)}(t)$$

is not null and in order that (4),…,(6) be solutions of (1), the next property should be true for all $k\ge 0$:

$$t_{2k+1}-t_{2k}>m_r\Rightarrow[t_{2k}+d_r,t_{2k+1}+d_r-m_r)\subset supp\ x$$

We have noted $supp\ x=\{t\mid x(t)=1\}$ the support set of x.

A special case of (1) is the one when $m_r=0$:

$$x(t-d_r)\le x(t) \quad (7)$$

and then for all $k\ge 0$ the next inclusion

$$[t_{2k}+d_r,t_{2k+1}+d_r)\subset supp\ x$$

is fulfilled. For example, the 'periodical' functions

$$x(t)=\chi_{[t_0,t_1)}(t)\oplus\chi_{[t_0+d_r,t_1+d_r)}(t)\oplus...\oplus\chi_{[t_0+n\cdot d_r,t_1+n\cdot d_r)}(t)\oplus...$$

where $0\le t_0<t_1\le t_0+d_r$ satisfy (7) because

$$x(t-d_r)=\chi_{[t_0+d_r,t_1+d_r)}(t)\oplus\chi_{[t_0+2d_r,t_1+2d_r)}(t)\oplus...\oplus\chi_{[t_0+(n+1)\cdot d_r,t_1+(n+1)\cdot d_r)}(t)\oplus...$$

An interesting situation in BDC+AIC is the special case $\delta_r\ge m_r,\delta_f=0$ when the inclusion

$$[t_{2k}+d_r,t_{2k+1}+d_r-m_r)\subset supp\ x$$

is true for all $k\ge 0$ and all solutions x, the hypothesis $t_{2k+1}-t_{2k}>\delta_r\ge m_r$ being satisfied due to AIC.

Adding RIC in the case $d_f-m_f=0,d_r>0$ of BDC, under the form

$$\overline{x(t-0)}\cdot x(t)\le\bigcap_{\xi\in[t-\delta_r,t-\delta_r+\mu_r]}x(\xi) \quad (8)$$

$$x(t-0)\cdot\overline{x(t)}\le\bigcap_{\xi\in[t-\delta_f,t-\delta_f+\mu_f]}\overline{x(\xi)} \quad (9)$$

implies if $\delta_r>0$ that $x(t)=0$. For $\delta_r=0$, inequality (8) becomes trivial: $\overline{x(t-0)}\cdot x(t)\le x(t)$ and then, if $\delta_f>0$, the restrictions corresponding to RIC on the solutions x of BDC are expressed under the form, see (4),…,(6)

$$\chi_{\{t_1,t_3,...\}}(t)=x(t-0)\cdot\overline{x(t)}\le$$

$$\le\bigcap_{\xi\in[t-\delta_f,t-\delta_f+\mu_f]}\overline{x(\xi)}=\chi_{(-\infty,t_0+\delta_f-\mu_f)\vee[t_1+\delta_f,t_2+\delta_f-\mu_f)\vee[t_3+\delta_f,t_4+\delta_f-\mu_f)\vee...}(t)$$

i.e. equivalently

$$\{t_1,t_3,...\}\subset(-\infty,t_0+\delta_f-\mu_f)\vee[t_1+\delta_f,t_2+\delta_f-\mu_f)\vee[t_3+\delta_f,t_4+\delta_f-\mu_f)\vee...$$

$\delta_r=\delta_f=0$ means triviality for RIC.

Case $d_f - m_f = 0, d_r = 0$

BDC consists in

$$x(t) \le x(t) \le \bigcup_{\xi \in [t-d_f, t]} x(\xi)$$

and all the signals x satisfy it.

By duality, the possibility $x(0-0)=1$ is analyzed. We observe for example that if $d_f - m_f > 0, d_r - m_r > 0$ then the only solutions of BDC are the constant functions.

FDC The equation to be solved is

$$x(t) = x(t-d), d \ge 0$$

If $d > 0$, then the solutions are the two constant functions and if $d = 0$ then the solutions are all the signals.

DBRIDC The system is

$$\overline{x(t-0)} \cdot x(t) = \overline{x(t-0)} \cdot \bigcap_{\xi \in [t-d_r, t-d_r+m_r]} x(\xi) \tag{10}$$

$$x(t-0) \cdot \overline{x(t)} = x(t-0) \cdot \bigcap_{\xi \in [t-d_f, t-d_f+m_f]} \overline{x(\xi)} \tag{11}$$

and we suppose like before that $x(0-0)=0$.

Case $d_r > 0$

The only solution is $x(t)=0$.

Case $d_r = 0, d_f = m_f > 0$

The switch from 0 to 1 is possible, because (10) takes the trivial form $\overline{x(t-0)} \cdot x(t) = \overline{x(t-0)} \cdot x(t)$. From this moment $\bigcap_{\xi \in [t-d_f, t]} \overline{x(\xi)}$ is null, thus the solutions have one of the forms (2), (3).

Case $d_r = 0, d_f = m_f = 0$

All the signals x satisfy the system, (10), (11) being both trivial.

Case $d_r = 0, d_f > m_f \ge 0$

The switch from 0 to 1 seems possible and let t_0 be the moment of the first such switch, thus $\overline{x(t_0 - 0)} \cdot x(t_0) = 1$. At the time instant $t_1 > t_0$ characterized by $[t_0, t_1) \subset supp\ x$, (11) becomes

$$\overline{x(t_1)} = \bigcap_{\xi \in [t_1-d_f, t_1-d_f+m_f]} \overline{x(\xi)} \tag{12}$$

For all $t_1 - d_f + m_f < t_0$, i.e. if $0 < t_1 - t_0 < d_f - m_f$, the right member of (12) is 1 and the switch of x from 1 to 0 necessary. We have reached a contradiction showing that DBRIDC has no solution $x(t) \ne 0$.

The analysis of the situation when $x(0-0)=1$ is similar.

SDBRIDC' The solutions of the equation

$$Dx(t) = 0$$

are the constant functions.

2.3 The Logical Gate NOT

The logical gate NOT that computes the complement in the set $\{0,1\}$ is symbolized like in the next figure

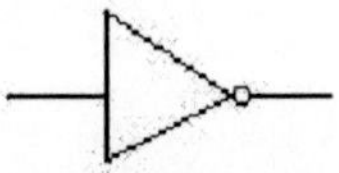

Fig 4

where the gate and the two wires are characterized by delays. It is modeled by one of the next circuits

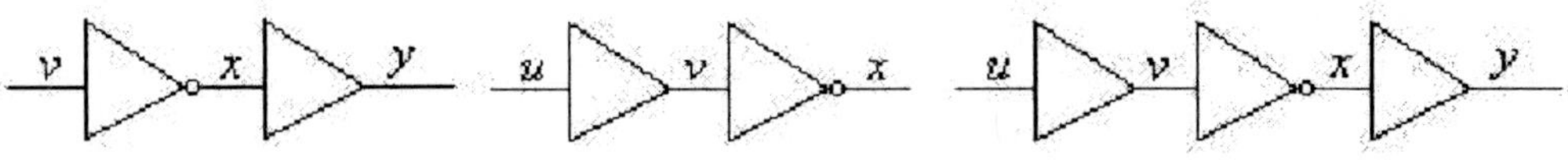

a) b) c)

Fig 5

In Fig 5 the logical gate is ideal

$$x(t) = x(0-0) \cdot \chi_{(-\infty,0)}(t) \oplus \overline{v(t)} \cdot \chi_{[0,\infty)}(t) \quad (1)$$

as well as the wires and the delays are localized in the delay circuits. Writing the relations between u, v, respectively between x, y follows, like at 2.1. The last step is the elimination (if possible) of the intermediary variables: x at a), v at b), v and x at c). We give some examples.

SC Fig 5 c)

The fact that u is of the form

$$u(t) = u(t) \cdot \chi_{(-\infty,t_0)}(t) \oplus u(t_0) \cdot \chi_{[t_0,\infty)}(t) \quad (2)$$

implies that v is of the form

$$v(t) = v(t) \cdot \chi_{(-\infty,t_1)}(t) \oplus u(t_0) \cdot \chi_{[t_1,\infty)}(t) \quad (3)$$

thus, from (1), x is given by

$$x(t) = x(t) \cdot \chi_{(-\infty,t_1)}(t) \oplus \overline{u(t_0)} \cdot \chi_{[t_1,\infty)}(t) \quad (4)$$

and by using SC again for the second delay circuit we get

$$y(t) = y(t) \cdot \chi_{(-\infty,t_2)}(t) \oplus \overline{u(t_0)} \cdot \chi_{[t_2,\infty)}(t) \quad (5)$$

In (2),...,(5) $t_0 \geq 0, t_1 \geq 0, t_2 \geq 0$.

BDC' Fig 5 a)

$$\bigcap_{\xi \in [t-d_r,t)} x(\xi) \leq y(t) \leq \bigcup_{\xi \in [t-d_f,t)} x(\xi) \quad (6)$$

$$\bigcap_{\xi \in [t-d_r,t)} (x(0-0) \cdot \chi_{(-\infty,0)}(\xi) \oplus \overline{v(\xi)} \cdot \chi_{[0,\infty)}(\xi)) \leq y(t) \leq$$

$$\leq \bigcup_{\xi \in [t-d_f,t)} (x(0-0) \cdot \chi_{(-\infty,0)}(\xi) \oplus \overline{v(\xi)} \cdot \chi_{[0,\infty)}(\xi)) \quad \text{(from (1), (6))} \quad (7)$$

BDC' Fig 5 b)

$$\bigcap_{\xi\in[t-d_r,t)} u(\xi) \le v(t) \le \bigcup_{\xi\in[t-d_f,t)} u(\xi) \tag{8}$$

$$\bigcap_{\xi\in[t-d_f,t)} \overline{u(\xi)} \le \overline{v(t)} \le \bigcup_{\xi\in[t-d_r,t)} \overline{u(\xi)} \quad \text{(from (8))} \tag{9}$$

$$x(0-0)\cdot\chi_{(-\infty,0)}(t)\oplus \bigcap_{\xi\in[t-d_f,t)} \overline{u(\xi)}\cdot\chi_{[0,\infty)}(t) \le x(t) \le$$

$$\le x(0-0)\cdot\chi_{(-\infty,0)}(t)\oplus \bigcup_{\xi\in[t-d_r,t)} \overline{u(\xi)}\cdot\chi_{[0,\infty)}(t) \quad \text{(from (1), (9))} \tag{10}$$

SDBRIDC' Fig 5a) Some of the next equations are better understood if we take into account the fact that $\forall a\in\{0,1\}, \overline{a}=a\oplus 1$:

$$x(t-0)=x(0-0)\cdot\chi_{(-\infty,0]}(t)\oplus \overline{v(t-0)}\cdot\chi_{(0,\infty)}(t) \quad \text{(from (1))} \tag{11}$$

$$v(t-0)=v(0-0)\cdot\chi_{(-\infty,0]}(t)\oplus v(t-0)\cdot\chi_{(0,\infty)}(t) \tag{12}$$

$$\overline{v(t-0)}=\overline{v(0-0)}\cdot\chi_{(-\infty,0]}(t)\oplus \overline{v(t-0)}\cdot\chi_{(0,\infty)}(t) \quad \text{(from (12))} \tag{13}$$

$$x(t-0)=(x(0-0)\oplus\overline{v(0-0)})\cdot\chi_{(-\infty,0]}(t)\oplus\overline{v(t-0)} \quad \text{(from (11),(13))} \tag{14}$$

$$Dx(t)=x(0-0)\cdot\chi_{(-\infty,0]}(t)\oplus x(0-0)\cdot\chi_{(-\infty,0)}(t)\oplus$$

$$\oplus\overline{v(t-0)}\cdot\chi_{(0,\infty)}(t)\oplus\overline{v(t)}\cdot\chi_{[0,\infty)}(t) \quad \text{(from (1),(11))}$$

$$=x(0-0)\cdot\chi_{\{0\}}(t)\oplus\overline{v(t-0)}\cdot\chi_{(0,\infty)}(t)\oplus\overline{v(0)}\cdot\chi_{\{0\}}(t)\oplus\overline{v(t)}\cdot\chi_{(0,\infty)}(t)$$

$$=(x(0-0)\oplus\overline{v(0)})\cdot\chi_{\{0\}}(t)\oplus(\overline{v(t-0)}\oplus\overline{v(t)})\cdot\chi_{(0,\infty)}(t)$$

$$=(x(0-0)\oplus\overline{v(0)})\cdot\chi_{\{0\}}(t)\oplus Dv(t)\cdot\chi_{(0,\infty)}(t) \tag{15}$$

$$Dv(t)=(v(0-0)\oplus v(0))\cdot\chi_{\{0\}}(t)\oplus Dv(t)\cdot\chi_{(0,\infty)}(t) \tag{16}$$

$$Dx(t)=(x(0-0)\oplus\overline{v(0)}\oplus v(0-0)\oplus v(0))\cdot\chi_{\{0\}}(t)\oplus Dv(t) \quad \text{(from (15),(16))}$$

$$=\overline{x(0-0)\oplus v(0-0)}\cdot\chi_{\{0\}}(t)\oplus Dv(t) \tag{17}$$

$$Dy(t)=(y(t-0)\oplus x(t-0))\cdot\overline{\bigcup_{\xi\in(t-d,t)} Dx(\xi)}\cdot\chi_{[d,\infty)}(t) \quad \text{(the hypothesis SDBRIDC')}$$

$$=(y(t-0)\oplus x(0-0)\cdot\chi_{(-\infty,0]}(t)\oplus\overline{v(t-0)}\cdot\chi_{(0,\infty)}(t))\cdot$$

$$\cdot\overline{\bigcup_{\xi\in(t-d,t)}(\overline{x(0-0)\oplus v(0-0)}\cdot\chi_{\{0\}}(\xi)\oplus Dv(\xi))}\cdot\chi_{[d,\infty)}(t) \quad \text{(from (11),(17))}$$

$$=(y(t-0)\oplus\overline{v(t-0)})\cdot\chi_{(0,\infty)}(t)\cdot \quad (y(0-0)=x(0-0))$$

$$\cdot\overline{\bigcup_{\xi\in(t-d,t)}(\overline{x(0-0)\oplus v(0-0)}\cdot\chi_{\{0\}}(\xi)\oplus Dv(\xi))}\cdot\chi_{[d,\infty)}(t)$$

$$=\overline{y(t-0)\oplus v(t-0)}\cdot\overline{\bigcup_{\xi\in(t-d,t)} Dv(\xi)}\cdot\chi_{[d,\infty)}(t) \tag{18}$$

SDBRIDC' Fig 5b)

$$Dv(t) = (v(t-0) \oplus u(t-0)) \cdot \overline{\bigcup_{\xi \in (t-d,t)} Du(\xi)} \cdot \chi_{[d,\infty)}(t) \quad \text{(the hypothesis SDBRIDC')} \tag{19}$$

$$v(t-0) = \overline{x(t-0)} \oplus \overline{x(0-0) \oplus v(0-0)} \cdot \chi_{(-\infty,0]}(t) \qquad \text{(from (14))} \tag{20}$$

$$u(t-0) = u(0-0) \cdot \chi_{(-\infty,0]}(t) \oplus u(t-0) \cdot \chi_{(0,\infty)}(t) \tag{21}$$

$$Dx(t) = (\overline{x(t-0)} \oplus \overline{x(0-0) \oplus v(0-0)} \cdot \chi_{(-\infty,0]}(t) \oplus u(t-0)) \cdot \overline{\bigcup_{\xi \in (t-d,t)} Du(\xi)} \cdot \chi_{[d,\infty)}(t)$$

$$\oplus\, \overline{x(0-0) \oplus v(0-0)} \cdot \chi_{\{0\}}(t) \qquad \text{(from (17),(19),(20))}$$

$$= (\overline{x(0-0)} \cdot \chi_{(-\infty,0]}(t) \oplus \overline{x(t-0)} \cdot \chi_{(0,\infty)}(t) \oplus$$

$$\oplus (\overline{x(0-0)} \oplus v(0-0)) \cdot \chi_{(-\infty,0]}(t) \oplus u(0-0) \cdot \chi_{(-\infty,0]}(t) \oplus u(t-0) \cdot \chi_{(0,\infty)}(t)) \cdot$$

$$\cdot \overline{\bigcup_{\xi \in (t-d,t)} Du(\xi)} \cdot \chi_{[d,\infty)}(t) \oplus \overline{x(0-0) \oplus v(0-0)} \cdot \chi_{\{0\}}(t) \quad \text{(from (21)}$$

$$= (\overline{x(t-0)} \oplus u(t-0)) \cdot \chi_{(0,\infty)}(t) \cdot \overline{\bigcup_{\xi \in (t-d,t)} Du(\xi)} \cdot \chi_{[d,\infty)}(t) \oplus \overline{x(0-0) \oplus u(0-0)} \cdot \chi_{\{0\}}(t)$$

$$(u(0-0) = v(0-0))$$

$$= \overline{x(t-0) \oplus u(t-0)} \cdot \overline{\bigcup_{\xi \in (t-d,t)} Du(\xi)} \cdot \chi_{[d,\infty)}(t) \oplus \overline{x(0-0) \oplus u(0-0)} \cdot \chi_{\{0\}}(t) \tag{22}$$

A comparison between the forms of (18) and (22) is interesting.

2.4 Circuit With Feedback Using a Logical Gate NOT

Let the next circuit, where the logical gate and the wires have delays

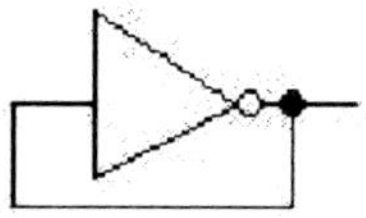

Fig 6

and the circuits to be analyzed are the next ones

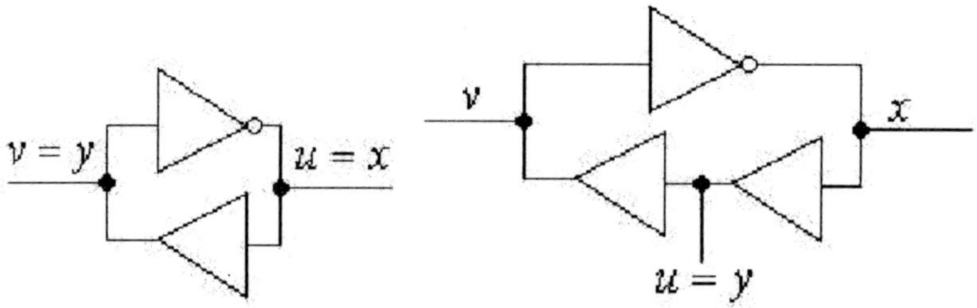

a) b)

Fig 7

Fig 7 a), respectively Fig 7 b) result from and keep the notations of Fig 5 a), b) (the modeling coincides), respectively of Fig 5 c). In Fig 7 the logical gate is supposed to be ideal

$$x(t) = x(0-0) \cdot \chi_{(-\infty,0)}(t) \oplus \overline{v(t)} \cdot \chi_{[0,\infty)}(t) \qquad (1)$$

as well as the wires and the delays are localized in the delay circuits. We shall write the relations between u, v, x, y and we shall try to eliminate three of the four variables.

SC Fig 7 a)

We suppose that x is of the form

$$x(t) = x(t) \cdot \chi_{(-\infty,t_0)}(t) \oplus x(t_0) \cdot \chi_{[t_0,\infty)}(t) \qquad (2)$$

and from SC this implies that v is of the form

$$v(t) = v(t) \cdot \chi_{(-\infty,t_1)}(t) \oplus v(t_1) \cdot \chi_{[t_1,\infty)}(t) \qquad (3)$$

where

$$x(t_0) = v(t_1) \qquad (4)$$

and $t_0 \geq 0, t_1 \geq 0$. On the other hand (1), (2) and (3) show that

$$x(t_0) = \overline{v(t_1)} \qquad (5)$$

(4) and (5) are contradictory, meaning the falsity of the hypothesis (2). A major difference exists between the facts from 2.2 and the present ones: SC did not bring there information on x, that circuit could be stable or unstable, unlike here where (2) is false, the circuit is unstable and instead of (2) we can write

$$x(t) = x(0-0) \cdot \chi_{(-\infty,t_0)}(t) \oplus \overline{x(0-0)} \cdot \chi_{[t_0,t_1)}(t) \oplus$$
$$\oplus\, x(0-0) \cdot \chi_{[t_1,t_2)}(t) \oplus \overline{x(0-0)} \cdot \chi_{[t_2,t_3)}(t) \oplus \ldots \qquad (6)$$

where $0 \leq t_0 < t_1 < t_2 < \ldots$ is unbounded.

BDC' Fig 7 a)

The system is the next one

$$\bigcap_{\xi \in [t-d_r,t)} x(\xi) \leq v(t) \leq \bigcup_{\xi \in [t-d_f,t)} x(\xi) \qquad (7)$$

thus from (1):

$$\bigcap_{\xi \in [t-d_r,t)} (x(0-0) \cdot \chi_{(-\infty,0)}(\xi) \oplus \overline{v(\xi)} \cdot \chi_{[0,\infty)}(\xi)) \leq v(t) \leq$$
$$\leq \bigcup_{\xi \in [t-d_f,t)} (x(0-0) \cdot \chi_{(-\infty,0)}(\xi) \oplus \overline{v(\xi)} \cdot \chi_{[0,\infty)}(\xi)) \qquad (8)$$

<u>Case</u> $x(0-0) = 0$

The functions $\bigcap_{\xi \in [t-d_r,t)} \overline{v(\xi)} \cdot \chi_{[0,\infty)}(\xi)$, $v(t)$, $\bigcup_{\xi \in [t-d_f,t)} \overline{v(\xi)} \cdot \chi_{[0,\infty)}(\xi)$ are all null for $t \leq 0$. At the right of 0, because $\overline{v(0)} = 1$, $\bigcup_{\xi \in [t-d_f,t)} \overline{v(\xi)} \cdot \chi_{[0,\infty)}(\xi)$ becomes 1 and if v continues to remain 0, in the point $t = d_r$, $\bigcap_{\xi \in [t-d_r,t)} \overline{v(\xi)} \cdot \chi_{[0,\infty)}(\xi)$ becomes 1, thus $0 < t_0 \leq d_r$ exists so that $v(t_0) = 1$. At the right of t_0, because $\overline{v(t_0)} = 0$, $\bigcap_{\xi \in [t-d_r, t)} \overline{v(\xi)} \cdot \chi_{[0,\infty)}(\xi)$ is 0 and if v continues to be 1, in the point $t_0 + d_f$, $\bigcup_{\xi \in [t-d_f, t)} \overline{v(\xi)} \cdot \chi_{[0,\infty)}(\xi)$ becomes 0, in other words $t_0 < t_1 \le t_0 + d_f$ exists so that $v(t_1) = 0$ etc. The conclusion is that the unbounded family $t_0, t_1, t_2, ...$ exists so that

$$\begin{aligned} & 0 < t_0 \le d_r \\ & t_0 < t_1 \le t_0 + d_f \\ & t_1 < t_2 \le t_1 + d_r \\ & t_2 < t_3 \le t_2 + d_f \\ & \ldots \end{aligned} \tag{9}$$

and

$$v(t) = \chi_{[t_0,t_1)}(t) \oplus \chi_{[t_2,t_3)}(t) \oplus ... \tag{10}$$

<u>Case</u> $x(0-0) = 1$

In similar conditions with the previous ones, the solutions v of (8) are of the form

$$v(t) = \chi_{(-\infty,t_0)}(t) \oplus \chi_{[t_1,t_2)}(t) \oplus \chi_{[t_3,t_4)}(t) \oplus ... \tag{11}$$

where

$$\begin{aligned} & 0 < t_0 \le d_f \\ & t_0 < t_1 \le t_0 + d_r \\ & t_1 < t_2 \le t_1 + d_f \\ & t_2 < t_3 \le t_2 + d_r \\ & \ldots \end{aligned} \tag{12}$$

Adding AIC to BDC' gives the minimal length of the 0-pulses, respectively of the 1-pulses

in (10):

$$\begin{aligned} & \delta_r < t_{2k+1} - t_{2k} \\ & \delta_f < t_{2k+2} - t_{2k+1} \end{aligned} \tag{13}$$

in (11):

$$\begin{aligned} & \delta_f < t_{2k+1} - t_{2k} \\ & \delta_r < t_{2k+2} - t_{2k+1} \end{aligned} \tag{14}$$

for all $k \ge 0$.

RIC is the next one:

$$\overline{v(t-0)} \cdot v(t) \le \bigcap_{\xi \in [t-\delta_r, t-\delta_r+\mu_r]} x(\xi) \tag{15}$$

$$v(t-0) \cdot \overline{v(t)} \le \bigcap_{\xi \in [t-\delta_f, t-\delta_f+\mu_f]} \overline{x(\xi)} \tag{16}$$

(10) gives (case $x(0-0) = 0$):

$$\overline{v(t-0)} \cdot v(t) = \chi_{\{t_0,t_2,t_4,...\}}(t) \tag{17}$$

$$\bigcap_{\xi \in [t-\delta_r, t-\delta_r+\mu_r]} \overline{v(\xi)} \cdot \chi_{[0,\infty)}(\xi) = \bigcap_{\xi \in [t-\delta_r, t-\delta_r+\mu_r]} (\chi_{[0,t_0)}(\xi) \oplus \chi_{[t_1,t_2)}(\xi) \oplus \chi_{[t_3,t_4)}(\xi) \oplus ...) =$$

$$= \chi_{[\delta_r, t_0+\delta_r-\mu_r)}(t) \oplus \chi_{[t_1+\delta_r, t_2+\delta_r-\mu_r)}(t) \oplus \chi_{[t_3+\delta_r, t_4+\delta_r-\mu_r)}(t) \oplus ... \tag{18}$$

and inequality (15)

$$\chi_{\{t_0,t_2,t_4,...\}}(t) \le \chi_{[\delta_r,t_0+\delta_r-\mu_r)}(t) \oplus \chi_{[t_1+\delta_r,t_2+\delta_r-\mu_r)}(t) \oplus \chi_{[t_3+\delta_r,t_4+\delta_r-\mu_r)}(t) \oplus ...$$

is equivalent with

$$\{t_0,t_2,t_4,...\} \subset [\delta_r,t_0+\delta_r-\mu_r) \vee [t_1+\delta_r,t_2+\delta_r-\mu_r) \vee [t_3+\delta_r,t_4+\delta_r-\mu_r) \vee ...$$

Similarly, from (10) and (16):

$$\{t_1,t_3,t_5,...\} \subset (-\infty,\delta_f-\mu_f) \vee [t_0+\delta_f,t_1+\delta_f-\mu_f) \vee [t_2+\delta_f,t_3+\delta_f-\mu_f) \vee ...$$

Equation (11) (case $x(0-0)=1$) combined with RIC gives restrictions of the same nature.

FDC Fig 7b)

(1) is true together with

$$u(t) = x(t-d_1) \quad (19)$$

$$v(t) = u(t-d_2) \quad (20)$$

where $d_1 \ge 0, d_2 \ge 0$ and by eliminating u, v we obtain

$$x(t) = x(0-0)\cdot\chi_{(-\infty,0)}(t) \oplus \overline{x(t-d_1-d_2)}\cdot\chi_{[0,\infty)}(t) \quad (21)$$

<u>Case</u> $d_1+d_2=0$

Equation (21) is incompatible.

<u>Case</u> $d_1+d_2>0$

The solution of (21) is

$$x(t) = x(0-0)\cdot\chi_{(-\infty,0)}(t) \oplus \overline{x(0-0)}\cdot\chi_{[0,d_1+d_2)}(t) \oplus$$

$$\oplus\, x(0-0)\cdot\chi_{[d_1+d_2,2(d_1+d_2))}(t) \oplus \overline{x(0-0)}\cdot\chi_{[2(d_1+d_2),3(d_1+d_2))}(t) \oplus ... \quad (22)$$

DBRIDC Fig 7 a)

(1) is true together with

$$\overline{v(t-0)}\cdot v(t) = \overline{v(t-0)}\cdot \bigcap_{\xi\in[t-d_r,t-d_r+m_r]} x(\xi) \quad (23)$$

$$v(t-0)\cdot\overline{v(t)} = v(t-0)\cdot \bigcap_{\xi\in[t-d_f,t-d_f+m_f]} \overline{x(\xi)} \quad (24)$$

where $0 \le m_r \le d_r, 0 \le m_f \le d_f, v(0-0) = x(0-0)$ and by eliminating x we get

$$\overline{v(t-0)}\cdot v(t) = \overline{v(t-0)}\cdot \bigcap_{\xi\in[t-d_r,t-d_r+m_r]} (x(0-0)\cdot\chi_{(-\infty,0)}(\xi) \oplus \overline{v(\xi)}\cdot\chi_{[0,\infty)}(\xi)) \quad (25)$$

$$v(t-0)\cdot\overline{v(t)} = v(t-0)\cdot \bigcap_{\xi\in[t-d_f,t-d_f+m_f]} (\overline{x(0-0)}\cdot\chi_{(-\infty,0)}(\xi) \oplus v(\xi)\cdot\chi_{[0,\infty)}(\xi)) \quad (26)$$

We suppose that $x(0-0)=0$.

<u>Case</u> $d_r-m_r>0, d_f-m_f>0$

Because in (25) we have $\forall\xi\in[0,d_r), v(\xi)=0$, the implication is $v(d_r)=1$. Because in (26) we have $\forall\xi\in[d_r,d_r+d_f), v(\xi)=1$, the implication is $v(d_r+d_f)=0$ etc. The solution is

$$v(t) = \chi_{[d_r,d_r+d_f)}(t) \oplus \chi_{[2d_r+d_f,2d_r+2d_f)}(t) \oplus \chi_{[3d_r+2d_f,3d_r+3d_f)}(t) \oplus ... \quad (27)$$

<u>Case</u> $d_r-m_r=0 \; or \; d_f-m_f=0$

We suppose that $d_r=m_r>0$ is true. (25) is in this situation

$$\overline{v(t-0)}\cdot v(t)=\overline{v(t-0)}\cdot\bigcap_{\xi\in[t-d_r,t]}\overline{v(\xi)}\cdot\chi_{[0,\infty)}(\xi)=\overline{v(t-0)}\cdot\bigcap_{\xi\in[t-d_r,t)}\overline{v(\xi)}\cdot\chi_{[0,\infty)}(\xi)\cdot\overline{v(t)} \quad (28)$$

For $t<d_r, v(t)=0$ and at $t=d_r$ we get the contradiction $v(d_r)=\overline{v(d_r)}$. The system is incompatible. The possibilities $d_r=m_r=0, d_f=m_f>0, d_f=m_f=0$ result in incompatible systems too.

The situation when $x(0-0)=1$ is to be treated similarly.

SDBRIDC' Fig 7b)

(1) is true together with

$$Dy(t)=(y(t-0)\oplus x(t-0))\cdot\overline{\bigcup_{\xi\in(t-d_1,t)}Dx(\xi)}\cdot\chi_{[d_1,\infty)}(t) \quad (29)$$

$$Dv(t)=(v(t-0)\oplus y(t-0))\cdot\overline{\bigcup_{\xi\in(t-d_2,t)}Dy(\xi)}\cdot\chi_{[d_2,\infty)}(t) \quad (30)$$

where $d_1>0, d_2>0$. We have $x(0-0)=y(0-0)=v(0-0)$.

We suppose that $x(0-0)=0$ and (30) used under the form $Dv(0)=0$ gives $v(0)=0$.

From (1), $x(0)=1$. From (29), y becomes 1 at the time instant d_1. From (30), v becomes 1 at the time instant d_1+d_2, when in (1) x becomes 0. The conclusion is:

$$x(t)=\chi_{[0,d_1+d_2)}(t)\oplus\chi_{[2d_1+2d_2,3d_1+3d_2)}(t)\oplus... \quad (31)$$

$$y(t)=\chi_{[d_1,2d_1+d_2)}(t)\oplus\chi_{[3d_1+2d_2,4d_1+3d_2)}(t)\oplus... \quad (32)$$

$$v(t)=\chi_{[d_1+d_2,2d_1+2d_2)}(t)\oplus\chi_{[3d_1+3d_2,4d_1+4d_2)}(t)\oplus... \quad (33)$$

The situation when $x(0-0)=1$ is similar.

The solutions are in this case the same like at FDC.

2.5 First Conclusions

Some of the facts that were presented in this section have been studied by us some time ago and they have brought a direction of research called pseudo-Boolean differential and integral calculus that is interesting by itself, being related with mathematical analysis ([22] and others). We can define for the functions $\boldsymbol{R}\rightarrow\{0,1\}$ derivatives, integrals, convolution products, distributions etc and many notions and results from the real mathematical analysis have analogues of this type. It is interesting also the study of the equations and of the inequalities written with such functions, in no direct relation with digital electrical engineering.

Another direction of research is the present one, related with the asynchronous circuits. Starting from the known models as well as using the intuition suggested by the literature, modeling is abstracted by defining the delay conditions, shortly the delays, as real time models of the delay circuits. From this moment, the construction of new models is natural. On the other hand, the way that the delay circuit is generalized by the C-element of Muller, the delays are generalized by the 2-delays and generally by the n-delays, that are the models of the C-elements of Muller. An example of this nature is sketched at 11.3.

3. Preliminaries

3.1 The Boole Algebra with Two Elements

3.1.1 Definition The set $\boldsymbol{B}=\{0,1\}$ is called the *binary Boole algebra*, or the *Boole algebra with two elements*. It is endowed with:

- the order $0<1$
- the laws:

unary: ' $\overline{\ }$ ', the *complement*

binary: '$\cup$' the *reunion*, '$\cdot$' the *intersection*, '$\oplus$' the *modulo 2 sum*

defined in the next table:

$-$	
0	1
1	0

$\cup$	0	1
0	0	1
1	1	1

$\cdot$	0	1
0	0	0
1	0	1

$\oplus$	0	1
0	0	1
1	1	0

Table 1

We give the usual meaning to the binary relations on $\boldsymbol{B}$: $>,\le,\ge$.

3.1.2 Remarks $(\boldsymbol{B},\overline{\ },\cup,\cdot)$ is a Boole algebra indeed and $(\boldsymbol{B},\oplus,\cdot)$ is a field, where the inverse of a relative to $\oplus$ is a itself: $a\oplus a=0$. The relation between the order and the laws of $\boldsymbol{B}$ is expressed by:

$$\forall a,b\in \boldsymbol{B}, a\le b \Leftrightarrow \overline{a}\ge \overline{b}$$

$$\forall a,b\in \boldsymbol{B}, a\cup b=\max(a,b),\ a\cdot b=\min(a,b)$$

$$\forall a,b,c\in \boldsymbol{B}, b\le c\Rightarrow (a\cup b\le a\cup c), b\le c\Rightarrow (a\cdot b\le a\cdot c)$$

3.1.3 Definition Let the binary generalized sequence $(x_j)_{j\in J}$. We define

$$\bigcup_{j\in J} x_j=\begin{cases}1, \textit{if } \exists j\in J, x_j=1\\ 0, \textit{otherwise}\end{cases},\ \bigcup_{j\in\emptyset} x_j=0$$

$$\bigcap_{j\in J} x_j=\begin{cases}0, \textit{if } \exists j\in J, x_j=0\\ 1, \textit{otherwise}\end{cases},\ \bigcap_{j\in\emptyset} x_j=1$$

3.1.4 Definition The functions $f:\boldsymbol{B}^n\to \boldsymbol{B}^m$, $n,m\ge 1$ and as a special case the functions $f:\boldsymbol{B}^n\to\boldsymbol{B}$ are called *Boolean functions*.

3.2 Generalities on the $\boldsymbol{R}\to\boldsymbol{B}$ Functions

3.2.1 Definition The next order and laws are induced on $\boldsymbol{B}^{\boldsymbol{R}}$ by those of $\boldsymbol{B}$:

$$f\le g \Leftrightarrow \forall t, f(t)\le g(t)$$

$$\forall t, \overline{f}(t)=\overline{f(t)}$$

$$\forall t,(f\cup g)(t)=f(t)\cup g(t)$$

$$\forall t,(f\cdot g)(t)=f(t)\cdot g(t)$$

$$\forall t,(f\oplus g)(t)=f(t)\oplus g(t)$$

where $f, g : \boldsymbol{R} \to \boldsymbol{B}$ and $t \in \boldsymbol{R}$. The fact that we have abusively used the same notations for different orders and laws will cause no misunderstanding.

3.2.2 Definition We note with $\chi_A : \boldsymbol{R} \to \boldsymbol{B}$, where $A \subset \boldsymbol{R}$, the *characteristic function* of the set A:

$$\chi_A(t) = \begin{cases} 1, t \in A \\ 0, t \notin A \end{cases}$$

3.2.3 Definition The *support* of the function $f : \boldsymbol{R} \to \boldsymbol{B}$ is the set $supp\ f \subset \boldsymbol{R}$ defined by

$$supp\ f = \{t \mid t \in \boldsymbol{R}, f(t) = 1\}$$

3.2.4 Remarks The next properties are true for all $t \in \boldsymbol{R}$ and all $f, g : \boldsymbol{R} \to \boldsymbol{B}$:

$$\chi_\varnothing(t) = 0,\ \chi_{\boldsymbol{R}}(t) = 1$$

$$f(t) = \chi_{supp\ f}(t)$$

$$f \le g \Leftrightarrow supp\ f \subset supp\ g$$

$$supp\ \overline{f} = \boldsymbol{R} - supp\ f$$

$$supp\ (f \cup g) = supp\ f \vee supp\ g$$

$$supp\ (f \cdot g) = supp\ f \wedge supp\ g$$

$$supp\ (f \oplus g) = supp\ f\ \Delta\ supp\ g$$

In fact we can identify $\boldsymbol{B}^{\boldsymbol{R}}$ and $2^{\boldsymbol{R}}$ from the point of view of the order and of the algebraical properties.

3.2.5 Definition We say that $f : \boldsymbol{R} \to \boldsymbol{B}$ *has a limit when* t *tends to infinite* if

$$\exists t', \forall t \ge t', f(t) = f(t')$$

The number $f(t')$ that does not depend on t' is noted with $\lim_{t \to \infty} f(t)$.

3.3 Limits and Derivatives. The Continuity and the Differentiability of the $R \to B$ Functions

3.3.1 Definition Let $f : \boldsymbol{R} \to \boldsymbol{B}$. If the function $f^- : \boldsymbol{R} \to \boldsymbol{B}$ exists so that

$$\forall t \in \boldsymbol{R}, \exists \varepsilon > 0, \forall \xi \in (t - \varepsilon, t), f(\xi) = f^-(t)$$

i.e. if for any t and any $\xi < t$ sufficiently close to t, $f(\xi)$ depends on t only and not on ξ, we say that f *has left limit* or that the *left limit of* f *exists*. Similarly if $f^+ : \boldsymbol{R} \to \boldsymbol{B}$ exists having the property that

$$\forall t \in \boldsymbol{R}, \exists \varepsilon > 0, \forall \xi \in (t, t + \varepsilon), f(\xi) = f^+(t)$$

is true, we say that f *has right limit* or that the *right limit of* f *exists*. In the hypothesis that both previous properties are satisfied, we use to say that f is *differentiable*. $f^-(t), f^+(t)$ are sometimes noted with $f(t-0), f(t+0)$ and are called the *left limit*, respectively the *right limit (function) of* f.

3.3.2 Definition The functions

$$D_{01}f(t) = \overline{f(t-0)} \cdot f(t),\ D_{10}f(t) = f(t-0) \cdot \overline{f(t)}$$

$$D_{10}^{*}f(t)=f(t)\cdot\overline{f(t+0)},\ D_{01}^{*}f(t)=\overline{f(t)}\cdot f(t+0)$$

are called the *left* and the *right semi-derivatives of* f and the functions

$$Df(t)=f(t-0)\oplus f(t)=\overline{f(t-0)}\cdot f(t)\cup f(t-0)\cdot\overline{f(t)}$$
$$D^{*}f(t)=f(t+0)\oplus f(t)=\overline{f(t+0)}\cdot f(t)\cup f(t+0)\cdot\overline{f(t)}$$

are called the *left*, respectively the *right derivative of* f.

3.3.3 Definition f is *left continuous*, respectively *right continuous*, if

$$\forall t, f(t)=f(t-0)$$
$$\forall t, f(t)=f(t+0)$$

3.3.4 Remark We can prove [22] that the only differentiable $\boldsymbol{R}\to\boldsymbol{B}$ functions that are both left continuous and right continuous (on an interval) are the two constant functions (on that interval). If the differentiable function f is right continuous, then it is constant (on an interval) iff $Df(t)=0$ (on that interval) and a dual property holds for the differentiable left continuous functions.

3.3.5 Examples

a) $$f(t)=\chi_{[0,1]}(t)\oplus\chi_{\{2\}}(t)$$

is a differentiable function, that is neither left, nor right continuous. More precisely

$$f(t-0)=\chi_{(0,1]}(t),\ f(t+0)=\chi_{[0,1)}(t)$$
$$Df(t)=\chi_{\{0\}}(t)\oplus\chi_{\{2\}}(t),\ D^{*}f(t)=\chi_{\{1\}}(t)\oplus\chi_{\{2\}}(t)$$

b) The function

$$f(t)=\bigcup_{n\geq 1}\chi_{(\frac{1}{2n+1},\frac{1}{2n}]}(t)$$

is left continuous, as it has the property that $f(t-0)$ exists and it is equal with $f(t)$. $f(t+0)$ does not exist however, because for $t=0$, we have

$$\forall\varepsilon>0,\exists\xi,\xi'\in(0,\varepsilon),f(\xi)\neq f(\xi')$$

3.4 The Properties of the Limits and of the Derivatives

3.4.1 Theorem If f,g have left limit, respectively right limit, then the next properties hold

a) $D\overline{f}=Df$

b) $D(f\oplus g)=Df\oplus Dg$

c) $D(f\cdot g)=f\cdot Dg\oplus g\cdot Df\oplus Df\cdot Dg$

respectively the dual properties.

Proof

a) $D\overline{f}(t)=\overline{f}(t-0)\oplus\overline{f}(t)=\overline{f(t-0)}\oplus\overline{f(t)}=1\oplus f(t-0)\oplus 1\oplus f(t)=$
$=f(t-0)\oplus f(t)=Df(t)$

3.4.2 Theorem

a) If f has left limit, then f^{-} has left limit and

$$(f^-)^- = f^-$$

b) If f is differentiable, then f^- has right limit and

$$(f^-)^+ = f^+$$

the dual statements of a), b) being also true.

Proof a) Let t arbitrary and fixed, $t' < t$ and f^- with the property

$$\forall \xi \in (t',t), f(\xi) = f^-(t)$$

We fix the numbers ξ, ω arbitrary with $t' < \xi < \omega < t$. We have $f(\xi) = f(\omega)$ and, as $f(\xi)$ depends only on ω -not on ξ- we get $f(\xi) = f^-(\omega)$. On the other hand $f^-(\omega) = f^-(t)$ thus $f^-(\omega)$ is independent on ω -it depends only on t-and we get $f^-(\omega) = (f^-)^-(t)$. We have obtained $(f^-)^-(t) = f^-(\omega) = f^-(t)$.

3.4.3 Corollary

a) For f with left limit, Df has left limit and

$$DDf = Df$$

b) If f is differentiable, then

$$D^* Df = Df$$

Proof

a) $DDf(t) = D(f(t-0) \oplus f(t)) = f(t-0) \oplus f(t-0) \oplus f(t-0) \oplus f(t) = Df(t)$

b) $D^* Df(t) = D^*(f(t-0) \oplus f(t)) = f(t+0) \oplus f(t+0) \oplus f(t-0) \oplus f(t) = Df(t)$

3.4.4 **Remark** The way that the left, respectively the right limits are iterated shows that we do not need to work with derivatives of the second or higher order.

3.4.5 **Notation** We note with $\tau^d : \boldsymbol{R} \to \boldsymbol{R}$ the translation with $d \in \boldsymbol{R}$:

$$\tau^d(t) = t - d$$

3.4.6 **Theorem** Let $d \in \boldsymbol{R}$ arbitrary. f has left limit iff $f \circ \tau^d$ has left limit. Similar properties hold for the left continuity, the differentiability etc.

Proof Obvious.

3.4.7 **Remark** The compatibility between the Boolean laws and the translation is given by

$$\overline{f} \circ \tau^d = \overline{f \circ \tau^d}$$

$$(f \cup g) \circ \tau^d = f \circ \tau^d \cup g \circ \tau^d$$

etc. and the compatibility between the limits, the derivatives and respectively the translation is expressed by the equations

$$f^- \circ \tau^d = (f \circ \tau^d)^-, \; f^+ \circ \tau^d = (f \circ \tau^d)^+$$

$$Df \circ \tau^d = D(f \circ \tau^d), \; D^* f \circ \tau^d = D^*(f \circ \tau^d)$$

3.5 Conventions Concerning the Drawings of the Graphics of the $\boldsymbol{R} \to \boldsymbol{B}$ Functions

3.5.1 Conventions In order to make easier the understanding of the $\boldsymbol{R} \to \boldsymbol{B}$ functions, we make the next *conventions* concerning the drawing of their graphics:

a) the two values 0,1 are not written on the vertical axis. They are supposed to be known, the only necessary convention is that the low value be associated with 0 and the high value be associated with 1

b) we draw vertical lines in these points where the function switches (the discontinuity points), even if the vertical lines do not belong to the graphic

c) we put bullets on the vertical lines that are drawn like at b), underlining this way the points that actually belong to the graphic (the value of the function in the switching point)

d) we avoid writing values on the time axis, i.e. the horizontal one, whenever this causes no misunderstanding.

3.5.2 Example We give the example of the next figure, where we have drawn the graphics of the functions from 3.3.5 a).

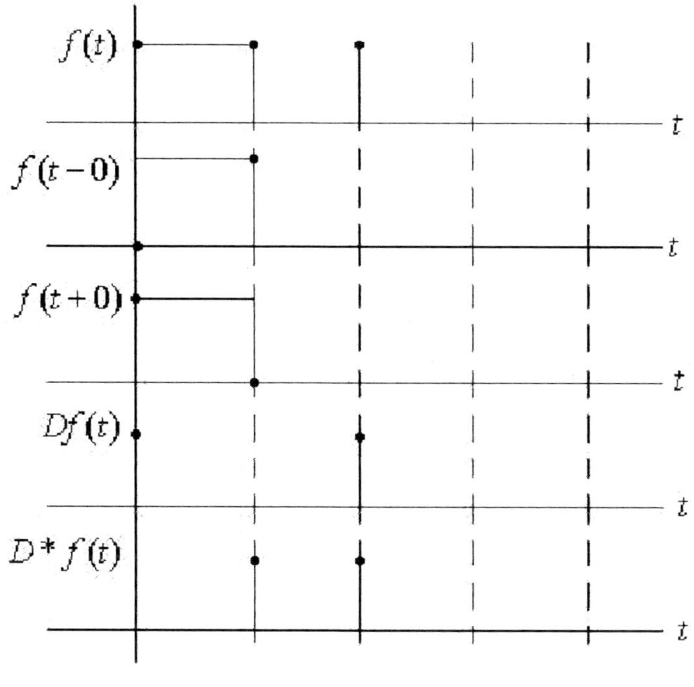

Fig 8

4. Signals

4.1 The Definition of the Signals

4.1.1 **Definition** A function $f : \boldsymbol{R} \to \boldsymbol{B}$ is called (*electrical*) *signal*[2], if

i) it is differentiable

ii) it is right continuous

---

2 These functions, or similar functions with the same role in modeling, have also been called in literature (see [1], [14], [16]) *Boolean signals*, *piecewise constant signals*, *piecewise continuous signals*, *non-zeno signals* and respectively *finite variability signals*.

iii) $supp\ Df \subset [0,\infty)$

The set of the signals is noted with S and the set of the non-empty subsets of S is noted $P^*(S)$.

4.1.2 **Remark** We give an interpretation to the previous definition. The next property, that can be inferred from i)

$$\forall t', t'' \in \mathbf{R}, t' < t'' \Rightarrow (t', t'') \wedge supp\ Df \text{ is a finite set}$$

is the *finite variability*, a signal switches finitely many times in any bounded time interval and it is an inertia request. The right continuity of f is a property of *causality*, or *non-anticipation* and it is related to the fact that the present depends on the past and maybe on the present itself, but not on the future. The request iii) is related to the initial time that is 0 -but this condition is also one of non-anticipation. The anticipative systems having an evolution with the time axis reversed and where the present depends on the future and maybe on the present itself, are modeled by differentiable left continuous functions f with

$$supp\ D^* f \subset (-\infty, 0]$$

We have just indicated how the dual notion to that of signal is to be defined.

4.1.3 Theorem The next conditions are equivalent for the function $f : \mathbf{R} \to \mathbf{B}$:

a) f is signal

b) the unbounded family $0 \le t_0 < t_1 < t_2 < ...$ exists so that

$$f(t) = f(-1) \cdot \chi_{(-\infty, t_0)}(t) \oplus f(t_0) \cdot \chi_{[t_0, t_1)}(t) \oplus f(t_1) \cdot \chi_{[t_1, t_2)}(t) \oplus ...$$

Sketch of proof

a) $\Rightarrow$ *b)* 4.1.1 i) implies the existence of an upper and lower unbounded family $... < t_{-1} < t_0 < t_1 < ...$ where t_0 can be taken ≥ 0 without loosing the generality, satisfying the property that $\forall t$,

$$f(t) = ... \oplus f(t_{-1}) \cdot \chi_{\{t_{-1}\}}(t) \oplus f(\tfrac{t_{-1}+t_0}{2}) \cdot \chi_{(t_{-1}, t_0)}(t) \oplus$$

$$\oplus f(t_0) \cdot \chi_{\{t_0\}}(t) \oplus f(\tfrac{t_0+t_1}{2}) \cdot \chi_{(t_0, t_1)}(t) \oplus f(t_1) \cdot \chi_{\{t_1\}}(t) \oplus ...$$

4.1.1 ii), 4.1.1 iii) and the previous equation imply b).

b) $\Rightarrow$ *a)* It is shown that $\forall t$, three possibilities exist:

i) $t < t_0$; then $f(t-0) = f(t+0) = f(t)$

ii) $t \ge t_0$ and $\exists k, t = t_k$; then $f(t-0) = \begin{cases} f(t_{k-1}), k \ge 1 \\ f(-1), \quad k = 0 \end{cases}$, $f(t+0) = f(t_k)$

iii) $t \ge t_0$ and $\exists k, t \in (t_k, t_{k+1})$; then $f(t-0) = f(t+0) = f(t_k)$

4.1.4 **Theorem** Let $f \in S$ an arbitrary signal and $d \in \mathbf{R}$. The following statements are true:

a) $f \circ \tau^d$ is differentiable and right continuous

b) $f \circ \tau^d \in S \Leftrightarrow supp\ Df \circ \tau^d \subset [0,\infty)$

c) if $d \ge 0$, then $f \circ \tau^d \in S$.

Proof a) results from 4.1.3 b), because $f \circ \tau^d$ has the same form like f except the request $0 \le t_0$. b) results from $Df \circ \tau^d = D(f \circ \tau^d)$ (see Remark 3.4.7) and from a). For c), we take in consideration the fact that

$$supp\ D(f \circ \tau^d) = \{t \mid Df(t-d) = 1\} = \{t+d \mid Df(t) = 1\} = d + supp\ Df$$

and b) also, implication $\Leftarrow$:

$$d \ge 0 \ and \ supp\ Df \subset [0,\infty) \Rightarrow d + supp\ Df \subset [0,\infty) \Rightarrow$$

$$\Rightarrow supp\ D(f \circ \tau^d) \subset [0,\infty) \Rightarrow f \circ \tau^d \in S$$

4.1.5 **Remarks** $(S,\le)$ is an ordered set, with $\le$ induced from $\boldsymbol{B}^{\boldsymbol{R}}$ and the constant functions 0, 1 are the null and respectively the universal element of S. $(S, \overline{\ \ }, \cup, \cdot)$ is a Boolean algebra and $(S,\oplus,\cdot)$ is a commutative ring.

In S, the next equivalence holds, see Remark 3.3.4:

a) f is constant (on certain intervals)

b) $Df = 0$ (on certain intervals).

4.1.6 **Definition** Let $f \in S$. By *1-pulse*, respectively *0-pulse* of the signal f we mean the existence of the numbers $t' < t''$ with the property that

$$\forall \xi \in [t',t''), f(\xi) = 1 \ and \ f(t'-0) = f(t'') = 0$$

$$\forall \xi \in [t',t''), f(\xi) = 0 \ and \ f(t'-0) = f(t'') = 1$$

is true. In this case we say that f has a 1-pulse, respectively a 0-pulse of *length* $t''-t'$.

4.2 Useful Lemmas

4.2.1 **Theorem** Let f some differentiable function and the numbers $0 \le m \le d$. The functions

$$\Phi(t) = \bigcap_{\xi \in [t-d,t-d+m]} f(\xi)$$

$$\Psi(t) = \bigcup_{\xi \in [t-d,t-d+m]} f(\xi)$$

are differentiable and they satisfy

$$\Phi(t-0) = f(t-d-0) \cdot \bigcap_{\xi \in [t-d,t-d+m)} f(\xi) \quad (1)$$

$$\Phi(t+0) = \bigcap_{\xi \in (t-d,t-d+m]} f(\xi) \cdot f(t-d+m+0) \quad (2)$$

$$\Psi(t-0) = f(t-d-0) \cup \bigcup_{\xi \in [t-d,t-d+m)} f(\xi) \quad (3)$$

$$\Psi(t+0) = \bigcup_{\xi \in (t-d,t-d+m]} f(\xi) \cup f(t-d+m+0) \quad (4)$$

Proof If $m = 0$, then $\Phi(t) = \Psi(t) = f(t-d)$ is differentiable and we use Definition 3.1.3 ($\bigcap_{\xi \in \varnothing} f(\xi) = 1, \bigcup_{\xi \in \varnothing} f(\xi) = 0$).

We suppose now that $m > 0$. Let t arbitrary and fixed. The left limit of f in $t-d$ shows the existence of $\varepsilon_1 > 0$ with

$$\forall \xi \in (t-d-\varepsilon_1, t-d), f(\xi) = f(t-d-0)$$

and the left limit of f in $t-d+m$ shows the existence of $\varepsilon_2 > 0$ so that

$$\forall \xi \in (t-d+m-\varepsilon_2, t-d+m), f(\xi) = f(t-d+m-0)$$

For any $0 < \varepsilon < \min(\varepsilon_1, \varepsilon_2, m)$ we infer

$$\Phi(t-\varepsilon) = \bigcap_{\xi\in[t-d-\varepsilon,t-d+m-\varepsilon]} f(\xi) = \bigcap_{\xi\in[t-d-\varepsilon,t-d)} f(\xi) \cdot \bigcap_{\xi\in[t-d,t-d+m-\varepsilon]} f(\xi) =$$

$$= f(t-d-0) \cdot \bigcap_{\xi\in[t-d,t-d+m-\varepsilon]} f(\xi) =$$

$$= f(t-d-0) \cdot \bigcap_{\xi\in[t-d,t-d+m-\varepsilon]} f(\xi) \cdot f(t-d+m-0) =$$

$$= f(t-d-0) \cdot \bigcap_{\xi\in[t-d,t-d+m-\varepsilon]} f(\xi) \cdot \bigcap_{\xi\in(t-d+m-\varepsilon,t-d+m)} f(\xi) =$$

$$= f(t-d-0) \cdot \bigcap_{\xi\in[t-d,t-d+m)} f(\xi)$$

Because the value of $\Phi(t-\varepsilon)$ does not depend on ε, we get $\Phi(t-\varepsilon) = \Phi(t-0)$ and because t was arbitrary, (1) is proved.

The right limit of f in $t-d$ shows the existence of $\varepsilon_3 > 0$ so that

$$\forall \xi \in (t-d, t-d+\varepsilon_3), f(\xi) = f(t-d+0)$$

and on the other hand the right limit of f in $t-d+m$ shows the existence of $\varepsilon_4 > 0$ with

$$\forall \xi \in (t-d+m, t-d+m+\varepsilon_4), f(\xi) = f(t-d+m+0)$$

We take some $0 < \varepsilon' < \min(\varepsilon_3, \varepsilon_4, m)$ for which we have

$$\Phi(t+\varepsilon') = \bigcap_{\xi\in[t-d+\varepsilon',t-d+m+\varepsilon']} f(\xi) = \bigcap_{\xi\in[t-d+\varepsilon',t-d+m]} f(\xi) \cdot \bigcap_{\xi\in(t-d+m,t-d+m+\varepsilon']} f(\xi) =$$

$$= \bigcap_{\xi\in[t-d+\varepsilon',t-d+m]} f(\xi) \cdot f(t-d+m+0) =$$

$$= f(t-d+0) \cdot \bigcap_{\xi\in[t-d+\varepsilon',t-d+m]} f(\xi) \cdot f(t-d+m+0) =$$

$$= \bigcap_{\xi\in(t-d,t-d+\varepsilon')} f(\xi) \cdot \bigcap_{\xi\in[t-d+\varepsilon',t-d+m]} f(\xi) \cdot f(t-d+m+0) =$$

$$= \bigcap_{\xi\in(t-d,t-d+m]} f(\xi) \cdot f(t-d+m+0)$$

The fact that $\Phi(t+\varepsilon')$ does not depend on ε' shows that $\Phi(t+\varepsilon') = \Phi(t+0)$ and because t was arbitrary, (2) is true. Φ is differentiable.

The proof for Ψ is similar.

4.2.2 Theorem In the previous conditions and with the previous notations, we have:

$$\overline{\Phi(t-0)} \cdot \Phi(t) = \overline{f(t-d-0)} \cdot \bigcap_{\xi\in[t-d,t-d+m]} f(\xi)$$

$$\Phi(t-0)\cdot\overline{\Phi(t)} = f(t-d-0)\cdot\overline{\bigcap_{\xi\in[t-d,t-d+m)} f(\xi)\cdot f(t-d+m)}$$

$$\overline{\Psi(t-0)}\cdot\Psi(t) = \overline{f(t-d-0)}\cdot\overline{\bigcup_{\xi\in[t-d,t-d+m)} f(\xi)}\cdot f(t-d+m)$$

$$\Psi(t-0)\cdot\overline{\Psi(t)} = f(t-d-0)\cdot\overline{\bigcup_{\xi\in[t-d,t-d+m]} f(\xi)}$$

Proof $$\overline{\Phi(t-0)}\cdot\Phi(t) = \overline{f(t-d-0)\cdot\bigcap_{\xi\in[t-d,t-d+m)} f(\xi)}\cdot\bigcap_{\xi\in[t-d,t-d+m]} f(\xi) =$$

$$= (\overline{f(t-d-0)}\cup\overline{\bigcap_{\xi\in[t-d,t-d+m)} f(\xi)})\cdot\bigcap_{\xi\in[t-d,t-d+m]} f(\xi) = \overline{f(t-d-0)}\cdot\bigcap_{\xi\in[t-d,t-d+m]} f(\xi)$$

$$\overline{\Psi(t-0)}\cdot\Psi(t) = \overline{f(t-d-0)\cup\bigcup_{\xi\in[t-d,t-d+m)} f(\xi)}\cdot\bigcup_{\xi\in[t-d,t-d+m]} f(\xi) =$$

$$= \overline{f(t-d-0)}\cdot\overline{\bigcup_{\xi\in[t-d,t-d+m)} f(\xi)}\cdot(\bigcup_{\xi\in[t-d,t-d+m)} f(\xi)\cup f(t-d+m)) =$$

$$= \overline{f(t-d-0)}\cdot\overline{\bigcup_{\xi\in[t-d,t-d+m)} f(\xi)}\cdot f(t-d+m)$$

4.2.3 **Theorem** If f is signal, then Φ,Ψ are signals.

Proof If $m=0$ and $\Phi(t)=\Psi(t)=f(t-d)$, then the differentiable function $f(t-d)$ is signal, from Theorem 4.1.4 c). We consider from this moment that $m>0$.

We know from Theorem 4.2.1 that Φ is differentiable and we must show that it satisfies 4.1.1 ii) and 4.1.1 iii). The right continuity of f in $t-d$ shows that $\varepsilon_1>0$ exists with

$$\forall\xi\in[t-d,t-d+\varepsilon_1), f(\xi)=f(t-d)$$

and the right continuity of f in $t-d+m$ shows the existence of $\varepsilon_2>0$ so that

$$\forall\xi\in(t-d+m,t-d+m+\varepsilon_2), f(\xi)=f(t-d+m)$$

Let $0<\varepsilon<\min(\varepsilon_1,\varepsilon_2,m)$ and we conclude

$$\Phi(t+\varepsilon) = \bigcap_{\xi\in[t-d+\varepsilon,t-d+m+\varepsilon]} f(\xi) = \bigcap_{\xi\in[t-d+\varepsilon,t-d+m]} f(\xi)\cdot\bigcap_{\xi\in(t-d+m,t-d+m+\varepsilon]} f(\xi) =$$

$$= \bigcap_{\xi\in[t-d+\varepsilon,t-d+m]} f(\xi)\cdot f(t-d+m) = \bigcap_{\xi\in[t-d+\varepsilon,t-d+m]} f(\xi) =$$

$$= f(t-d)\cdot\bigcap_{\xi\in[t-d+\varepsilon,t-d+m]} f(\xi) =$$

$$= \bigcap_{\xi\in[t-d,t-d+\varepsilon)} f(\xi)\cdot\bigcap_{\xi\in[t-d+\varepsilon,t-d+m]} f(\xi) = \bigcap_{\xi\in[t-d,t-d+m]} f(\xi) = \Phi(t)$$

Thus $\Phi(t+\varepsilon) = \Phi(t+0) = \Phi(t)$. Φ is right continuous.

Moreover, the property 4.1.1 iii) is fulfilled since from 4.2.2:

$$D\Phi(t) = \overline{\Phi(t-0)}\cdot\Phi(t)\cup\Phi(t-0)\cdot\overline{\Phi(t)} =$$

$$= \overline{f(t-d-0)}\cdot\bigcap_{\xi\in[t-d,t-d+m]} f(\xi)\cup f(t-d-0)\cdot\overline{\bigcap_{\xi\in[t-d,t-d+m)} f(\xi)\cdot f(t-d+m)} \le$$

$$\leq \overline{f(t-d-0)} \cdot f(t-d) \cup f(t-d+m-0) \cdot \overline{f(t-d+m)} \leq$$

$$\leq \overline{f(t-d-0)} \cdot f(t-d) \cup f(t-d-0) \cdot \overline{f(t-d)} \cup$$

$$\cup \overline{f(t-d+m-0)} \cdot f(t-d+m) \cup f(t-d+m-0) \cdot \overline{f(t-d+m)} =$$

$$= D(f \circ \tau^{d})(t) \cup D(f \circ \tau^{d-m})(t)$$

and, because $f \circ \tau^{d}, f \circ \tau^{d-m}$ are signals

$$supp\ D(f \circ \tau^{d}) \subset [0,\infty),\ supp\ D(f \circ \tau^{d-m}) \subset [0,\infty)$$

we have

$$supp\ D\Phi \subset supp\ D(f \circ \tau^{d}) \vee supp\ D(f \circ \tau^{d-m}) \subset [0,\infty)$$

Φ is signal.

The proof for Ψ is dual.

5. An Overview of the Delays: Informal Definitions

5.1 We present now some of the intuitive knowledge that has generated the efforts represented by the present work.

At least two things are understood by the word *delay*: a *real non-negative number* d see 5.2, 5.3 and a *logical condition* see 5.4 and the following. These two occur usually together in definitions, since a complete separation is very difficult.

5.2 Informal definitions As real non-negative number, the word *delay* is a short form for one of the following i), ii).

i) *propagation delay*, or *transport delay* [10] representing the '*time interval between a transition in an input to the gate and a corresponding output transition. If the output transition changes from 0 to 1, the delay is rising, otherwise falling*'. The same notion is called in [12], [13] *transmission delay for transitions*.

ii) *inertial delay* representing [10] the '*minimum amount of time during which an input signal must persist to affect a change at the output*''. In [12], [13] the same notion is called *threshold for cancellation* and in [14] *latency delay*.

5.3 **Convention** The distinct numbers 5.2 i) and 5.2 ii) are generally taken to be equal [14] when the last exists, i.e. in the presence of inertia. We quote the next opinion:[12], [13]: '*A common form of implementation of the inertial delay model is the one in which the transmission delay d for transitions is the same as the threshold for cancellation. In other words, when a transition appears at the input, the transition will appear at the output after d unless a second transition occurs within that period*'.

5.4 **Classification of delays** The logical condition called *delay condition* defines a model and idioms like '*fixed delay*' will often be used as a short form for '*fixed delay condition*' or '*fixed delay model*' etc. The 'delays' to follow are all logical conditions defined informally.

Thus, from the *timing properties* point of view, we have

a) *unbounded delays*

b) *bounded delays*

c) *fixed delays*

and from the *memory properties* point of view, the delays are:

i) *pure delays*, i.e. delays without memory

ii) *inertial delays*, i.e. delays with memory.

5.5 Informal definition The *unbounded delays* are defined

a) [7]: '*a delay may take on any finite value*'

b) [11]: '*no bound on the magnitude is known a priori, except that it is positive and finite*'.

5.6 Remark The unbounded delay model is evaluated in [5] to be '*robust to delay variations*', but '*unrealistically conservative*'.

5.7 Informal definition The *bounded delays* are defined in the next manner:

a) [7]: '*a delay may have any value in a given time interval*'

b) [11]: a delay is bounded '*if an upper and lower bound on its magnitude are known before the synthesis or analysis of the circuit is begun*'

c) [5] '*every component is assumed to have an uncertain delay, that lies between given upper and lower bounds. The delay bounds take into account potential delay variations due to statistical fluctuations in the fabrication process, variations in ambient temperature, power supply etc*'.

d) [10]: '*In practice, manufactured circuits of the same design may have different gate delays due to manufacturing fluctuations in delay related parameters such as capacitance, resistivity and transistors sizes. To be practical, we need to provide an analysis for not just a manufactured instance of a design but the entire family of manufactured circuits of the same design. To model manufacturing uncertainties, we assume the gate delays to be variable within closed intervals. Therefore a complete delay analysis determines the delays of circuits with variable gate delays...*'

5.8 Remarks The bounded delay model is considered to be the most realistic one from the three: unbounded, bounded and fixed delays.

To be remarked in this context the necessary supplementary conditions (of speed-independence, or delay insensitiveness for example) of invariance relative to the variation of the delays, required in the synthesis procedure of the circuits.

On the other hand, non-conflicting differences occur in the approaches when defining and using the unbounded and the bounded delays: from having no lower bounds or upper bounds, the poorest case of the delay model, to having four such bounds $d_{r,\min} \leq d_{r,\max}$, $d_{f,\min} \leq d_{f,\max}$, the richest case of bounded delay that makes use of the distinction between the rising and the falling delays. The more detailed the model is, the more difficult is its handling and the more realistic are its results.

5.9 Informal definition The *fixed delays* are a special case of bounded delays, when '*a delay is assumed to have a fixed value*', [7] and the lower bounds of the delays are equal with the upper bounds of the delays making the delay be fixed, known.

5.10 Remark The fixed delay model is considered to be very unrealistic, in the sense that small variations of the delays due to variations in the ambient temperature, power supply,... cause great, unacceptable differences between the model and the modeled circuit. [5]: '*Since it is almost impossible to obtain a precise delay of a component in a chip, this is not a realistic model for timing verification purpose*'.

5.11 Informal definition The *pure delays*, or *ideal delays* are defined like this.

a) [11]: a delay is considered to be pure '*if it transmits each event on its input to its output, i.e. it corresponds to a pure translation in time of the input waveform*'.

b) [5]: '*a pure delay simply shifts a waveform in time without altering its shape*'.

The same idea is found in [10], where the pure delay timed Boolean functions are defined.

5.12 Remark [13] refers to the pure delays, by considering that '*This model is unrealistic in the sense that practical gates will not transit a pulse caused by two transitions very close together whereas the model guarantees that every transition will be at the output irrespective of the proximity of the successive pulses*'.

5.13 Informal definition The *inertial delays* (or *latency delays*) have generated the most controversies, see also [5], [10]. The next opinions are generally accepted.

a) [12], [13] The inertial delays '*model the fact that the practical circuits will not respond to two transitions which are very close together. The inertial delay model is one in which input transitions are replicated at the output after some period of time unless two transitions occur at the input within some defined period, in which case neither transition is transmitted*'.

b) [11]: '*pulses shorter than or equal to the delay magnitude are not transmitted*', see also Convention 5.3.

c) [7] '*an inertial delay has a threshold period* d. *Pulses of duration less than* d *are filtered out*', compatible with Convention 5.3 again.

5.14 Alternative definition In [1], [14] the authors show intuitively, like above, what inertia is and then two variants of fixed, respectively bounded inertial delays are mentioned. We reproduce only the second variant from [1], called there *non-deterministic inertial delay*, for making the exposure as simple as possible and for the same reason we have changed the language and the notations. $x^0 \in \boldsymbol{B}$ and the real numbers $0 \le d_{\min} \le d_{\max}$ are given and the requests are

i) $\forall t \in [0, d_{\min}), x(t) = x^0$ initialization

ii) $\forall t \ge d_{\min}$, $Dx(t) = 1 \Rightarrow \exists t' \in supp\ Du \wedge [t - d_{\max}, t - d_{\min}]$ such that $x(t) = u(t')\ and\ (t', t) \wedge supp\ Du = \emptyset$

iii) $\forall t \in supp\ Du, (t, t + d_{\max}] \wedge supp\ Du \ne \emptyset\ or\ [t + d_{\min}, t + d_{\max}] \wedge supp\ Dx \ne \emptyset$

5.15 **Remark** In [1] we can find the next observation relative to definition 5.14: '*one could assume that changes should persist for at least* l_1 *time units but propagated after* $l_2, l_2 > l_1$ *time*', in other words one could abandon for the sake of accuracy the 'common form of implementation of the inertial delay model' from Convention 5.3.

5.16 **Alternative definition** We refer now to the approach from [4], where two variants of fixed, respectively of bounded inertial delays are given also, from which we reproduce the second one under the form:

i) $Dx(t) = 1 \Rightarrow \forall \xi \in [t - d_{\min}, t), u(\xi) = x(t)$

ii) $\forall a \in \boldsymbol{B}, ((\forall \xi \in [t, t + d_{\max}), u(\xi) = a) \Rightarrow$

$$\Rightarrow (\exists \tau \in [t, t + d_{\max}), \forall \xi \in [\tau, t + d_{\max}), x(\xi) = a))$$

5.17 **Remark** We make brief comments and a comparison between 5.14 and 5.16:

- terminological differences with our work occur, that the reader is asked to pay not very much attention at his first reading of this text.

- in the second definition, initialization is missing. If we start by definition from null initial conditions, then initialization is not necessary and if we reason for any possible initial value, then initialization is missing too. The possibility that initialization is missing at 5.14 also is given by the value $d_{\min} = 0$.

-5.14 ii) and 5.16 i) essentially express the same idea, the first condition being stronger.

-5.14 iii) is a negligent way of expressing the idea 5.16 ii). This negligence is symptomatic in the sense that in the non-formalized theories that we refer to, it produces no effects (we quote in this context with amusement one of our mentors, professor A. C. Albu from Timisoara that is specialized in the Foundations of Mathematics who called our attention once that '*all the research is made in a non-formalized manner*').

6. Delays

6.1 Stability. Rising and Falling Transmission Delays for Transitions

6.1.1 Definition Let u, x two signals, called *input* (or *control*) and respectively *state* (or *output*). The next property

$$\forall a \in \boldsymbol{B}, (\exists t_1, \forall t \geq t_1, u(t) = a) \Longrightarrow (\exists t_2, \forall t \geq t_2, x(t) = a)$$

is called the *stability condition* (SC). We say that the couple (u, x) satisfies SC.

We also call stability condition the function $Sol_{SC} : S \to P^*(S)$ defined by:

$$Sol_{SC}(u) = \{x \mid (u, x)\ satisfies\ SC\}$$

6.1.2 **Remark** SC states the next cause-effect relation between u and x: if $\lim_{t\to\infty} u(t)$ does not exist, then $Sol_{SC}(u) = S$ and if $\lim_{t\to\infty} u(t)$ exists then, whichever it might be, $\lim_{t\to\infty} x(t)$ exists and $\lim_{t\to\infty} x(t) = \lim_{t\to\infty} u(t)$. On the other hand, the next 'non-anticipative' statement

$$\forall a \in \boldsymbol{B}, (\exists t_1, \forall t \geq t_1, u(t) = a) \Longrightarrow (\exists t_2 \geq t_1, \forall t \geq t_2, x(t) = a)$$

is equivalent with SC.

6.1.3 **Definition** We suppose that (u, x) satisfies SC, that $\lim_{t\to\infty} u(t)$ exists and that $supp\ Du \neq \emptyset$, $supp\ Dx \neq \emptyset$ [3]. We note

$$t_1 = \max\ supp\ Du, t_2 = \max\ supp\ Dx$$

The *transmission delay for transitions* (of x relative to u) is the number $d \geq 0$ given by

$$d = \max(0, t_2 - t_1)$$

If

$$\overline{u(t_1 - 0)} \cdot u(t_1) = \overline{x(t_2 - 0)} \cdot x(t_2) = 1$$

then d is called *rising* and if

$$u(t_1 - 0) \cdot \overline{u(t_1)} = x(t_2 - 0) \cdot \overline{x(t_2)} = 1$$

then it is called *falling*. If $supp\ Du$, respectively $supp\ Dx$ is empty, then t_1, respectively t_2 is by definition 0 and if $\lim_{t\to\infty} u(t)$ does not exist, then d is not defined.

6.2 Delays

6.2.1 **Definition** A *delay condition* (DC) or shortly a *delay* is a function $i : S \to P^*(S)$ with

[3] *supp Dx, supp Dy* are finite, non-empty in this case.

$$\forall u, i(u) \subset Sol_{SC}(u)$$

6.2.2 **Remark** The delays are the models of the delay circuits, i.e. of the circuits that compute the identity 1_B. In practice, we usually work with systems of equations or inequalities in u, x and for each u, $i(u)$ represents the set of solutions of these systems. Definition 6.2.1 asks that such solutions always exist and that the systems be stable.

6.2.3 **Examples** of DC's.

a) $i(u) = \{u\}$ is usually noted with I. More general, the equation $i(u) = \{u \circ \tau^d\}$ defines a DC when $d \geq 0$ (see Theorem 4.1.4 c)) noted with I_d.

b) $i(u) = \{x \mid \exists d \geq 0, x(t) = u(t) \cdot \chi_{[d,\infty)}(t)\}$ and

$$i(u) = \{x \mid \exists d \geq 0, x(t) = \chi_{(-\infty,d)}(t) \oplus u(t) \cdot \chi_{[d,\infty)}(t)\}$$

are DC's.

c) $i(u) = Sol_{SC}(u)$ is a DC called the *unbounded delay*.

6.2.4 Theorem Let $U \subset S$, the DC's i, j and the arbitrary function $\varphi : S \to P^*(S)$.

a) If $\forall u, i(u) \wedge U \neq \varnothing$, then the next equation defines a DC:

$$(i \wedge U)(u) = i(u) \wedge U$$

b) If i, j satisfy $\forall u, i(u) \wedge j(u) \neq \varnothing$, then $i \wedge j$ is a DC defined by:

$$(i \wedge j)(u) = i(u) \wedge j(u)$$

c) Items a), b) are generalized by: if $\forall u, i(u) \wedge \varphi(u) \neq \varnothing$, then $i \wedge \varphi$ is a DC

$$(i \wedge \varphi)(u) = i(u) \wedge \varphi(u)$$

d) The function $i \vee j$ that is defined in the next manner is a DC:

$$(i \vee j)(u) = i(u) \vee j(u)$$

Proof c) The fact that $i \wedge \varphi$ takes values in $P^*(S)$ is assured by the hypothesis $\forall u, i(u) \wedge \varphi(u) \neq \varnothing$. Furthermore, for all u we have

$$(i \wedge \varphi)(u) = i(u) \wedge \varphi(u) \subset i(u) \subset Sol_{SC}(u)$$

6.3 Determinism

6.3.1 **Definition** Let the DC i. If $\forall u, i(u)$ has a single element, then it is called *deterministic* and otherwise it is called *non-deterministic*.

6.3.2 **Remark** By interpreting i as the set of the solutions of a system, its determinism indicates that the solution is unique for all u and this allows identifying a deterministic DC with a function $i : S \to S$. The meaning of the non-deterministic delays consists in the fact that in an electrical circuit to one input u there correspond several possible outputs $x \in i(u)$ depending on the variations in ambient temperature, power supply, on the technology etc.

6.3.3 **Examples** At 6.2.3 I, I_d are deterministic and the other DC's are non-deterministic.

Let $U \subset S$ and the DC's i, j. At 6.2.4 a) and respectively at 6.2.4 b), if i is deterministic then $i \wedge U (= i)$ is deterministic and respectively $i \wedge j (= i)$ is deterministic.

6.3.4 **Theorem** For $0 \le m \le d$, the next functions are deterministic DC's

$$x(t) = \bigcap_{\xi \in [t-d, t-d+m]} u(\xi)$$

$$x(t) = \bigcup_{\xi \in [t-d, t-d+m]} u(\xi)$$

Proof They are signals from Theorem 4.2.3. If $\exists d', \forall t \ge d', u(t) = 0$ and this is equivalent with $u(t) \le \chi_{(-\infty, d')}(t)$ then

$$x(t) = \bigcap_{\xi \in [t-d, t-d+m]} u(\xi) \le \bigcap_{\xi \in [t-d, t-d+m]} \chi_{(-\infty, d')}(\xi) = \chi_{(-\infty, d+d'-m)}(t)$$

i.e. $\forall t \ge d + d' - m, x(t) = 0$. Similarly, if $\exists d', \forall t \ge d', u(t) = 1$ and this is equivalent with $u(t) \ge \chi_{[d', \infty)}(t)$, then

$$x(t) = \bigcap_{\xi \in [t-d, t-d+m]} u(\xi) \ge \bigcap_{\xi \in [t-d, t-d+m]} \chi_{[d', \infty)}(\xi) = \chi_{[d+d', \infty)}(t)$$

in other words $\forall t \ge d + d', x(t) = 1$. We have shown that $x \in Sol_{SC}(u)$.

The proof for $x(t) = \bigcup_{\xi \in [t-d, t-d+m]} u(\xi)$ is dual.

6.4 Order

6.4.1 **Definition** For the DC's i, j we define $i \subset j$ by

$$\forall u, i(u) \subset j(u)$$

6.4.2 **Remarks** The inclusion $\subset$ defines an order –that is not total- in the set of the DC's. Sol_{SC} is the unit of this ordered set: any DC i satisfies $i \subseteq Sol_{SC}$.

We interpret the inclusion $i \subset j$ by the fact that the first system contains more restrictive conditions than the second and modeling in the first case is more precise than in the second case. In particular, a deterministic DC i contains the maximal information and the DC Sol_{SC} contains the minimal information about the modeled delay circuit.

6.4.3 **Theorem** Any DC j includes a deterministic DC i.

Proof For any u, the axiom of choice allows choosing from the set $j(u)$ a point x and we define $i(u) = \{x\}$. $i(u)$ is non-empty and satisfies $i(u) \subset j(u) \subset Sol_{SC}(u)$, in other words i is a deterministic DC.

6.4.4 **Corollary** In the inclusion $i \subset j$ of DC's, if j is deterministic, then $i = j$.

Proof In the previous proof, the only possibility of choosing i is

$$\forall u, i(u) = j(u)$$

6.4.5 **Examples** Let $U \subset S$ and the DC's i, j. If $\forall u, i(u) \wedge U \neq \emptyset$, then $i \wedge U \subset i$ and if $\forall u, i(u) \wedge j(u) \neq \emptyset$, then $i \wedge j \subset i \subset i \vee j$.

6.5 Time Invariance

6.5.1 **Definition** The DC i is called *time invariant* if

$$\forall u, \forall x, \forall d \in \boldsymbol{R}, (u \circ \tau^d \in S \; and \; x \in i(u)) \Rightarrow (x \circ \tau^d \in S \; and \; x \circ \tau^d \in i(u \circ \tau^d))$$

and if the previous property is not true, then i is called *time variable.*

6.5.2 **Remarks** We mention also a weaker version of time invariance, that we shall not use:

$$\forall u, \forall x, \forall d \in \boldsymbol{R}, (u \circ \tau^d \in S \; and \; x \in i(u) \; and \; x \circ \tau^d \in S) \Rightarrow (x \circ \tau^d \in i(u \circ \tau^d))$$

Let us suppose now that the signals $f : \boldsymbol{R} \to \boldsymbol{B}$ would have been defined more generally by any of the next equivalent conditions, see Theorem 4.1.3:

a) f is differentiable, right continuous and $\exists t_0, supp\ Df \subset [t_0, \infty)$

b) the unbounded family $t_0 < t_1 < t_2 < ...$ exists so that

$$f(t) = f(t_0 - 0) \cdot \chi_{(-\infty, t_0)}(t) \oplus f(t_0) \cdot \chi_{[t_0, t_1)}(t) \oplus f(t_1) \cdot \chi_{[t_1, t_2)}(t) \oplus ...$$

i.e. we relax the condition $supp\ Df \subset [0, \infty)$ at a) and respectively we omit the condition $0 \leq t_0$ at b). We keep the conditions of lower boundness of $supp\ Df$ and respectively of (t_n), that both mean the existence of *some* initial time instant t_0 and let us note with $\widetilde{S}$ the set of these signals. Obviously $S \subset \widetilde{S}$. In such conditions, a time invariant DC $\widetilde{i}$ is a function $\widetilde{i} : \widetilde{S} \to P^*(\widetilde{S})$ ($P^*(\widetilde{S}) = \{A \mid A \subset \widetilde{S}, A \neq \emptyset\}$) satisfying

i) $\forall u \in \widetilde{S}, \forall x \in \widetilde{i}(u), \forall a \in \boldsymbol{B}, (\exists t_1, \forall t \geq t_1, u(t) = a) \Rightarrow (\exists t_2, \forall t \geq t_2, x(t) = a)$

ii) $\forall u \in S, \forall x \in S, \forall d \in \boldsymbol{R},$

$$(u \circ \tau^d \in S \; and \; x \in \widetilde{i}(u)) \Rightarrow (x \circ \tau^d \in S \; and \; x \circ \tau^d \in \widetilde{i}(u \circ \tau^d))$$

i.e. ii) reproduces 6.5.1 written with S not with $\widetilde{S}$. We note with $i = \widetilde{i}_{|S}$ the restriction of $\widetilde{i}$ at S. We have the next

6.5.3 **Theorem**

a) $\forall u \in S, \widetilde{i}(u) \subset S$

b) i is a time invariant DC

Proof a) We suppose against all reason the existence of some $u \in S$ and $x \in \widetilde{i}(u)$ so that $x \notin S$, thus $supp\ Dx \neq \emptyset$ and $t_0 = \min supp\ Dx$ satisfies $t_0 < 0$. Then for any $d \in (t_0, 0)$ we have that $u \circ \tau^{-d} \in S$ and $x \in \widetilde{i}(u)$ are both true, but $x \circ \tau^{-d} \in S$ is false because, see also the proof of Theorem 4.1.4 c)

$$\min supp\ D(x \circ \tau^{-d}) = -d + \min supp\ Dx = -d + t_0 < 0$$

This is in contradiction with the fact that $\widetilde{i}$ satisfies the time invariance condition 6.5.2 ii).

b) We take into account a). The three properties that must be fulfilled, i.e. the fact that $\forall u \in S, i(u) \neq \emptyset$, that $\forall u \in S, i(u) \subset Sol_{SC}(u)$ and the condition of time invariance 6.5.1 are satisfied by i because they are satisfied by $\widetilde{i}$.

6.5.4 **Remark** If we try to replace 6.5.2 ii) with 6.5.1 written with $\widetilde{S}$ instead of S, then this time invariance condition becomes, see also Theorem 6.5.6 for something similar:

$$\forall u \in \widetilde{S}, \forall x \in \widetilde{S}, \forall d \in \mathbf{R}, x \in \widetilde{i}(u) \Rightarrow x \circ \tau^d \in \widetilde{i}(u \circ \tau^d)$$

The property is reasonable and it constitutes an alternative definition of time invariance for the DC's $\widetilde{i} : \widetilde{S} \to P^*(\widetilde{S})$, but it is too weak to produce the validity of the statement 6.5.3 a).

On the other hand, all the important delay conditions that we are interested in are time invariant. Theorem 6.5.3 allows choosing for them the initial time instant be 0 and this was already anticipated by Definition 4.1.1. We shall always use from this moment S in our work, not $\widetilde{S}$.

6.5.5 **Examples**

a) We show that I_d is time invariant, where $d \geq 0$: for $d' \in \mathbf{R}$ arbitrary, $u \circ \tau^{d'} \in S$ and $x \in I_d(u)$, i.e. $x = u \circ \tau^d$ imply

$$x \circ \tau^{d'} = (u \circ \tau^d) \circ \tau^{d'} = u \circ \tau^{d+d'} = (u \circ \tau^{d'}) \circ \tau^d \in S$$

from Theorem 4.1.4 c), resulting the fact that $x \circ \tau^{d'} \in I_d(u \circ \tau^{d'})$ too.

b) We show that Sol_{SC} is time variable and we give the next counterexample. For $u = 1, d = -1$ and $x = \chi_{[0,\infty)}$, the prerequisites of 6.5.1 is fulfilled under the form $1 = 1 \circ \tau^{-1} \in S$ and $\chi_{[0,\infty)} \in Sol_{SC}(1)$, but the conclusion is false, since $\chi_{[0,\infty)} \circ \tau^{-1} = \chi_{[-1,\infty)} \notin S$.

c) Let the time invariant DC's i, j. Then $i \vee j$ is time invariant and if $\forall u, i(u) \wedge j(u) \neq \emptyset$, then $i \wedge j$ is time invariant too.

6.5.6 **Theorem** Let i a time invariant DC. We have the next equivalence:

$$\forall u, \forall x, \forall d \geq 0, x \in i(u) \Leftrightarrow x \circ \tau^d \in i(u \circ \tau^d)$$

Proof $\Rightarrow$ $u \circ \tau^d \in S$ and $x \in i(u)$ are both true, taking into account Theorem 4.1.4 c). We apply the time invariance of i.

$\Leftarrow$ $(u \circ \tau^d) \circ \tau^{-d} \in S$ and $x \circ \tau^d \in i(u \circ \tau^d)$ are true. By using 6.5.1 we get $(x \circ \tau^d) \circ \tau^{-d} \in i((u \circ \tau^d) \circ \tau^{-d})$.

6.6 Constancy

6.6.1 **Definition** A DC i is called *constant*, if $d_r \geq 0, d_f \geq 0$ exist so that for any u and any $x \in i(u)$ we have

$$\overline{x(t-0)} \cdot x(t) \leq u(t - d_r) \tag{1}$$

$$x(t-0) \cdot \overline{x(t)} \leq \overline{u(t - d_f)} \tag{2}$$

If the previous property is not satisfied then i is called *non-constant*.

6.6.2 **Examples**

a) I_d is constant, $d \geq 0$ because from $x(t) = u(t-d)$ we infer

$$\overline{x(t-0)} \cdot x(t) = \overline{u(t-d-0)} \cdot u(t-d) \leq u(t-d)$$

$$x(t-0) \cdot \overline{x(t)} = u(t-d-0) \cdot \overline{u(t-d)} \leq \overline{u(t-d)}$$

b) Let $U \subset S$ and the DE's i, j from which i is constant. If defined, $i \wedge U$ and $i \wedge j$ are constant and in general a DC included in a constant DC is constant. If j is constant, then the property $\forall u, i(u) \wedge j(u) = \varnothing$ makes $i \vee j$ be not constant in general due to the possibility $d_r^i \neq d_r^j$, respectively $d_f^i \neq d_f^j$, but if $\exists u, i(u) \wedge j(u) \neq \varnothing$, then d_r, d_f uniquely exist so that $\forall x \in i(u) \wedge j(u)$ 6.6.1 (1), 6.6.1 (2) are fulfilled and in such circumstances $i \vee j$ is constant.

6.6.3 **Theorem** The deterministic DC's (see Theorem 6.3.4) defined by the next equations

$$x(t) = \bigcap_{\xi \in [t-d, t-d+m]} u(\xi) \tag{1}$$

$$x(t) = \bigcup_{\xi \in [t-d, t-d+m]} u(\xi) \tag{2}$$

where $0 \leq m \leq d$ are time invariant and constant.

Proof We give the proof for (1) and the proof for (2) is similar.

The time invariance Let $d' \in \boldsymbol{R}$ arbitrary so that $u \circ \tau^{d'} \in S$. Then

$$(x \circ \tau^{d'})(t) = x(t-d') = \bigcap_{\xi \in [t-d-d', t-d-d'+m]} u(\xi) = \bigcap_{\xi + d' \in [t-d, t-d+m]} u(\xi) =$$

$$= \bigcap_{\xi \in [t-d, t-d+m]} u(\xi - d') = \bigcap_{\xi \in [t-d, t-d+m]} (u \circ \tau^{d'})(\xi) \tag{3}$$

shows that $x \circ \tau^{d'} \in S$ and $x \circ \tau^{d'} \in i(u \circ \tau^{d'})$, i.e. i defined by (1) is time invariant.

The constancy From 4.2.2 we get

$$\overline{x(t-0)} \cdot x(t) = \overline{u(t-d-0)} \cdot \bigcap_{\xi \in [t-d, t-d+m]} u(\xi) \leq u(t-d)$$

$$x(t-0) \cdot \overline{x(t)} = u(t-d-0) \cdot \bigcap_{\xi \in [t-d, t-d+m)} u(\xi) \cdot \overline{u(t-d+m)} \leq \overline{u(t-d+m)}$$

6.6.4 **Remark** Constancy means that x is allowed to switch only if u has anticipated that possibility d_r, respectively d_f time units before. It does not imply the uniqueness of d_r, d_f and at 6.6.3 (1) we have an example when d_r is not unique.

6.7 Rising-Falling Symmetry

6.7.1 **Definition** The DC i is called (*rising-falling*) *symmetrical* if one of the next equivalent properties is true:

a) $\forall u, i(\overline{u}) = \{\overline{x} \mid x \in i(u)\}$

b) $\forall u, \forall x, x \in i(u) \Leftrightarrow \overline{x} \in i(\overline{u})$

and respectively (*rising-falling*) *asymmetrical* otherwise.

6.7.2 **Examples**

a) I_d with $d \geq 0$ arbitrary is symmetrical because

$$\overline{x} \in I_d(\overline{u}) \Leftrightarrow \overline{x(t)} = \overline{u(t-d)} \Leftrightarrow x(t) = u(t-d) \Leftrightarrow x \in I_d(u)$$

is true for all u and all x.

b) Sol_{SC} is symmetrical also and let for this an arbitrary u. If $\lim_{t\to\infty} u(t)$ does not exist, then $\lim_{t\to\infty} \overline{u(t)}$ does not exist and

$$Sol_{SC}(\overline{u}) = Sol_{SC}(u) = S$$

from where we infer the desired property. Let us suppose now that $\lim_{t\to\infty} u(t)$ exists, thus $\lim_{t\to\infty} \overline{u(t)}$ exists and we note with $c, \overline{c} \in \boldsymbol{B}$ these limits. We take an $x \in Sol_{SC}(u)$ and we have the existence of $d \geq 0$ with $x(t) = x(t) \cdot \chi_{(-\infty,d)}(t) \oplus c \cdot \chi_{[d,\infty)}(t)$. Because $\overline{x(t)} \cdot \chi_{(-\infty,d)}(t) \oplus \overline{c} \cdot \chi_{[d,\infty)}(t) \in Sol_{SC}(\overline{u})$, we infer $\overline{x} \in Sol_{SC}(\overline{u})$ resulting that $x \in Sol_{SC}(u) \Rightarrow \overline{x} \in Sol_{SC}(\overline{u})$. The inverse implication is similarly proved.

c) The DC's defined at 6.2.3 b) are asymmetrical. We suppose for the first of them that $x \in i(u)$, i.e. $d \geq 0$ exists so that $x(t) = u(t) \cdot \chi_{[d,\infty)}(t)$. Because $\overline{x(t)} = \chi_{(-\infty,d)}(t) \oplus \overline{u(t)} \cdot \chi_{[d,\infty)}(t) \notin i(\overline{u})$, we infer that the symmetry is not fulfilled.

d) Let $U \subset S$ with $x \in U \Rightarrow \overline{x} \in U$ and i, j symmetrical DC's. Then $i \vee j$ is symmetrical and, when defined, the DC's $i \wedge U$ and $i \wedge j$ are symmetrical too.

6.8 Serial Connection

6.8.1 **Definition** For the DC's i, j we note with $k = i \circ j$ the function $k : S \to P^*(S)$ defined in the next way

$$k(u) = \{y \mid \exists x, x \in j(u) \; and \; y \in i(x)\}$$

k is called the *serial connection* of the DC's i and j.

6.8.2 **Theorem** (*the compatibility between the serial connection and consistency, stability, determinism, time invariance and symmetry*)

a) k is a DC.

b) If i, j are deterministic, then k is deterministic.

c) If i, j are time invariant, then k is time invariant.

d) If i, j are symmetrical, then k is symmetrical.

Proof

a) Let u arbitrary for which $j(u)\neq\emptyset$ shows that $x\in j(u)$ exists and $i(x)\neq\emptyset$ shows that $y\in i(x)$ exists, thus $y\in k(u)$ exists. On the other hand, if $\lim\limits_{t\to\infty}u(t)$ exists, then $\lim\limits_{t\to\infty}x(t)$ exists and $\lim\limits_{t\to\infty}y(t)$ exists also and the three limits are equal.

b) The determinism of k is equivalent with the fact that the composition of the $S\to S$ functions (see Remark 6.3.2) is a $S\to S$ function.

c) We must show that for any $u,y\in S,d\in \mathbf{R}$ we have the implication

$$(u\circ\tau^d\in S\ and\ y\in k(u))\Rightarrow(y\circ\tau^d\in S\ and\ y\circ\tau^d\in k(u\circ\tau^d))$$

true. If $y\in k(u)$, let $x\in S$ whose existence is guaranteed by the definition of k so that $x\in j(u)$ and $y\in i(x)$. By applying 6.5.1 to j, because $u\circ\tau^d\in S$, we have that $x\circ\tau^d\in S$ and $x\circ\tau^d\in j(u\circ\tau^d)$. We apply again 6.5.1 to i and we obtain $y\circ\tau^d\in S$ and $y\circ\tau^d\in i(x\circ\tau^d)$. Thus $y\circ\tau^d\in k(u\circ\tau^d)$.

d) $\overline{y}\in k(\overline{u})\Leftrightarrow\exists\overline{x},\overline{x}\in j(\overline{u})\ and\ \overline{y}\in i(\overline{x})\Leftrightarrow\exists x,x\in j(u)\ and\ y\in i(x)\Leftrightarrow y\in k(u)$

6.8.3 **Counterexample** showing that the serial connection k of the constant DC's i,j is not necessarily constant and we consider for this the DC defined by

$$i(u)=Sol_{SC}(u)\wedge\{x\mid\overline{x(t-0)}\cdot x(t)\le u(t-d_r)\ and\ x(t-0)\cdot\overline{x(t)}\le\overline{u(t-d_f)}\}$$

where $d_r\ge 0,d_f\ge 0$. i is obviously constant.

Let $u=\chi_{[\tau,\infty)}$ for which $1\in i(u)$ and $\chi_{[d,\infty)}\in i(1)$ take place for any $\tau\ge 0$ and any $d\ge 0$. In order that $k=i\circ i$ be constant, $d_r^{''}\ge 0$ must exist so that for any $u=\chi_{[\tau,\infty)}$, the signal $y=\chi_{[d,\infty)}$ should satisfy

$$\chi_{\{d\}}(t)=\overline{y(t-0)}\cdot y(t)\le u(t-d_r^{''})=\chi_{[d_r^{''}+\tau,\infty)}(t) \qquad (1)$$

Let such a $d_r^{''}$ fixed; by choosing d and τ so that $d<d_r^{''}+\tau$ be true, (1) is false. k is not constant.

6.8.4 **Remark** The set of the DC's is a non-commutative semi-group relative to the serial connection having the unit I:

$$i\circ I=I\circ i=i$$

Three of its important sub-semi-groups are represented by the deterministic, the time invariant and respectively the symmetrical DC's.

6.8.5 **Theorem** (*the compatibility between the serial connection and the order*) Let the DC's i,j,k. The next implications are true:

$$i\subset j\Rightarrow i\circ k\subset j\circ k$$
$$j\subset k\Rightarrow i\circ j\subset i\circ k$$

Proof Let u and $y\in(i\circ k)(u)$, meaning that some x exists with $x\in k(u)$ and $y\in i(x)$; because $y\in j(x)$, we obtain $y\in(j\circ k)(u)$.

On the other hand, if we suppose that $y\in(i\circ j)(u)$, then x exists so that $x\in j(u)$ and $y\in i(x)$. We get $x\in k(u)$ implying $y\in(i\circ k)(u)$.

6.8.6 **Theorem** (*the compatibility between the serial connection and* $\wedge,\vee$) Let $U \subset S$ and the DC's i, j, k .

a) If $\forall u, i(u) \wedge U \neq \emptyset$, then $\forall u, (i \circ j)(u) \wedge U \neq \emptyset$ and

$$(i \wedge U) \circ j = (i \circ j) \wedge U$$

If $\forall u, j(u) \wedge U \neq \emptyset$, then we have

$$i \circ (j \wedge U) \subset i \circ j$$

b) If $\forall u, i(u) \wedge j(u) \neq \emptyset$, then $\forall u, (i \circ k)(u) \wedge (j \circ k)(u) \neq \emptyset$ and

$$(i \wedge j) \circ k \subset (i \circ k) \wedge (j \circ k)$$

If $\forall u, j(u) \wedge k(u) \neq \emptyset$, then $\forall u, (i \circ j)(u) \wedge (i \circ k)(u) \neq \emptyset$ and

$$i \circ (j \wedge k) \subset (i \circ j) \wedge (i \circ k)$$

c) We have

$$(i \vee j) \circ k = (i \circ k) \vee (j \circ k)$$

$$i \circ (j \vee k) = (i \circ j) \vee (i \circ k)$$

Proof

a) $\forall u, ((i \wedge U) \circ j)(u) = \{y \mid \exists x, y \in i(x) \text{ and } y \in U \text{ and } x \in j(u)\} = ((i \circ j) \wedge U)(u)$

$\forall u, (i \circ (j \wedge U))(u) = \{y \mid \exists x, y \in i(x) \text{ and } x \in j(u) \text{ and } x \in U\} \subset$

$\subset \{y \mid \exists x, y \in i(x) \text{ and } x \in j(u)\} = (i \circ j)(u)$

b) $\forall u, ((i \wedge j) \circ k)(u) = \{y \mid \exists x, y \in i(x) \text{ and } y \in j(x) \text{ and } x \in k(u)\} \subset$

$\subset \{y \mid \exists x, \exists x', y \in i(x) \text{ and } x \in k(u) \text{ and } y \in j(x') \text{ and } x' \in k(u)\} = ((i \circ k) \wedge (j \circ k))(u)$

$\forall u, (i \circ (j \wedge k))(u) = \{y \mid \exists x, y \in i(x) \text{ and } x \in j(u) \text{ and } x \in k(u)\} \subset$

$\subset \{y \mid \exists x, \exists x', y \in i(x) \text{ and } x \in j(u) \text{ and } y \in i(x') \text{ and } x' \in k(u)\} = ((i \circ j) \wedge (i \circ k))(u)$

c) $\forall u, ((i \vee j) \circ k)(u) = \{y \mid \exists x, (y \in i(x) \text{ or } y \in j(x)) \text{ and } x \in k(u)\} =$

$= \{y \mid \exists x, (y \in i(x) \text{ and } x \in k(u)) \text{ or } (y \in j(x) \text{ and } x \in k(u))\} = ((i \circ k) \vee (j \circ k))(u)$

$\forall u, (i \circ (j \vee k))(u) = \{y \mid \exists x, y \in i(x) \text{ and } (x \in j(u) \text{ or } x \in k(u))\} =$

$= \{y \mid \exists x, (y \in i(x) \text{ and } x \in j(u)) \text{ or } (y \in i(x) \text{ and } x \in k(u))\} = ((i \circ j) \vee (i \circ k))(u)$

7. Bounded Delays

7.1 The Consistency Condition

7.1.1 Theorem Let $0 \le m_r \le d_r, 0 \le m_f \le d_f$ be given. The following statements are equivalent:

a) $$\forall u \in S, \quad \bigcap_{\xi \in [t-d_r, t-d_r+m_r]} u(\xi) \le \bigcup_{\xi \in [t-d_f, t-d_f+m_f]} u(\xi)$$

7.2.3 Theorem

a) The next system

$$\bigcap_{\xi\in[t-d_{r,\max},t-d_{f,\min}]} u(\xi) \le x(t) \le \bigcup_{\xi\in[t-d_{f,\max},t-d_{r,\min}]} u(\xi) \quad (1)$$

where $u,x\in S$, $0\le d_{r,\min}\le d_{r,\max}$, $0\le d_{f,\min}\le d_{f,\max}$ defines a DC if and only if

$$d_{r,\min}\le d_{f,\max} \quad (2)$$

$$d_{f,\min}\le d_{r,\max} \quad (3)$$

b) When (2), (3) are fulfilled, the system (1) and BDC from 7.2.1 (1) are equivalent, in the sense that by a suitable choice of the parameters $m_r, d_r, m_f, d_f, d_{r,\min}, d_{r,\max}$, $d_{f,\min}, d_{f,\max}$ their solutions coincide for all u.

Proof a) <u>If</u> (2), (3) show that the sets $[t-d_{r,\max},t-d_{f,\min}]$, $[t-d_{f,\max},t-d_{r,\min}]$ are non-empty and the inequalities $0\le d_{r,\min}\le d_{r,\max}$, $0\le d_{f,\min}\le d_{f,\max}$ show that the meet $[t-d_{r,\max},t-d_{f,\min}]\wedge[t-d_{f,\max},t-d_{r,\min}]$ is non-empty because

$$t-d_{f,\max}\le t-d_{f,\min} \textit{ and } t-d_{r,\max}\le t-d_{r,\min}$$

thus (1) has a solution for any u, similarly with the proof of 7.1.1. It is shown that for any u and any solution x of (1) we have $x\in Sol_{SC}(u)$.

<u>Only if</u> If $d_{r,\min}>d_{f,\max}$ then $[t-d_{f,\max},t-d_{r,\min}]=\varnothing$ shows that $\forall t, x(t)=0$ in (1) implying the existence of some u so that (1) has no solutions. Similarly for $d_{f,\min}>d_{r,\max}$.

b) We define

$$d_r = d_{r,\max} \quad (4)$$

$$d_f = d_{f,\max} \quad (5)$$

$$m_r = d_{r,\max} - d_{f,\min} \quad (6)$$

$$m_f = d_{f,\max} - d_{r,\min} \quad (7)$$

7.2.4 Theorem (*the property of compatibility between the initial values of the input and of the output for BDC*) If $x\in Sol_{BDC}^{m_r,d_r,m_f,d_f}(u)$, then $x(0-0)=u(0-0)$.

Proof $u(0-0)=0$ is equivalent with $u(t)\le\chi_{[0,\infty)}(t)$. We have in this case

$$x(t)\le \bigcup_{\xi\in[t-d_f,t-d_f+m_f]} u(\xi) \le \bigcup_{\xi\in[t-d_f,t-d_f+m_f]} \chi_{[0,\infty)}(\xi) = \chi_{[d_f-m_f,\infty)}(t)\le\chi_{[0,\infty)}(t)$$

i.e. $x(0-0)=0$.

$u(0-0)=1$ is equivalent with $u(t)\ge\chi_{(-\infty,0)}(t)$ and we have

$$x(t) \geq \bigcap_{\xi \in [t-d_r, t-d_r+m_r]} u(\xi) \geq \bigcap_{\xi \in [t-d_r, t-d_r+m_r]} \chi_{(-\infty,0)}(\xi) = \chi_{(-\infty,d_r-m_r)}(t) \geq \chi_{(-\infty,0)}(t)$$

i.e. $x(0-0) = 1$.

7.2.5 Theorem $Sol_{BDC}^{m_r,d_r,m_f,d_f}(c) = \{c\}, \forall c \in \boldsymbol{B}$.

Proof If $\forall t, u(t) = c$, then $\forall t, \bigcap_{\xi \in [t-d_r, t-d_r+m_r]} u(\xi) = \bigcup_{\xi \in [t-d_f, t-d_f+m_f]} u(\xi) = c$.

7.2.6 Remark We analyze BDC in the hypothesis that $m_r > 0$ in the following manner.

a) $x(0-0) = 0$ and $u(t) = \chi_{[0,\tau)}(t)$, with $0 < \tau \leq m_r$, i.e. we apply at the input a '*short*', '*insufficiently persistent*' 1-pulse. The situation is the one from the next figure, where we remark that $\bigcap_{\xi \in [t-d_r, t-d_r+m_r]} u(\xi)$ is identically null.

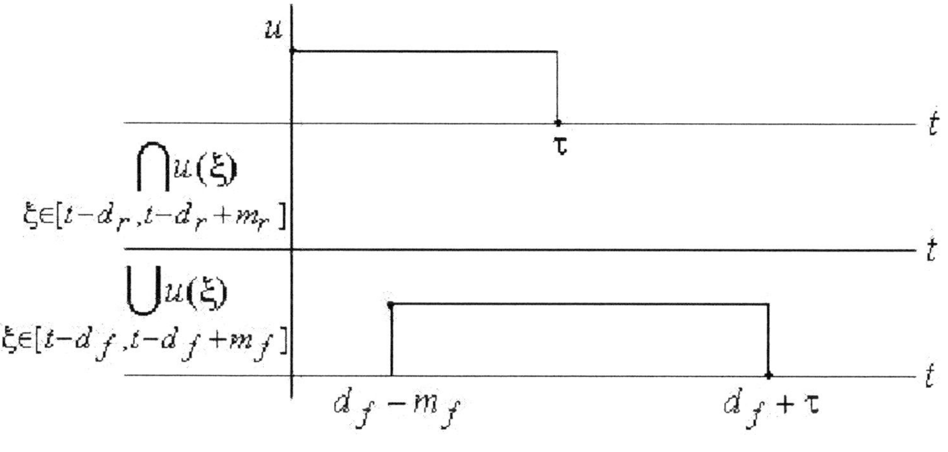

Fig 9

$$x(t) = x(t) \cdot \chi_{[d_f-m_f, d_f+\tau)}(t)$$

$t \in (-\infty, d_f - m_f)$; $x(t) = 0$ necessarily, the pulse from the input did not alter the output, that keeps the initial value

$t \in [d_f - m_f, d_f + \tau)$; $x(t) = 0$ or $x(t) = 1$, 0 and 1 are both possible values of the output, that could be altered by the pulse from the input

$t \in [d_f + \tau, \infty)$; $x(t) = 0$ necessarily, the value 1 from the input cannot alter the output any longer

We observe that the 1-pulses of length shorter than or equal to m_r (the dual situation is true also) at the input are not necessarily transmitted to the output, thus BDC includes the special case when such pulses are surely not transmitted. The last property strengthens the inertial character of

BDC.

b) $x(0-0)=0$ and $u(t)=\chi_{[0,\tau)}(t)$, with $\tau > m_r$, in other words a '*long*', '*persistent*' 1-pulse is applied at the input. This corresponds to the drawing in Fig 10, where $\bigcap_{\xi\in[t-d_r,t-d_r+m_r]} u(\xi)$ is not null:

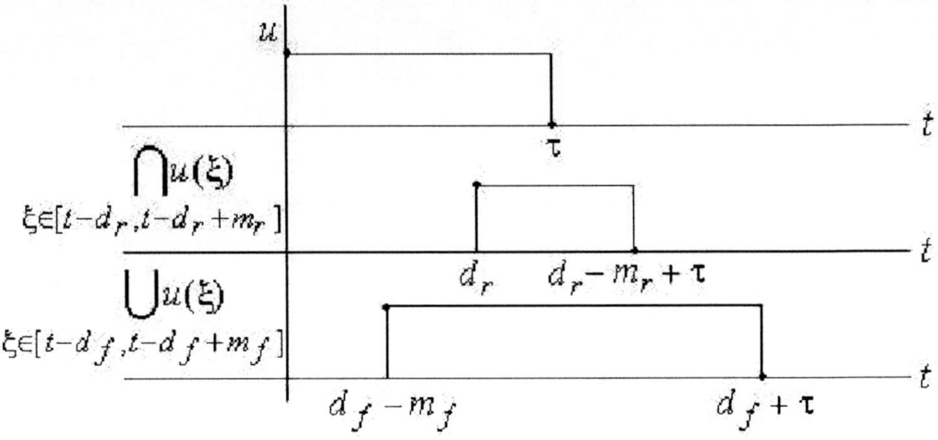

Fig 10

$$x(t)=x(t)\cdot\chi_{[d_f-m_f,d_r)}(t)\oplus\chi_{[d_r,d_r-m_r+\tau)}(t)\oplus x(t)\cdot\chi_{[d_r-m_r+\tau,d_f+\tau)}(t)$$

$t\in(-\infty,d_f-m_f)$; $x(t)=0$ necessarily, the input pulse did not alter the output

$t\in[d_f-m_f,d_r)$; $x(t)=0$ or $x(t)=1$, 0 and 1 are possible values of the output, that could be altered by the input pulse

$t\in[d_r,d_r-m_r+\tau)$; $x(t)=1$ necessarily, the persistent input pulse has propagated to the output

$t\in[d_r-m_r+\tau,d_f+\tau)$; $x(t)=0$ or $x(t)=1$, 0 and 1 are possible values of x, that could still be influenced by the input pulse

$t\in[d_f+\tau,\infty)$; $x(t)=0$ necessarily, the state of balance=stability when x depends only on the value $\lim_{t\to\infty} u(t)=0$ and not on the input pulse.

We conclude that if u is 1 for strictly more than m_r time units, then x becomes 1 with a delay of $d\in[d_f-m_f,d_r]$ time units and, in a dual manner, that if u is 0 for strictly more than m_f time units then x becomes 0 with a delay of $d\in[d_r-m_r,d_f]$ time units. Fig 10 best shows why $d_f-m_f=d_{r,\min}$ and $d_r=d_{r,\max}$, see 7.2.3 (4),..., 7.2.3 (7), were previously called the rising lower bound and upper bound of the delays, together with the dual taxonomy.

This analysis has shown, by the use of the words *possible* and *necessary* that was made on purpose, the existence of interference not only with temporal logic –this was obvious from the very beginning- but also with modal logic. The idea is natural to all these authors that consider temporal logic be a '*modal logic aiming to express time dependent processes*', together with Mihaela Malita and Mircea Malita ('*The Foundations of Artificial Intelligence, 1 Propositional Logics*', ed. Tehnica, Bucuresti, 1987, in Romanian).

Two interpretations of BDC exist, that we shall call the positive and the negative interpretation.

The *positive interpretation* of BDC is the following: it is natural that the value of the output be arbitrary when the input is not sufficiently persistent (in the previous case a) for $t \in [d_f - m_f, d_f + \tau)$ and in the previous case b), for $t \in [d_f - m_f, d_r) \vee [d_r - m_r + \tau, d_f + \tau)$). This fact could also be modeled by the replacement of the set $\{0,1\}$ with $\{0, \frac{1}{2}, 1\}$ -some authors do so- but this has algebraical disadvantages, because the set $\{0, \frac{1}{2}, 1\}$ is poorer algebraically than $\{0,1\}$. Non-determinism is another way (ours!) of solving this problem.

The *negative interpretation* of BDC: it is not natural that at some time moment t_1 we should have $x(t_1 - 0) \cdot \overline{x(t_1)} = 1$, while $\forall t \le t_1, u(t-0) \cdot \overline{u(t)} = 0$ in the sense that x switches in a manner that is not compatible with the (more or less) (left) local behavior of u.

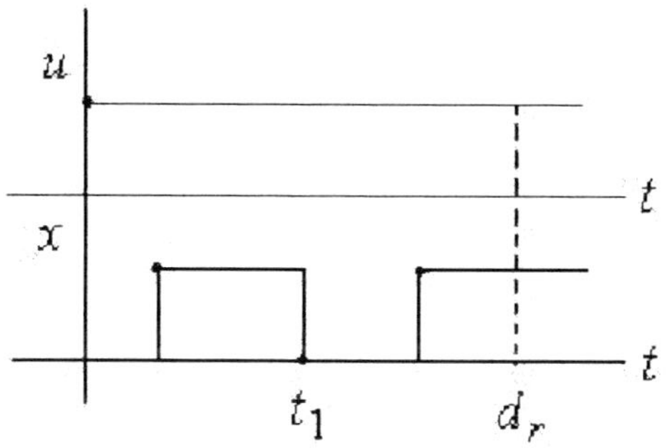

Fig 11

In other words, pulses on the output may exist that do not reproduce the pulses on the input.

7.3 The Properties of the Bounded Delays

7.3.1 Theorem (*The representation of the solutions of BDC*). Let $u, x \in S$ and the numbers $0 \le m_r \le d_r, 0 \le m_f \le d_f$ so that CC_{BDC} is fulfilled. The following statements are equivalent:

a) $$x \in Sol_{BDC}^{m_r, d_r, m_f, d_f}(u)$$

b) $\exists y \in S$ so that x satisfies

$$x(t) = \bigcap_{\xi \in [t-d_r, t-d_r+m_r]} u(\xi) \cup y(t) \cdot \bigcup_{\xi \in [t-d_f, t-d_f+m_f]} u(\xi)$$

Proof We can take $y(t) = x(t)$.

7.3.2 Remark Let $0 \leq m_r \leq d_r, 0 \leq m_f \leq d_f$ and $0 \leq m_r^{'} \leq d_r^{'}, 0 \leq m_f^{'} \leq d_f^{'}$ so that CC$_{BDC}$ is fulfilled twice: $d_r \geq d_f - m_f, d_f \geq d_r - m_r$, respectively $d_r^{'} \geq d_f^{'} - m_f^{'}, d_f^{'} \geq d_r^{'} - m_r^{'}$. The next statements are equivalent:

a) $\forall u, Sol_{BDC}^{m_r, d_r, m_f, d_f}(u) \wedge Sol_{BDC}^{m_r^{'}, d_r^{'}, m_f^{'}, d_f^{'}}(u) \neq \emptyset$

b) $d_r^{'} \geq d_f - m_f, d_f^{'} \geq d_r - m_r, d_r \geq d_f^{'} - m_f^{'}, d_f \geq d_r^{'} - m_r^{'}$

and if one of them is satisfied, then $Sol_{BDC}^{m_r, d_r, m_f, d_f} \wedge Sol_{BDC}^{m_r^{'}, d_r^{'}, m_f^{'}, d_f^{'}}$ exists under the form

$$\bigcap_{\xi \in [t-d_r, t-d_r+m_r]} u(\xi) \cup \bigcap_{\xi \in [t-d_r^{'}, t-d_r^{'}+m_r^{'}]} u(\xi) \leq x(t) \leq \bigcup_{\xi \in [t-d_f, t-d_f+m_f]} u(\xi) \cdot \bigcup_{\xi \in [t-d_f^{'}, t-d_f^{'}+m_f^{'}]} u(\xi)$$

but it is not a BDC. On the other hand $Sol_{BDC}^{m_r, d_r, m_f, d_f} \vee Sol_{BDC}^{m_r^{'}, d_r^{'}, m_f^{'}, d_f^{'}}$ exists without other consistency requirements than those represented by the validity of the two CC$_{BDC}$'s and it is not a BDC either:

$$\bigcap_{\xi \in [t-d_r, t-d_r+m_r]} u(\xi) \cdot \bigcap_{\xi \in [t-d_r^{'}, t-d_r^{'}+m_r^{'}]} u(\xi) \leq x(t) \leq \bigcup_{\xi \in [t-d_f, t-d_f+m_f]} u(\xi) \cup \bigcup_{\xi \in [t-d_f^{'}, t-d_f^{'}+m_f^{'}]} u(\xi)$$

7.3.3 Theorem Let $0 \leq m_r \leq d_r, 0 \leq m_f \leq d_f$ so that CC$_{BDC}$ is true. The next statements are equivalent:

a) $Sol_{BDC}^{m_r, d_r, m_f, d_f}$ is deterministic

b) the upper bounds and the lower bounds of the delays coincide

$$d_r = d_f - m_f, d_f = d_r - m_r$$

c) the memories are null

$$m_r = m_f = 0$$

d) the bounded delay degenerates in a translation

$$\exists d \geq 0, Sol_{BDC}^{m_r, d_r, m_f, d_f} = I_d$$

Proof $a) \Rightarrow b)$ The hypothesis states that $Sol_{BDC}^{m_r, d_r, m_f, d_f}$ has exactly one element, i.e.

$$\forall u, \quad \bigcap_{\xi\in[t-d_r,t-d_r+m_r]} u(\xi) = \bigcup_{\xi\in[t-d_f,t-d_f+m_f]} u(\xi) \tag{1}$$

We give u the values $\chi_{[0,\infty)}, \chi_{(-\infty,0)}$ and we obtain

$$\bigcap_{\xi\in[t-d_r,t-d_r+m_r]} \chi_{[0,\infty)}(\xi) = \chi_{[d_r,\infty)}(t) \tag{2}$$

$$\bigcup_{\xi\in[t-d_f,t-d_f+m_f]} \chi_{[0,\infty)}(\xi) = \chi_{[d_f-m_f,\infty)}(t) \tag{3}$$

$$\bigcap_{\xi\in[t-d_r,t-d_r+m_r]} \chi_{(-\infty,0)}(\xi) = \chi_{(-\infty,d_r-m_r)}(t) \tag{4}$$

$$\bigcup_{\xi\in[t-d_f,t-d_f+m_f]} \chi_{(-\infty,0)}(\xi) = \chi_{(-\infty,d_f)}(t) \tag{5}$$

(1) implies the equality of the functions from (2) and (3) and of the functions from (4) and (5) and this indicates the satisfaction of b).

$b) \Rightarrow c)$ We add the two relations term by term and we get $m_r + m_f = 0$. c) is true.

$c) \Rightarrow d)$ From the hypothesis $c)$ and from CC$_{BDC}$ we infer $d_r \geq d_f, d_f \geq d_r$ i.e. $d_r = d_f = d$ and 7.2.1 (1) becomes

$$u(t-d) \leq x(t) \leq u(t-d)$$

in other words $Sol_{BDC}^{0,d,0,d}(u) = \{u(t-d)\}$.

$d) \Rightarrow a)$ Obvious, since I_d is deterministic.

7.3.4 Theorem Let $0 \leq m_r \leq d_r, 0 \leq m_f \leq d_f$ and $0 \leq m'_r \leq d'_r, 0 \leq m'_f \leq d'_f$ so that CC$_{BDC}$ is fulfilled for each of them. The next statements are equivalent

a) $$Sol_{BDC}^{m_r,d_r,m_f,d_f} \subset Sol_{BDC}^{m'_r,d'_r,m'_f,d'_f}$$

b) $$\forall u, \quad \bigcap_{\xi\in[t-d'_r,t-d'_r+m'_r]} u(\xi) \leq \bigcap_{\xi\in[t-d_r,t-d_r+m_r]} u(\xi) \leq \bigcup_{\xi\in[t-d_f,t-d_f+m_f]} u(\xi) \leq \bigcup_{\xi\in[t-d'_f,t-d'_f+m'_f]} u(\xi)$$

c) $$[t-d'_r, t-d'_r+m'_r] \supset [t-d_r, t-d_r+m_r]$$
$$[t-d_f, t-d_f+m_f] \subset [t-d'_f, t-d'_f+m'_f]$$

d) $$d'_r - m'_r \leq d_r - m_r \leq d_f \leq d'_f$$
$$d'_f - m'_f \leq d_f - m_f \leq d_r \leq d'_r$$

Proof Obvious

7.3.5 Theorem $Sol_{BDC}^{m_r,d_r,m_f,d_f}$ is time invariant.

Proof: We choose $u,x \in S$ and $d \in \mathbf{R}$ arbitrary so that $u \circ \tau^d \in S$ and $x \in Sol_{BDC}^{m_r,d_r,m_f,d_f}(u)$ be true. From the supposition that $u(0-0)=0$, i.e. $u \circ \tau^d(t) \le \chi_{[0,\infty)}(t)$ and from

$$(x \circ \tau^d)(t) \le \bigcup_{\xi \in [t-d_f,t-d_f+m_f]} (u \circ \tau^d)(\xi) \le \bigcup_{\xi \in [t-d_f,t-d_f+m_f]} \chi_{[0,\infty)}(\xi) = \chi_{[d_f-m_f,\infty)}(t) \le \chi_{[0,\infty)}(t)$$

we infer $supp\ D_{01}(x \circ \tau^d) \subset [0,\infty)$; and if $u(0-0)=1$, i.e. $u \circ \tau^d(t) \ge \chi_{(-\infty,0)}(t)$, then

$$(x \circ \tau^d)(t) \ge \bigcap_{\xi \in [t-d_r,t-d_r+m_r]} (u \circ \tau^d)(\xi) \ge \bigcap_{\xi \in [t-d_r,t-d_r+m_r]} \chi_{(-\infty,0)}(\xi) = \chi_{(-\infty,d_r-m_r)}(t) \ge \chi_{(-\infty,0)}(t)$$

from where $supp\ D_{10}(x \circ \tau^d) \subset [0,\infty)$. Because

$$supp\ D(x \circ \tau^d) = supp\ D_{01}(x \circ \tau^d) \vee supp\ D_{10}(x \circ \tau^d) \subset [0,\infty)$$

we conclude that $x \circ \tau^d \in S$. The inequalities

$$\bigcap_{\xi \in [t-d_r,t-d_r+m_r]} (u \circ \tau^d)(\xi) \le (x \circ \tau^d)(t) \le \bigcup_{\xi \in [t-d_f,t-d_f+m_f]} (u \circ \tau^d)(\xi)$$

that we have already made use of show that $x \circ \tau^d \in Sol_{BDC}^{m_r,d_r,m_f,d_f}(u \circ \tau^d)$.

7.3.6 Theorem $Sol_{BDC}^{m_r,d_r,m_f,d_f}$ is symmetrical if and only if $d_r = d_f$ and $m_r = m_f$.

Proof <u>If</u> we note with d the common value of $d_r = d_f$ and with m the common value of $m_r = m_f$. We get

$$\overline{x} \in Sol_{BDC}^{m,d,m,d}(\overline{u}) \Leftrightarrow \bigcap_{\xi \in [t-d,t-d+m]} \overline{u(\xi)} \le \overline{x(t)} \le \bigcup_{\xi \in [t-d,t-d+m]} \overline{u(\xi)}$$

$$\Leftrightarrow \overline{\bigcup_{\xi \in [t-d,t-d+m]} u(\xi)} \le \overline{x(t)} \le \overline{\bigcap_{\xi \in [t-d,t-d+m]} u(\xi)}$$

$$\Leftrightarrow \bigcap_{\xi \in [t-d,t-d+m]} u(\xi) \le x(t) \le \bigcup_{\xi \in [t-d,t-d+m]} u(\xi) \Leftrightarrow x \in Sol_{BDC}^{m,d,m,d}(u)$$

<u>Only if</u> For $u = \chi_{[0,\tau)}$ with $\tau > m_r$, $\tau > m_f$, we have

$$\bigcap_{\xi \in [t-d_r,t-d_r+m_r]} \overline{u(\xi)} = \chi_{(-\infty,d_r-m_r) \vee [\tau+d_r,\infty)}(t)$$

$$\bigcup_{\xi\in[t-d_f,t-d_f+m_f]}\overline{u(\xi)} = \chi_{(-\infty,d_f)\vee[\tau+d_f-m_f,\infty)}(t)$$

$$\bigcap_{\xi\in[t-d_r,t-d_r+m_r]}u(\xi) = \chi_{[d_r,\tau+d_r-m_r)}(t)$$

$$\bigcup_{\xi\in[t-d_f,t-d_f+m_f]}u(\xi) = \chi_{[d_f-m_f,\tau+d_f)}(t)$$

The systems of inequalities that are inferred from $\overline{x}\in Sol_{BDC}^{m_r,d_r,m_f,d_f}(\overline{\chi_{[0,\tau)}})$:

$$\chi_{(-\infty,d_r-m_r)\vee[\tau+d_r,\infty)}(t)\le\overline{x(t)}\le\chi_{(-\infty,d_f)\vee[\tau+d_f-m_f,\infty)}(t) \text{ i.e.}$$

$$\chi_{[d_f,\tau+d_f-m_f)}(t)\le x(t)\le\chi_{[d_r-m_r,\tau+d_r)}(t)$$

and respectively from $x\in Sol_{BDC}^{m_r,d_r,m_f,d_f}(\chi_{[0,\tau)})$:

$$\chi_{[d_r,\tau+d_r-m_r)}(t)\le x(t)\le\chi_{[d_f-m_f,\tau+d_f)}(t)$$

are equivalent –i.e. they have the same solutions- only if $d_r=d_f$ and $m_r=m_f$.

7.3.7 Theorem Let the numbers $0\le m_r\le d_r, 0\le m_f\le d_f$ and $0\le m_r^{'}\le d_r^{'}, 0\le m_f^{'}\le d_f^{'}$ so that $d_r\ge d_f-m_f, d_f\ge d_r-m_r$ and $d_r^{'}\ge d_f^{'}-m_f^{'}, d_f^{'}\ge d_r^{'}-m_r^{'}$ are true. Then $Sol_{BDC}^{m_r+m_r^{'},d_r+d_r^{'},m_f+m_f^{'},d_f+d_f^{'}}$ is a BDC and we have

$$Sol_{BDC}^{m_r^{'},d_r^{'},m_f^{'},d_f^{'}}\circ Sol_{BDC}^{m_r,d_r,m_f,d_f}=Sol_{BDC}^{m_r+m_r^{'},d_r+d_r^{'},m_f+m_f^{'},d_f+d_f^{'}}$$

Proof We observe that $d_f+d_f^{'}\ge d_r+d_r^{'}-m_r-m_r^{'},\ d_r+d_r^{'}\ge d_f+d_f^{'}-m_f-m_f^{'}$, thus CC_{BDC} is fulfilled again and $Sol_{BDC}^{m_r+m_r^{'},d_r+d_r^{'},m_f+m_f^{'},d_f+d_f^{'}}$ makes sense.

We prove

$$Sol_{BDC}^{m_r^{'},d_r^{'},m_f^{'},d_f^{'}}\circ Sol_{BDC}^{m_r,d_r,m_f,d_f}\subset Sol_{BDC}^{m_r+m_r^{'},d_r+d_r^{'},m_f+m_f^{'},d_f+d_f^{'}}$$

Let u arbitrary and $y\in Sol_{BDC}^{m_r^{'},d_r^{'},m_f^{'},d_f^{'}}\circ Sol_{BDC}^{m_r,d_r,m_f,d_f}(u)$, i.e. $x\in Sol_{BDC}^{m_r,d_r,m_f,d_f}(u)$ exists so that $y\in Sol_{BDC}^{m_r^{'},d_r^{'},m_f^{'},d_f^{'}}(x)$. We infer $u(0-0)=x(0-0)=y(0-0)$, i.e. the compatibility with the initial conditions is satisfied. Moreover:

$$\bigcap_{\omega\in[\xi-d_r,\xi-d_r+m_r]} u(\omega) \le x(\xi) \le \bigcup_{\omega\in[\xi-d_f,\xi-d_f+m_f]} u(\omega) \quad (1)$$

$$\bigcap_{\xi\in[t-d'_r,t-d'_r+m'_r]} x(\xi) \le y(t) \le \bigcup_{\xi\in[t-d'_f,t-d'_f+m'_f]} x(\xi) \quad (2)$$

from where

$$\bigcap_{\xi\in[t-d_r-d'_r,t-d_r-d'_r+m_r+m'_r]} u(\xi) = \bigcap_{\xi\in[t-d'_r,t-d'_r+m'_r]}\bigcap_{\omega\in[\xi-d_r,\xi-d_r+m_r]} u(\omega) \le$$

$$\le \bigcap_{\xi\in[t-d'_r,t-d'_r+m'_r]} x(\xi) \le y(t) \le \bigcup_{\xi\in[t-d'_f,t-d'_f+m'_f]} x(\xi) \le$$

$$\le \bigcup_{\xi\in[t-d'_f,t-d'_f+m'_f]}\bigcup_{\omega\in[\xi-d_f,\xi-d_f+m_f]} u(\omega) = \bigcup_{\xi\in[t-d_f-d'_f,t-d_f-d'_f+m_f+m'_f]} u(\xi)$$

thus $y \in Sol_{BDC}^{m_r+m'_r,d_r+d'_r,m_f+m'_f,d_f+d'_f}(u)$.

We prove

$$Sol_{BDC}^{m_r+m'_r,d_r+d'_r,m_f+m'_f,d_f+d'_f} \subset Sol_{BDC}^{m'_r,d'_r,m'_f,d'_f} \circ Sol_{BDC}^{m_r,d_r,m_f,d_f}$$

and we must show that for any y with

$$\bigcap_{\xi\in[t-d_r-d'_r,t-d_r-d'_r+m_r+m'_r]} u(\xi) \le y(t) \le \bigcup_{\xi\in[t-d_f-d'_f,t-d_f-d'_f+m_f+m'_f]} u(\xi) \quad (3)$$

some x exists so that (1), (2) be fulfilled. The property is true for $t<0$ and let against all reason $t_0 \ge 0$ be the first time instant when the property is false. We suppose that $y(t_0)=0$. From (3)

$$\bigcap_{\xi\in[t_0-d'_r,t_0-d'_r+m'_r]}\bigcap_{\omega\in[\xi-d_r,\xi-d_r+m_r]} u(\omega) = 0$$

i.e.

$$\exists \xi_0 \in [t_0-d'_r, t_0-d'_r+m'_r], \quad \bigcap_{\omega\in[\xi_0-d_r,\xi_0-d_r+m_r]} u(\omega) = 0$$

(1) shows that we can choose $x(\xi_0)=0$ and (2) is true, because

$$\bigcap_{\xi\in[t_0-d'_r,t_0-d'_r+m'_r]} x(\xi) = x(\xi_0) = 0$$

in contradiction with the supposition that was made on the existence of t_0. The same result is obtained if we suppose $y(t_0)=1$.

7.3.8 Corollary The set of the BDC's is, relative to the serial connection, a commutative semi-group where the unit is I.

7.3.9 Remarks If i is an arbitrary DC, then by its serial connection with a BDC we obtain an arbitrary DC (not a BDC).

We combine now the order of the BDC's from 7.3.4 with Theorem 6.8.5 of compatibility between the serial connection and the order and with Theorem 7.3.7 related with the serial connection of the BDC's in the next manner. Let the BDC's $Sol_{BDC}^{m_r,d_r,m_f,d_f}$, $Sol_{BDC}^{m_r',d_r',m_f',d_f'}$ and $Sol_{BDC}^{m_r'',d_r'',m_f'',d_f''}$, where $0 \le m_r \le d_r$, $0 \le m_f \le d_f$, $0 \le m_r' \le d_r'$, $0 \le m_f' \le d_f'$, $0 \le m_r'' \le d_r''$, $0 \le m_f'' \le d_f''$ and CC$_{BDC}$ is fulfilled three times. The implication

$$Sol_{BDC}^{m_r',d_r',m_f',d_f'} \subset Sol_{BDC}^{m_r'',d_r'',m_f'',d_f''} \Rightarrow$$

$$\Rightarrow Sol_{BDC}^{m_r',d_r',m_f',d_f'} \circ Sol_{BDC}^{m_r,d_r,m_f,d_f} \subset Sol_{BDC}^{m_r'',d_r'',m_f'',d_f''} \circ Sol_{BDC}^{m_r,d_r,m_f,d_f}$$

means that

$$d_r'' - m_r'' \le d_r' - m_r' \le d_f' \le d_f''$$

$$d_f'' - m_f'' \le d_f' - m_f' \le d_r' \le d_r''$$

implies

$$d_r + d_r'' - m_r - m_r'' \le d_r + d_r' - m_r - m_r' \le d_f + d_f' \le d_f + d_f''$$

$$d_f + d_f'' - m_f - m_f'' \le d_f + d_f' - m_f - m_f' \le d_r + d_r' \le d_r + d_r''$$

The other situation from 6.8.5 is similar

$$Sol_{BDC}^{m_r',d_r',m_f',d_f'} \subset Sol_{BDC}^{m_r'',d_r'',m_f'',d_f''} \Rightarrow$$

$$\Rightarrow Sol_{BDC}^{m_r,d_r,m_f,d_f} \circ Sol_{BDC}^{m_r',d_r',m_f',d_f'} \subset Sol_{BDC}^{m_r,d_r,m_f,d_f} \circ Sol_{BDC}^{m_r'',d_r'',m_f'',d_f''}$$

7.3.10 Theorem If $x \in Sol_{BDC}^{m_r,d_r,m_f,d_f}(u)$, the next inequalities are fulfilled:

$$u(t-d_r-0) \cdot \bigcap_{\xi \in [t-d_r, t-d_r+m_r)} u(\xi) \le x(t-0) \le$$

$$u(t-d_f-0) \cup \bigcup_{\xi \in [t-d_f, t-d_f+m_f)} u(\xi)$$

Proof We take the left limit in BDC and use 4.2.1.

7.4 Fixed and Inertial Delays

7.4.1 Corollary of Theorem 7.3.3. The deterministic BDC's are given by the equatio

$$x(t) = u(t-d) \quad (1)$$

where $d \geq 0$; the non-deterministic BDC's consist in the system 7.2.1 (1), where $m_r + m_f > 0$.

7.4.2 Definition For $u, x \in S$ and $d \geq 0$, the relation 7.4.1 (1) is called the *fixed delay condition* (FDC). The delay defined by this equation is also called *pure, ideal* or *non-inertial.*

We also call fixed delay condition the function I_d.

A delay different from FDC is called *inertial.*

7.4.3 Remark A special case of inclusion at 7.3.4 consists in the situation when the left BDC is deterministic. Let $d \in [d_r - m_r, d_r] \wedge [d_f - m_f, d_f]$; then the statements

$$t - d_r \leq t - d \leq t - d_r + m_r, t - d_f \leq t - d \leq t - d_f + m_f$$

$$\bigcap_{\xi \in [t-d_r, t-d_r+m_r]} u(\xi) \leq u(t-d) \leq \bigcup_{\xi \in [t-d_f, t-d_f+m_f]} u(\xi)$$

make us conclude that $I_d \subset Sol_{BDC}^{m_r, d_r, m_f, d_f}$.

7.4.4 Corollary FDC is deterministic (Example 6.3.3, Theorem 7.3.3), time invariant (Example 6.5.5, Theorem 7.3.5), constant (Example 6.6.2) and symmetrical (Example 6.7.2, Theorem 7.3.6). The serial connection of the FDC's coincides with the composition of the translations: for $d \geq 0, d' \geq 0$ we have

$$I_d \circ I_{d'} = I_{d'} \circ I_d = I_{d+d'}$$

7.4.5 Remark At Definition 7.4.2 inertia was defined to be the property of the DC's of being not ideal. In particular the non-deterministic DC's, for example the non-trivial BDC's where $m_r + m_f > 0$ are inertial.

8. Absolute Inertial Delays

8.1 Absolute Inertia

8.1.1 Theorem Let the numbers $\delta_r \geq 0, \delta_f \geq 0$. When $x \in S$, the next conditions are equivalent:

a) $\overline{x(t-0)} \cdot x(t) \leq \bigcap_{\xi \in [t, t+\delta_r]} x(\xi)$

$$x(t-0)\cdot\overline{x(t)}\leq\bigcap_{\xi\in[t,t+\delta_f]}\overline{x(\xi)}$$

b) $$\overline{x(t-0)}\cdot x(t)\leq\overline{x(t-0)}\cdot\bigcap_{\xi\in[t,t+\delta_r]}x(\xi)$$

$$x(t-0)\cdot\overline{x(t)}\leq x(t-0)\cdot\bigcap_{\xi\in[t,t+\delta_f]}\overline{x(\xi)}$$

c) $$\overline{x(t-0)}\cdot x(t)=\overline{x(t-0)}\cdot\bigcap_{\xi\in[t,t+\delta_r]}x(\xi)$$

$$x(t-0)\cdot\overline{x(t)}=x(t-0)\cdot\bigcap_{\xi\in[t,t+\delta_f]}\overline{x(\xi)}$$

d) $$\overline{x(t-0)}\cdot x(t)\leq\overline{x(t-\delta_f-0)}\cdot\bigcap_{\xi\in[t-\delta_f,t)}\overline{x(\xi)}$$

$$x(t-0)\cdot\overline{x(t)}\leq x(t-\delta_r-0)\cdot\bigcap_{\xi\in[t-\delta_r,t)}x(\xi)$$

e) $$\forall d<d',\overline{x(d-0)}\cdot x(d)=1\ and\ x(d'-0)\cdot\overline{x(d')}=1\Rightarrow d'-d>\delta_r$$

$$\forall d<d',x(d-0)\cdot\overline{x(d)}=1\ and\ \overline{x(d'-0)}\cdot x(d')=1\Rightarrow d'-d>\delta_f$$

Proof $a)\Rightarrow b)$ Both terms of the first inequality from a) are multiplied with $\overline{x(t-0)}$ and the first inequality from b) results.

$b)\Rightarrow a)$ $$\overline{x(t-0)}\cdot x(t)\leq\overline{x(t-0)}\cdot\bigcap_{\xi\in[t,t+\delta_r]}x(\xi)\leq\bigcap_{\xi\in[t,t+\delta_r]}x(\xi)$$

$a)\Rightarrow c)$ In the system

$$\overline{x(t-0)}\cdot x(t)\leq\bigcap_{\xi\in[t,t+\delta_r]}x(\xi)\leq x(t)$$

we multiply all the terms with $\overline{x(t-0)}$.

$c)\Rightarrow a)$ $$\overline{x(t-0)}\cdot x(t)=\overline{x(t-0)}\cdot\bigcap_{\xi\in[t,t+\delta_r]}x(\xi)\leq\bigcap_{\xi\in[t,t+\delta_r]}x(\xi)$$

$a)\Rightarrow e)$ Let $d<d'$ arbitrary so that

$$\overline{x(d-0)}\cdot x(d)=1\ and\ x(d'-0)\cdot\overline{x(d')}=1$$

a) states that $\bigcap_{\xi\in[d,d+\delta_r]}u(\xi)=1$ and $\bigcap_{\xi\in[d',d'+\delta_f]}\overline{u(\xi)}=1$, thus

$[d,d+\delta_r]\wedge[d',d'+\delta_f]=\varnothing$ from where $d+\delta_r<d'$ and the conclusion is $d'-d>\delta_r$.

$e)\Rightarrow a)$ We suppose that a) is not true, i.e. d exists with

$$\overline{x(d-0)}\cdot x(d)=1 \; and \; \bigcap_{\xi\in[d,d+\delta_r]} x(\xi)=0$$

meaning the existence of $d'\in(d,d+\delta_r]$ where x switches from 1 to 0

$$x(d'-0)\cdot\overline{x(d')}=1$$

We have $d'-d\le\delta_r$, contradiction with e).

$d)\Rightarrow e)$ Let us take two numbers $d<d'$ so that

$$\overline{x(d-0)}\cdot x(d)=1 \; and \; x(d'-0)\cdot\overline{x(d')}=1$$

resulting

$$\overline{x(d-\delta_f-0)}\cdot \bigcap_{\xi\in[d-\delta_f,d)} \overline{x(\xi)}=1 \; and \; x(d'-\delta_r-0)\cdot \bigcap_{\xi\in[d'-\delta_r,d')} x(\xi)=1$$

In other words $\varepsilon_1>0$ and $\varepsilon_2>0$ exist with the property

$$\forall\xi\in[d-\delta_f-\varepsilon_1,d),x(\xi)=0$$

$$\forall\xi\in[d'-\delta_r-\varepsilon_2,d'),x(\xi)=1$$

$$[d-\delta_f-\varepsilon_1,d)\wedge[d'-\delta_r-\varepsilon_2,d')=\varnothing$$

The last empty intersection gives the conclusion that

$$d\le d'-\delta_r-\varepsilon_2$$

is true, i.e. $d'-d\ge\delta_r+\varepsilon_2>\delta_r$.

$e)\Rightarrow d)$ If d) is not true then d' exists so that

$$\overline{x(d'-0)}\cdot x(d')=1 \; and \; \overline{x(d'-\delta_f-0)}\cdot \bigcap_{\xi\in[d'-\delta_f,d')} \overline{x(\xi)}=0$$

This means that for any $\varepsilon>0$ some $d\in[d'-\delta_f-\varepsilon,d')$ exists with

$$x(d-0)\cdot\overline{x(d)}=1$$

The inequality $d'-\delta_f-\varepsilon\le d$ that is true for all $\varepsilon>0$ gives $d'-d\le\delta_f$, thus e) is not true.

8.1.2 Definition Any of the properties 8.1.1 a),..., 8.1.1 e) is called the *absolute inertial condition* (AIC). δ_r,δ_f are called the (*rising, falling*) *inertial parameters*. If AIC is fulfilled, we say that the tuple (δ_r,δ_f,x) satisfies AIC. When $\delta_r=\delta_f=0$, AIC is called *trivial* and if $\delta_r>0$ or $\delta_f>0$, then AIC is called *non-trivial*.

We also call absolute inertial condition the set $Sol_{AIC}^{\delta_r,\delta_f}\subset S$ defined by

$$Sol_{AIC}^{\delta_r,\delta_f}=\{x\,|\,(\delta_r,\delta_f,x)\; satisfies\; AIC\}$$

8.1.3 Remarks For all $t<0$ and all x, AIC is trivially fulfilled since $\overline{x(t-0)}\cdot x(t)=x(t-0)\cdot\overline{x(t)}=0$. This property represents the compatibility between AIC and the initial value of x.

The interpretation of AIC results from Fig 12. We observe how the switch $\overline{x(t_2-0)}\cdot x(t_2)=1$ in the 8.1.1 a) version assures that x will remain 1 for a time interval of length $t_3-t_2>\delta_r$ and in the 8.1.1 d) version assures that x has remained 0 for a time interval of length $t_2-t_1>\delta_f$. When t runs in $\boldsymbol{R}$, the two conditions are equivalent.

To be remarked the way that any of 8.1.1 a),..., 8.1.1 c) degenerates in the trivial situation $\delta_r=\delta_f=0$: $Sol_{AIC}^{0,0}=S$. To be remarked also the intermediary situations

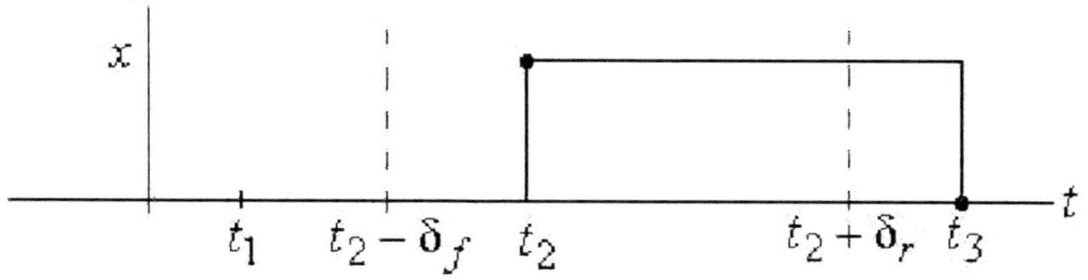

Fig 12

when one of $\delta_r>0,\delta_f=0$, respectively $\delta_r=0,\delta_f>0$ is true and the inclusions $Sol_{AIC}^{\delta_r,\delta_f}\subset S$ are strict. In fact we have

$$Sol_{AIC}^{\delta_r,\delta_f}\subset Sol_{AIC}^{\delta_r',\delta_f'}\Leftrightarrow\delta_r\geq\delta_r'\ and\ \delta_f\geq\delta_f'$$

$$Sol_{AIC}^{\delta_r,\delta_f}\wedge Sol_{AIC}^{\delta_r',\delta_f'}=Sol_{AIC}^{\max(\delta_r,\delta_r'),\max(\delta_f,\delta_f')}$$

$$Sol_{AIC}^{\delta_r,\delta_f}\vee Sol_{AIC}^{\delta_r',\delta_f'}=Sol_{AIC}^{\min(\delta_r,\delta_r'),\min(\delta_f,\delta_f')}$$

The set $Sol_{AIC}^{\delta_r,\delta_f}$ is not closed under the Boolean laws if $\delta_r>0$ or $\delta_f>0$, for example $\chi_{[0,2)},\chi_{[1,3)}\in Sol_{AIC}^{1,0}$ and $\chi_{[1,2)}=\chi_{[0,2)}\cdot\chi_{[1,3)}\notin Sol_{AIC}^{1,0}$.

8.2 Absolute Inertial Delays

8.2.1 Definition Let the numbers $\delta_r \geq 0$, $\delta_f \geq 0$. If the DC i satisfies $\forall u, i(u) \subset Sol_{AIC}^{\delta_r,\delta_f}$, then it is called *absolute inertial delay condition* (AIDC). We also say that i *satisfies AIC* (represented by $Sol_{AIC}^{\delta_r,\delta_f}$).

8.2.2 Remark Intuitively, we say that AIDC expresses a cause-effect relationship between an input and an inertial state, so that for any form of u, the variations of the delayed signal x cannot be faster than the satisfaction of AIC allows.

8.2.3 Examples A DC i with the property $\forall u, i(u) \wedge Sol_{AIC}^{\delta_r,\delta_f} \neq \emptyset$ defines the AIDC $i \wedge Sol_{AIC}^{\delta_r,\delta_f}$. For example $Sol_{SC} \wedge Sol_{AIC}^{\delta_r,\delta_f}$ is AIDC for any $\delta_r \geq 0, \delta_f \geq 0$ and $I_d \wedge Sol_{AIC}^{\delta_r,\delta_f}$, $d \geq 0$ is AIDC for $\delta_r = \delta_f = 0$ only.

On the other hand, the next functions

$$i(u) = \begin{cases} 1, \textit{if } \exists \lim_{t\to\infty} u(t) \textit{ and } \lim_{t\to\infty} u(t) = 1 \\ 0, \textit{otherwise} \end{cases}$$

$$i(u) = \begin{cases} 0, \textit{if } \exists \lim_{t\to\infty} u(t) \textit{ and } \lim_{t\to\infty} u(t) = 0 \\ 1, \textit{otherwise} \end{cases}$$

$$i(u) = \begin{cases} \{1\} \vee \{\chi_{[\tau,\infty)} \mid \tau \geq 0\}, \textit{if } \exists \lim_{t\to\infty} u(t) \textit{ and } \lim_{t\to\infty} u(t) = 1 \\ \{0\} \vee \{\chi_{(-\infty,\tau)} \mid \tau \geq 0\}, \textit{otherwise} \end{cases}$$

$$i(u) = \begin{cases} \{0\} \vee \{\chi_{(-\infty,\tau)} \mid \tau \geq 0\}, \textit{if } \exists \lim_{t\to\infty} u(t) \textit{ and } \lim_{t\to\infty} u(t) = 0 \\ \{1\} \vee \{\chi_{[\tau,\infty)} \mid \tau \geq 0\}, \textit{otherwise} \end{cases}$$

are DC's satisfying AIC for all $\delta_r \geq 0, \delta_f \geq 0$.

8.2.4 Theorem Let $0 \leq m \leq d$. The deterministic DC (see Theorem 6.3.4) $x(t) = \bigcap_{\xi\in[t-d,t-d+m]} u(\xi)$ satisfies

$$x(t-0) \cdot \overline{x(t)} \leq \bigcap_{\xi\in[t,t+m]} \overline{x(\xi)}$$

and its dual $x(t) = \bigcup_{\xi\in[t-d,t-d+m]} u(\xi)$ satisfies

$$\overline{x(t-0)} \cdot x(t) \leq \bigcap_{\xi \in [t,t+m]} x(\xi)$$

Proof We show the first of these two properties. The hypothesis states

$$d'' > d' \text{ and } x(d'-0) \cdot \overline{x(d')} = 1 \text{ and } \overline{x(d''-0)} \cdot x(d'') = 1$$

from where we infer (see 4.2.2)

$$u(d'-d-0) \cdot \bigcap_{\xi \in [d'-d, d'-d+m)} u(\xi) \cdot \overline{u(d'-d+m)} = 1$$

$$\overline{u(d''-d-0)} \cdot \bigcap_{\xi \in [d''-d, d''-d+m]} u(\xi) = 1$$

i.e. $d'-d+m = d''-d-\varepsilon$ for some $\varepsilon > 0$ and eventually $d''-d' > m$.

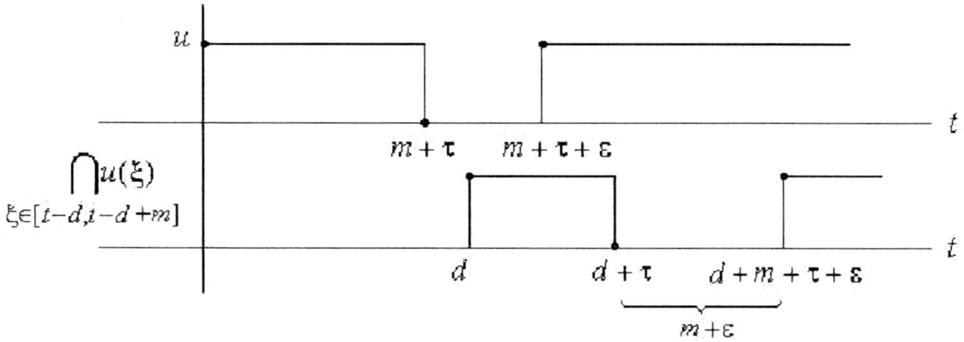

Fig 13

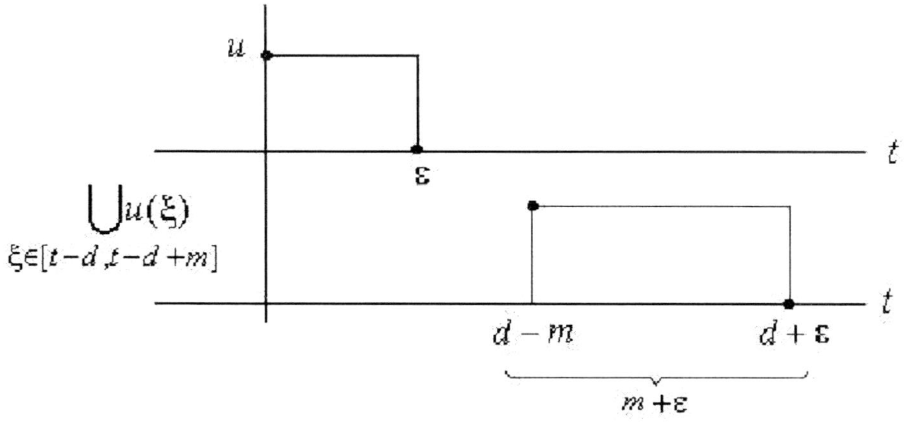

Fig 14

8.2.5 Theorem Let $0 \le m_r \le d_r, 0 \le m_f \le d_f$ so that $d_f \ge d_r - m_r, d_r \ge d_f - m_f$ is true. The system

$$\overline{x(t-0)} \cdot x(t) = \overline{x(t-0)} \cdot \bigcap_{\xi \in [t-d_r, t-d_r+m_r]} u(\xi) \quad (1)$$

$$x(t-0) \cdot \overline{x(t)} = x(t-0) \cdot \bigcap_{\xi \in [t-d_f, t-d_f+m_f]} \overline{u(\xi)} \quad (2)$$

satisfies the next properties:

a) (*the property of compatibility of (1), (2) with the initial conditions*) $x(0-0) = u(0-0)$ and for any $t < 0$ we have

$$\overline{x(t-0)} \cdot x(t) = \overline{x(t-0)} \cdot \bigcap_{\xi \in [t-d_r, t-d_r+m_r]} u(\xi) = 0 \quad (3)$$

$$x(t-0) \cdot \overline{x(t)} = x(t-0) \cdot \bigcap_{\xi \in [t-d_f, t-d_f+m_f]} \overline{u(\xi)} = 0 \quad (4)$$

b) (1), (2) have a unique solution $x \in S$.

c) (*the property of compatibility of the system with the final conditions*) (1), (2) define a deterministic DC i: $x \in Sol_{SC}(u)$ and if $\exists \lim\limits_{t \to \infty} u(t)$, then t_1 exists so that $\forall t \ge t_1$ we have (3), (4) fulfilled.

d) $x \in Sol_{AIC}^{d_f - d_r + m_r, d_r - d_f + m_f}$

e) $x \in Sol_{BDC}^{m_r, d_r, m_f, d_f}$

f) (1), (2) are time invariant

g) (1), (2) are constant

h) (1), (2) are symmetrical iff $d_r = d_f$ *and* $m_r = m_f$.

Proof a) If $x(0-0) \ne u(0-0)$, then we suppose $x(0-0) = 0, u(0-0) = 1$. This implies that for any $t < 0 \le d_r - m_r$ we have

$$0 = \overline{x(t-0)} \cdot x(t) \ne \overline{x(t-0)} \cdot \bigcap_{\xi \in [t-d_r, t-d_r+m_r]} u(\xi) = 1$$

contradiction and similarly for $x(0-0) = 1, u(0-0) = 0$. Thus $x(t-0) = u(t-0) = c$ for any $t < 0$, where $c \in \boldsymbol{B}$ is some constant and we get $\overline{x(t-0)} \cdot x(t) = x(t-0) \cdot \overline{x(t)} = c \cdot \overline{c} = 0$. At the same time, $t < 0$ implies that $\bigcap\limits_{\xi \in [t-d_r, t-d_r+m_r]} u(\xi)$ is equal with c and $\bigcap\limits_{\xi \in [t=d_f, t-d_f+m_f]} \overline{u(\xi)}$ is equal with $\overline{c}$ so that

$$\overline{x(t-0)} \cdot \bigcap_{\xi \in [t-d_r, t-d_r+m_r]} u(\xi) = \overline{c} \cdot c = 0$$

$$x(t-0)\cdot\bigcap_{\xi\in[t-d_f,t-d_f+m_f]}\overline{u(\xi)}=c\cdot\bar{c}=0$$

and the truth of a) results.

b) The solution is unique for $t<0$ and is given by $x(t)=u(0-0)$. The non-uniqueness means the existence of a time instant $t_1\geq 0$ with the property that $\forall t<t_1$ the solution is unique and on the other hand $x(t_1)=0, x(t_1)=1$ satisfy both (1), (2). We suppose $x(t_1-0)=0$ and (1) becomes

$$x(t_1)=\bigcap_{\xi\in[t_1-d_r,t_1-d_r+m_r]}u(\xi)$$

from where either $x(t_1)=0$, or $x(t_1)=1$ is true but not both. Similarly for $x(t_1-0)=1$. As t_1 was arbitrary, the solution is unique.

c) We suppose without loosing the generality that $\exists t_1\geq 0,\forall t\geq t_1,u(t)=1$ and we have two possibilities:

c.i) $x(t_1+d_r-0)=0$. From (1) we have $x(t_1+d_r)=1$ and $\forall t>t_1+d_r$, $x(t)=1$ and (3), (4) are fulfilled

c.ii) $x(t_1+d_r-0)=1$. Then $\forall t\geq t_1+d_r$, $x(t)=1$ and (3), (4) are fulfilled too.

d) The hypothesis is

$$d'>d \; and \; \overline{x(d-0)}\cdot x(d)=1 \; and \; x(d'-0)\cdot\overline{x(d')}=1$$

resulting

$$\bigcap_{\xi\in[d-d_r,d-d_r+m_r]}u(\xi)\cdot\bigcap_{\xi\in[d'-d_f,d'-d_f+m_f]}\overline{u(\xi)}=1$$

$$\Rightarrow[d-d_r,d-d_r+m_r]\wedge[d'-d_f,d'-d_f+m_f]=\varnothing$$

$$\Rightarrow d-d_r+m_r<d'-d_f \; or \; d'-d_f+m_f<d-d_r$$

$$\Rightarrow d'-d>d_f-d_r+m_r$$

(the inequality $d'-d<d_f-m_f-d_r$ represents a contradiction, because the left term is strictly positive and from $d_f-m_f\leq d_r$, we get that the right term is non-positive).

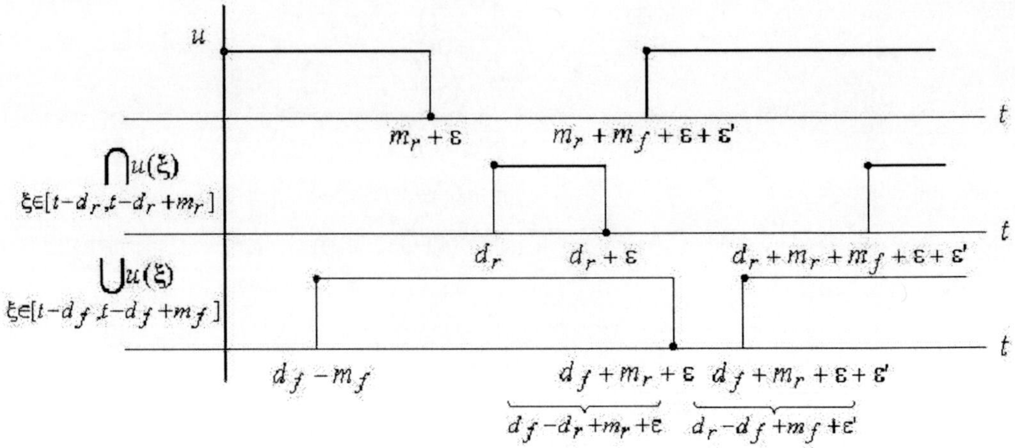

Fig 15

e) We suppose against all reason that t,u exist so that $\bigcap\limits_{\xi\in[t-d_r,t-d_r+m_r]} u(\xi) = 1$ and $x(t)=0$; we get from (1) $\overline{x(t-0)}=0$ and $x(t-0)=1$ and on the other hand, because $\bigcap\limits_{\xi\in[t-d_f,t-d_f+m_f]} \overline{u(\xi)} = 0$ (from CC$_{\mathrm{BDC}}$) equation (2) gives $\overline{x(t)}=0$, thus $x(t)=1$, contradiction. In other words $\bigcap\limits_{\xi\in[t-d_r,t-d_r+m_r]} u(\xi) \le x(t)$. The inequality $x(t) \le \bigcup\limits_{\xi\in[t-d_f,t-d_f+m_f]} u(\xi)$ is similarly proved.

f) We show that i is time invariant and the hypothesis is $u\circ\tau^d \in S$ and $x=i(u)$, where $d\in\boldsymbol{R}$ is arbitrary. Because $i(u\circ\tau^d)\in S$ and $x\circ\tau^d = i(u\circ\tau^d)$ (as resulted by the replacement in (1), (2) of u,x with $x\circ\tau^d, u\circ\tau^d$), the fulfillment of this property follows.

g) The inequalities

$$\overline{x(t-0)}\cdot x(t) = \overline{x(t-0)}\cdot \bigcap_{\xi\in[t-d_r,t-d_r+m_r]} u(\xi) \le u(t-d_r)$$

$$x(t-0)\cdot \overline{x(t)} = x(t-0)\cdot \bigcap_{\xi\in[t-d_f,t-d_f+m_f]} \overline{u(\xi)} \le \overline{u(t-d_f)}$$

show that i is constant.

h) $\overline{x}\in i(\overline{u}) \Leftrightarrow x\in i(u)$ is equivalent, from the form of (1), (2) with the fact that

$$\bigcap_{\xi\in[t-d_r,t-d_r+m_r]} u(\xi) = \bigcap_{\xi\in[t-d_f,t-d_f+m_f]} u(\xi)$$

and with the fact that $d_r = d_f, m_r = m_f$.

8.2.6 Remark If in 8.2.5 we put $m_r = m_f = 0$, then CC_{BDC} implies $d_r = d_f = d$ and the system

$$\overline{x(t-0)} \cdot x(t) = \overline{x(t-0)} \cdot u(t-d)$$
$$x(t-0) \cdot \overline{x(t)} = x(t-0) \cdot \overline{u(t-d)}$$

is equivalent with FDC (it has the same solution).

8.2.7 Theorem

a) $Sol_{SC} \wedge Sol_{AIC}^{\delta_r,\delta_f}$ is time variable.

b) $Sol_{SC} \wedge Sol_{AIC}^{\delta_r,\delta_f}$ is symmetrical iff $\delta_r = \delta_f$.

Proof a) See Example 6.5.5 b) where the time variability of Sol_{SC} is shown.

b) If Like at 6.7.2 b), by replacing Sol_{SC} with $Sol_{SC} \wedge Sol_{AIC}^{\delta,\delta}$.

Only if We suppose against all reason that $\delta_r < \delta_f$; by taking a $\delta \in (\delta_r, \delta_f)$ we have for some u (with $\lim_{t \to \infty} u(t) = 1$ false) that $\chi_{[0,\delta)} \in Sol_{AIC}^{\delta_r,\delta_f}$ and $\overline{\chi_{[0,\delta)}} \notin Sol_{AIC}^{\delta_r,\delta_f}$, contradiction with the symmetry request:

$$\forall u, Sol_{SC}(\overline{u}) \wedge Sol_{AIC}^{\delta_r,\delta_f} = \{\overline{x} \mid x \in Sol_{SC}(u) \wedge Sol_{AIC}^{\delta_r,\delta_f}\}$$

Similarly for $\delta_f < \delta_r$.

8.2.8 Theorem Being given the non-negative numbers $\delta_r, \delta_f, \delta_r', \delta_f'$ and the DC's i, j, the next properties are true:

a)

$$(i \wedge Sol_{AIC}^{\delta_r',\delta_f'}) \circ (j \wedge Sol_{AIC}^{\delta_r,\delta_f}) = (i \circ (j \wedge Sol_{AIC}^{\delta_r,\delta_f})) \wedge Sol_{AIC}^{\delta_r',\delta_f'} \subset (i \circ j) \wedge Sol_{AIC}^{\delta_r',\delta_f'}$$

b) If $\forall u, i(u) \subset Sol_{AIC}^{\delta_r',\delta_f'}$, $j(u) \subset Sol_{AIC}^{\delta_r,\delta_f}$ then $\forall u, (i \circ j)(u) \subset Sol_{AIC}^{\delta_r',\delta_f'}$.

Proof a) From 6.8.6 a).

b)

$$\forall u, (i \circ j)(u) = ((i \wedge Sol_{AIC}^{\delta_r',\delta_f'}) \circ (j \wedge Sol_{AIC}^{\delta_r,\delta_f}))(u) \overset{a)}{\subset} ((i \circ j) \wedge Sol_{AIC}^{\delta_r',\delta_f'})(u) \subset (i \circ j)(u)$$

thus $i \circ j = (i \circ j) \wedge Sol_{AIC}^{\delta_r',\delta_f'}$. The conclusion follows.

8.3 The Consistency Condition

8.3.1 Theorem The numbers $0 \le m_r \le d_r$, $0 \le m_f \le d_f$ are given so that $d_f \ge d_r - m_r, d_r \ge d_f - m_f$ is true and let also $\delta_r \ge 0, \delta_f \ge 0$. The next statements are equivalent:

a) $\delta_r + \delta_f \le m_r + m_f$

b) For any $u \in S$, the system of inequalities

$$\bigcap_{\xi \in [t-d_r, t-d_r+m_r]} u(\xi) \le x(t) \le \bigcup_{\xi \in [t-d_f, t-d_f+m_f]} x(\xi)$$

$$\overline{x(t-0)} \cdot x(t) \le \bigcap_{\xi \in [t, t+\delta_r]} x(\xi)$$

$$x(t-0) \cdot \overline{x(t)} \le \bigcap_{\xi \in [t, t+\delta_f]} \overline{x(\xi)}$$

has a solution $x \in S$.

Proof $a) \Rightarrow b)$ The next possibilities exist:

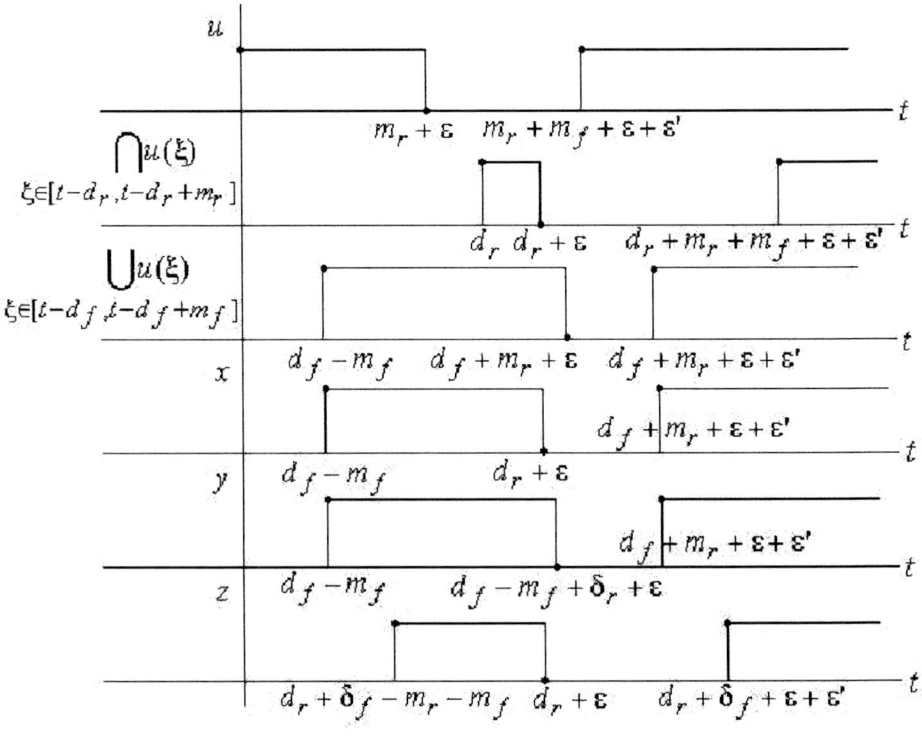

Fig 16

i) $d_r - d_f + m_f \geq \delta_r, d_f - d_r + m_r \geq \delta_f$

ii) $d_r - d_f + m_f < \delta_r, d_f - d_r + m_r \geq \delta_f$

iii) $d_r - d_f + m_f \geq \delta_r, d_f - d_r + m_r < \delta_f$

because the fourth possibility, i.e. $d_r - d_f + m_f < \delta_r, d_f - d_r + m_r < \delta_f$ gives the contradiction $\delta_r + \delta_f > m_r + m_f$. It is sufficient without restricting the generality to consider the input

$$u(t) = \chi_{[0,m_r+\varepsilon)\vee[m_r+m_f+\varepsilon+\varepsilon',\infty)}(t)$$

that produces a 1-pulse followed by a 0-pulse at the output, where $\varepsilon, \varepsilon' > 0$ are arbitrary, for which the existing solutions of the system in the three cases i), ii), iii) have been noted in Fig 16 with x, y, z. For $d_r - d_f + m_f \geq \delta_r,\ d_f - d_r + m_r \geq \delta_f$ (case i)) and

$$x(t) = \chi_{[d_f - m_f, d_r+\varepsilon)\vee[d_f+m_r+\varepsilon+\varepsilon',\infty)}(t)$$

it is obvious that BDC and AIC:

$$d_r + \varepsilon - d_f + m_f > \delta_r, d_f + m_r + \varepsilon + \varepsilon' - d_r - \varepsilon > \delta_f$$

are fulfilled. In the case of

$$y(t) = \chi_{[d_f - m_f, d_f - m_f + \delta_r + \varepsilon)\vee[d_f + m_r + \varepsilon + \varepsilon',\infty)}(t)$$

if $d_r - d_f + m_f < \delta_r$ (consequence of case ii)) we have BDC and AIC fulfilled under the form

$$d_r + \varepsilon < d_f - m_f + \delta_r + \varepsilon \leq d_f + m_r + \varepsilon$$

$$d_f - m_f + \delta_r + \varepsilon - d_f + m_f > \delta_r, d_f + m_r + \varepsilon + \varepsilon' - d_f + m_f - \delta_r - \varepsilon > \delta_f$$

and similarly for

$$z(t) = \chi_{[d_r + \delta_f - m_r - m_f, d_r+\varepsilon)\vee[d_r+\delta_f+\varepsilon+\varepsilon',\infty)}(t)$$

if $d_f - d_r + m_r < \delta_f$ (consequence of case iii)) where BDC and AIC are fulfilled again:

$$d_f - m_f < d_r + \delta_f - m_r - m_f \leq d_r$$

$$d_r + \varepsilon - d_r - \delta_f + m_r + m_f > \delta_r, d_r + \delta_f + \varepsilon + \varepsilon' - d_r - \varepsilon > \delta_f$$

$b) \Rightarrow a)$ We consider the input

$$u(t) = \chi_{[0,m_r+\varepsilon)\vee[m_r+m_f+2\varepsilon,2m_r+m_f+3\varepsilon)\vee[2(m_r+m_f)+4\varepsilon,3m_r+2m_f+5\varepsilon)\vee\ldots}(t)$$

where $\varepsilon > 0$ is arbitrary

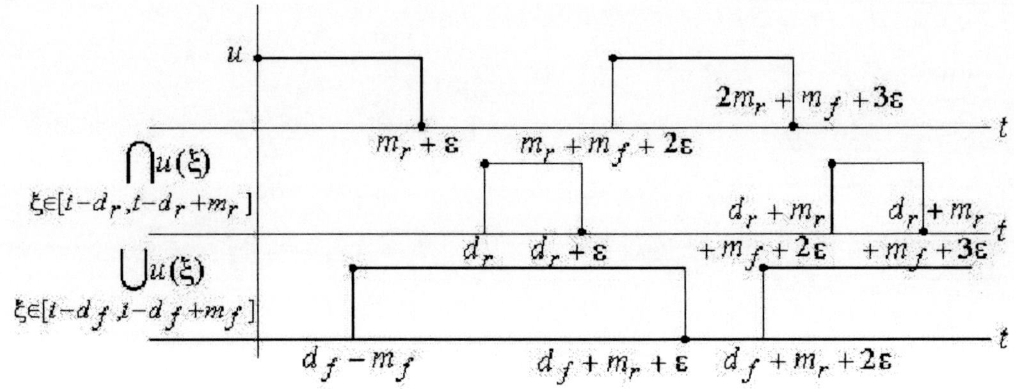

Fig 17

The hypothesis states the existence of a state x of the form

$$x(t)=\chi_{[t_1,t_2)\vee[t_3,t_4)\vee\ldots}(t)$$

where

$$\delta_r<t_2-t_1$$
$$\delta_f<t_3-t_2$$
$$\delta_r<t_4-t_3$$
$$\ldots$$

and $t_1<t_2<t_3<t_4<\ldots$ are arbitrary numbers so that

$$d_f-m_f\le t_1\le d_r$$
$$d_r+\varepsilon\le t_2\le d_f+m_r+\varepsilon$$
$$d_f+m_r+2\varepsilon\le t_3\le d_r+m_r+m_f+2\varepsilon$$
$$d_r+m_r+m_f+3\varepsilon\le t_4\le d_f+2m_r+m_f+3\varepsilon$$
$$d_f+2m_r+m_f+4\varepsilon\le t_5\le d_r+2m_r+2m_f+4\varepsilon$$
$$\ldots$$

We infer

$$\delta_r+\delta_f<t_3-t_1\le d_r-d_f-m_r+2(m_r+m_f)+2\varepsilon\le 2(m_r+m_f)+2\varepsilon$$
$$2(\delta_r+\delta_f)<t_5-t_1\le d_r-d_f-m_r+3(m_r+m_f)+4\varepsilon\le 3(m_r+m_f)+4\varepsilon$$
$$3(\delta_r+\delta_f)<t_7-t_1\le d_r-d_f-m_r+4(m_r+m_f)+6\varepsilon\le 4(m_r+m_f)+6\varepsilon$$
$$\ldots$$

and thus

$$\forall n\ge 1,\forall\varepsilon>0,\delta_r+\delta_f<\tfrac{n+1}{n}(m_r+m_f)+2\varepsilon$$

8.3.2 Definition Given the numbers $0\le m_r\le d_r, 0\le m_f\le d_f$ and $\delta_r\ge 0,\delta_f\ge 0$, the system of inequalities

$$d_r \geq d_f - m_f, d_f \geq d_r - m_r$$
$$\delta_r + \delta_f \leq m_r + m_f$$

is called the *consistency condition* (of the bounded absolute inertial delay condition) (CC_{BAIDC}).

8.3.3 Remark (*Special cases of* CC_{BAIDC}) If $m_r = m_f = 0$ then CC_{BAIDC} becomes $d_r = d_f$ and $\delta_r = \delta_f = 0$ and the system 8.3.1 b) is equivalent with FDC. For $m_r = d_r, m_f = d_f$ CC_{BAIDC} becomes $\delta_r + \delta_f \leq d_r + d_f$; and in the symmetrical case $m_r = m_f = m$, $d_r = d_f = d, \delta_r = \delta_f = \delta$, CC_{BAIDC} means $\delta \leq m$.

8.4 Bounded Absolute Inertial Delays

8.4.1 Definition Let $u, x \in S$ and the numbers $0 \leq m_r \leq d_r, 0 \leq m_f \leq d_f, 0 \leq \delta_r, 0 \leq \delta_f$ so that $d_f \geq d_r - m_r, d_r \geq d_f - m_f$ and $\delta_r + \delta_f \leq m_r + m_f$ are true. The system of inequalities

$$\bigcap_{\xi \in [t-d_r, t-d_r+m_r]} u(\xi) \leq x(t) \leq \bigcup_{\xi \in [t-d_f, t-d_f+m_f]} u(\xi) \quad (1)$$

$$\overline{x(t-0)} \cdot x(t) \leq \bigcap_{\xi \in [t, t+\delta_r]} x(\xi) \quad (2)$$

$$x(t-0) \cdot \overline{x(t)} \leq \bigcap_{\xi \in [t, t+\delta_f]} \overline{x(\xi)} \quad (3)$$

is called the *bounded absolute inertial delay condition* (BAIDC). When BAIDC is fulfilled, we say that the tuple $(u, m_r, d_r, m_f, d_f, \delta_r, \delta_f, x)$ satisfies BAIDC.

We also call bounded absolute inertial delay condition the DC $Sol_{BDC}^{m_r, d_r, m_f, d_f} \wedge Sol_{AIC}^{\delta_r, \delta_f}$.

8.4.2 Remark BAIDC is a DC indeed, from Theorem 8.3.1. Its interpretation is obvious: x is a solution of BAIDC if it switches from 0 to 1 with a delay $d \in [d_f - m_f, d_r]$ and then it keeps the value 1 for strictly more than δ_r time units and dually if it switches from 1 to 0 with a delay $d \in [d_r - m_r, d_f]$ and, after the switch, a new switch may happen after strictly more than δ_f time units.

BAIDC keeps the negative interpretation of BDC, see 7.2.6.

8.4.3 Theorem We suppose that $0 \le m_r \le d_r$, $0 \le m_f \le d_f$, $0 \le m_r^{'} \le d_r^{'}$, $0 \le m_f^{'} \le d_f^{'}$ and $\delta_r \ge 0$, $\delta_f \ge 0$, $\delta_r^{'} \ge 0$, $\delta_f^{'} \ge 0$ are given and they satisfy CC_{BAIDC} twice. In such conditions $Sol_{BDC}^{m_r,d_r,m_f,d_f} \wedge Sol_{AIC}^{\delta_r,\delta_f}$, $Sol_{BDC}^{m_r^{'},d_r^{'},m_f^{'},d_f^{'}} \wedge Sol_{AIC}^{\delta_r^{'},\delta_f^{'}}$, $Sol_{BDC}^{m_r+m_r^{'},d_r+d_r^{'},m_f+m_f^{'},d_f+d_f^{'}} \wedge Sol_{AIC}^{\delta_r^{'},\delta_f^{'}}$ are BAIDC's and the next property of serial connection holds:

$$(Sol_{BDC}^{m_r^{'},d_r^{'},m_f^{'},d_f^{'}} \wedge Sol_{AIC}^{\delta_r^{'},\delta_f^{'}}) \circ (Sol_{BDC}^{m_r,d_r,m_f,d_f} \wedge Sol_{AIC}^{\delta_r,\delta_f}) \subset$$

$$\subset Sol_{BDC}^{m_r+m_r^{'},d_r+d_r^{'},m_f+m_f^{'},d_f+d_f^{'}} \wedge Sol_{AIC}^{\delta_r^{'},\delta_f^{'}}$$

Proof We observe that $\delta_r^{'} + \delta_f^{'} \le m_r^{'} + m_f^{'}$ implies $\delta_r^{'} + \delta_f^{'} \le m_r + m_r^{'} + m_f + m_f^{'}$ thus, taking into account Theorems 7.3.7 and 8.2.8, the result follows.

9. Relative Inertial Delays

9.1 Relative Inertia

9.1.1 Theorem Let the real numbers $0 \le \mu_r \le \delta_r, 0 \le \mu_f \le \delta_f$. The next statements are equivalent

a) $$\overline{x(t-0)} \cdot x(t) \le \bigcap_{\xi \in [t-\delta_r, t-\delta_r+\mu_r]} u(\xi)$$

$$x(t-0) \cdot \overline{x(t)} \le \bigcap_{\xi \in [t-\delta_f, t-\delta_f+\mu_f]} \overline{u(\xi)}$$

b) $$\overline{x(t-0)} \cdot x(t) \le \overline{x(t-0)} \cdot \bigcap_{\xi \in [t-\delta_r, t-\delta_r+\mu_r]} u(\xi)$$

$$x(t-0) \cdot \overline{x(t)} \le x(t-0) \cdot \bigcap_{\xi \in [t-\delta_f, t-\delta_f+\mu_f]} \overline{u(\xi)}$$

where $u, x \in S$.

Proof Similar with the $a) \Leftrightarrow b)$ part of the proof from 8.1.1.

9.1.2 Definition Any of the properties 9.1.1 a), 9.1.1 b) is called the *relative inertial condition* (RIC). u, x are the *input*, respectively the *state* (or *output*) and $\mu_r, \delta_r, \mu_f, \delta_f$ are the (*rising, falling*) *inertia parameters*. We say that the tuple $(u, \mu_r, \delta_r, \mu_f, \delta_f, x)$ satisfies RIC.

We call also relative inertial condition the function $Sol_{RIC}^{\mu_r,\delta_r,\mu_f,\delta_f} : S \to P^*(S)$ defined by

$$Sol_{RIC}^{\mu_r,\delta_r,\mu_f,\delta_f}(u) = \{x \mid (u, \mu_r, \delta_r, \mu_f, \delta_f, x) \text{ satisfies } RIC\}$$

9.1.3 Remarks The compatibility between RIC and the initial values $u(0-0), x(0-0)$ is given by the fact that for any $t<0$ we have $\overline{x(t-0)}\cdot x(t) = x(t-0)\cdot\overline{x(t)} = 0$, thus RIC is fulfilled trivially.

The word '*relative*' in our terminology refers to the fact that u, x occur both in RIC. We interpret this condition now by recalling some quotations.

[12], [13], see 5.13 a): the inertial delays '*model the fact that the practical circuits will not respond* (at the output) *to two transitions* (on the input) *which are very close together*'. In case that two transitions of u are 'very close together', i.e. if u has a 1-pulse of length $\le \mu_r$, respectively a 0-pulse of length $\le \mu_f$, then the function $\bigcap_{\xi\in[t-\delta_r, t-\delta_r+\mu_r]} u(\xi)$, respectively $\bigcap_{\xi\in[t-\delta_f, t-\delta_f+\mu_f]} \overline{u(\xi)}$ is null, thus the function $\overline{x(t-0)}\cdot x(t)$, respectively $x(t-0)\cdot\overline{x(t)}$ is null too.

In this context we rewrite a quotation from [11], see 5.13 b): '*pulses shorter than or equal to the delay magnitude are not transmitted*' in the next manner: '*pulses shorter than or equal to* μ_r (respectively μ_f) *are not transmitted and pulses strictly longer than* μ_r (respectively than μ_f) *may be transmitted*'.

On the other hand 5.14 ii) and 5.16 i) look like RIC with $\delta_r = \delta_f = d_{\min}$, $\mu_r = \mu_f = d_{\min} - 0$ in the latter, point of view that agrees with the one from [12], [13] see Convention 5.3 stating that : '*the transmission delay for transitions is the same as the threshold for cancellation*'. Here δ_r, δ_f act as 'transmission delays for transitions' even if they are rather 'minimum transmission delays for transitions' and μ_r, μ_f act as 'thresholds for cancellation'. 'The same as' means that the two quantities differ by a small infinitesimal.

Furthermore, let us recall [1], see 5.15 with: '*changes should persist for at least* l_1 *time units but propagated after* $l_2, l_2 > l_1$ *time*'. In our formalism, if we accept the rising-falling symmetry, we have: $l_1 = \mu_r = \mu_f, l_2 = \delta_r = \delta_f$ and '*changes should persist for strictly more than* l_1 *time units but propagated after more than or equal with* $l_2, l_2 \ge l_1$ *time*'.

9.1.4 Theorem (*The relation between RIC and AIC*) Let $0 \le \mu_r \le \delta_r, 0 \le \mu_f \le \delta_f$ arbitrary. If $\delta_f \ge \delta_r - \mu_r, \delta_r \ge \delta_f - \mu_f$ then $\forall u, Sol_{RIC}^{\mu_r,\delta_r,\mu_f,\delta_f}(u) \subset Sol_{AIC}^{\delta_f-\delta_r+\mu_r,\delta_r-\delta_f+\mu_f}$.

Proof Let $d < d'$, u and $x \in Sol_{RIC}^{\mu_r,\delta_r,\mu_f,\delta_f}(u)$ so that

$$\overline{x(d-0)} \cdot x(d) = 1 \; and \; x(d'-0) \cdot \overline{x(d')} = 1$$

We get

$$\bigcap_{\xi \in [d-\delta_r, d-\delta_r+\mu_r]} u(\xi) = \bigcap_{\xi \in [d'-\delta_f, d'-\delta_f+\mu_f]} \overline{u(\xi)} = 1$$

$$\Rightarrow [d-\delta_r, d-\delta_r+\mu_r] \wedge [d'-\delta_f, d'-\delta_f+\mu_f] = \varnothing$$

$$\Rightarrow d-\delta_r+\mu_r < d'-\delta_f \; or \; d'-\delta_f+\mu_f < d-\delta_r$$

$$\Rightarrow d'-d > \delta_f-\delta_r+\mu_r \; or \; d'-d < \delta_f-\mu_f-\delta_r$$

$$\Rightarrow d'-d > \delta_f-\delta_r+\mu_r$$

(The inequality $d'-d < \delta_f-\mu_f-\delta_r$ is false, because the left term is strictly positive and the right term is non-positive).

The proof is similar for the second inequality.

9.1.5 Definition In the next property:

$\forall \varepsilon > 0, \exists d, \exists d', \exists u, \; \exists x \in Sol_{RIC}^{\mu_r,\delta_r,\mu_f,\delta_f}(u)$ so that

$$\overline{x(d-0)} \cdot x(d) = 1 \; and \; x(d'-0) \cdot \overline{x(d')} = 1 \; and \; |d-d'| < \varepsilon$$

the signal x whose existence is stated is called *Zeno solution of RIC* (expressed by $Sol_{RIC}^{\mu_r,\delta_r,\mu_f,\delta_f}$).

9.1.6 Theorem The necessary and the sufficient condition in order that $Sol_{RIC}^{\mu_r,\delta_r,\mu_f,\delta_f}$ has no Zeno solutions is that $\delta_f > \delta_r - \mu_r, \delta_r > \delta_f - \mu_f$.

Proof The necessity We suppose against all reason that $\delta_f \le \delta_r - \mu_r$ and let $u = \chi_{(-\infty,0)}$ for which

$$\bigcap_{\xi \in [t-\delta_r, t-\delta_r+\mu_r]} \chi_{(-\infty,0)}(\xi) = \chi_{(-\infty,\delta_r-\mu_r)}(t)$$

$$\bigcap_{\xi \in [t-\delta_f, t-\delta_f+\mu_f]} \chi_{[0,\infty)}(\xi) = \chi_{[\delta_f,\infty)}(t)$$

We have for any $\varepsilon > 0$ that $x = \chi_{[\delta_f-\varepsilon,\delta_f)} \in Sol_{RIC}^{\mu_r,\delta_r,\mu_f,\delta_f}(u)$, contradiction with the hypothesis. The supposition that $\delta_r \le \delta_f - \mu_f$ is similar.

The sufficiency results from Theorem 9.1.4.

9.1.7 Remarks We have for any $a \in \mathbf{B}$ that $Sol_{RIC}^{\mu_r,\delta_r,\mu_f,\delta_f}(a) = \{0,1\} \vee \{\overline{a} \oplus \chi_{[\tau,\infty)} \mid \tau \geq 0\}$.

On the other hand RIC is a constancy condition, in the sense that

$$\overline{x(t-0)} \cdot x(t) \leq u(t-\delta_r)$$
$$x(t-0) \cdot \overline{x(t)} \leq \overline{u(t-\delta_f)}$$

9.2 Relative Inertial Delays

9.2.1 Definition Let the numbers $0 \leq \mu_r \leq \delta_r, 0 \leq \mu_f \leq \delta_f$ and the DC i. If i satisfies the condition $\forall u, i(u) \subset Sol_{RIC}^{\mu_r,\delta_r,\mu_f,\delta_f}(u)$, then it is called *relative inertial delay condition* (RIDC). We also say that i satisfies RIC (represented by $Sol_{RIC}^{\mu_r,\delta_r,\mu_f,\delta_f}$).

9.2.2 Examples

a) If the DC i fulfills $\forall u, i(u) \wedge Sol_{RIC}^{\mu_r,\delta_r,\mu_f,\delta_f}(u) \neq \emptyset$, then it defines (see Theorem 6.2.4 c)) the RIDC $i \wedge Sol_{RIC}^{\mu_r,\delta_r,\mu_f,\delta_f}$. The extreme situations are expressed by Sol_{SC} and respectively by I_d, that define in this manner RIDC's for all $\mu_r, \delta_r, \mu_f, \delta_f$, respectively for $\mu_r = \mu_f = 0, \delta_r = \delta_f = d$.

b) The next functions

$$i(u) = \begin{cases} 1, if \ \exists \lim\limits_{t \to \infty} u(t) \ and \ \lim\limits_{t \to \infty} u(t) = 1 \\ 0, otherwise \end{cases}$$

$$i(u) = \begin{cases} 0, if \ \exists \lim\limits_{t \to \infty} u(t) \ and \ \lim\limits_{t \to \infty} u(t) = 0 \\ 1, otherwise \end{cases}$$

and more general the next functions

$$i(u) = \begin{cases} \{1\} \vee \{\chi_{[\tau,\infty)} \mid \tau \geq \delta\}, \delta = \begin{cases} \delta_r + \max supp\ Du, supp\ Du \neq \emptyset \\ 0, supp\ Du = \emptyset \end{cases}, \\ \qquad if \ \exists \lim\limits_{t \to \infty} u(t) \ and \ \lim\limits_{t \to \infty} u(t) = 1 \\ 0, otherwise \end{cases}$$

$$i(u)=\begin{cases}\{0\}\vee\{\chi_{(-\infty,\tau)}\mid\tau\geq\delta\},\delta=\begin{cases}\delta_f+\max supp\, Du, supp\, Du\neq\emptyset\\ 0, supp\, Du=\emptyset\end{cases}, \\ \qquad if\ \exists\lim_{t\to\infty}u(t)\ and\ \lim_{t\to\infty}u(t)=0\\ 1, otherwise\end{cases}$$

are DC's defining RIDC's like at a) for all $\mu_r,\delta_r,\mu_f,\delta_f$.

c) Let $0\leq m\leq d$. From 4.2.2 we have that the DC $x(t)=\bigcap_{\xi\in[t-d,t-d+m]}u(\xi)$ satisfies RIC

$$\overline{x(t-0)}\cdot x(t)\leq\bigcap_{\xi\in[t-d,t-d+m]}u(\xi)$$

$$x(t-0)\cdot\overline{x(t)}\leq\overline{u(t-d+m)}$$

and dually for $x(t)=\bigcup_{\xi\in[t-d,t-d+m]}u(\xi)$.

d) The DC that is defined by 8.2.5 (1), 8.2.5 (2) satisfies the relative inertial condition

$$\overline{x(t-0)}\cdot x(t)\leq\bigcap_{\xi\in[t-d_r,t-d_r+m_r]}u(\xi)$$

$$x(t-0)\cdot\overline{x(t)}\leq\bigcap_{\xi\in[t-d_f,t-d_f+m_f]}\overline{u(\xi)}$$

9.2.3 Theorem Let $0\leq\mu_r\leq\delta_r,0\leq\mu_f\leq\delta_f$.

a) $Sol_{SC}\wedge Sol_{RIC}^{\mu_r,\delta_r,\mu_f,\delta_f}$ is time variable.

b) $Sol_{SC}\wedge Sol_{RIC}^{\mu_r,\delta_r,\mu_f,\delta_f}$ is symmetrical iff $\mu_r=\mu_f,\delta_r=\delta_f$.

Proof a) Like at Example 6.5.5 b), $1=1\circ\tau^{-1}\in S$ and $\chi_{[0,\infty)}\in Sol_{SC}(1)\wedge Sol_{RIC}^{\mu_r,\delta_r,\mu_f,\delta_f}(1)$, but $\chi_{[0,\infty)}\circ\tau^{-1}=\chi_{[-1,\infty)}\notin S$.

b) Only if For $u=\chi_{[0,\infty)}$ we compute

$$\bigcap_{\xi\in[t-\delta_r,t-\delta_r+\mu_r]}\chi_{[0,\infty)}(\xi)=\chi_{[\delta_r,\infty)}(t)$$

$$\bigcap_{\xi\in[t-\delta_f,t-\delta_f+\mu_f]}\chi_{(-\infty,0)}(\xi)=\chi_{(-\infty,\delta_f-\mu_f)}(t)$$

$$\bigcap_{\xi\in[t-\delta_r,t-\delta_r+\mu_r]}\chi_{(-\infty,0)}(\xi)=\chi_{(-\infty,\delta_r-\mu_r)}(t)$$

$$\bigcap_{\xi\in[t-\delta_f,t-\delta_f+\mu_f]}\chi_{[0,\infty)}(\xi)=\chi_{[\delta_f,\infty)}(t)$$

The systems of inequalities

$$\begin{cases}\overline{x(t-0)}\cdot x(t)\le\chi_{[\delta_r,\infty)}(t)\\ x(t-0)\cdot\overline{x(t)}\le\chi_{(-\infty,\delta_f-\mu_f)}(t)\end{cases}\qquad\begin{cases}x(t-0)\cdot\overline{x(t)}\le\chi_{(-\infty,\delta_r-\mu_r)}(t)\\ \overline{x(t-0)}\cdot x(t)\le\chi_{[\delta_f,\infty)}(t)\end{cases}$$

are equivalent only if $\delta_r=\delta_f$ and $\mu_r=\mu_f$.

9.2.4 **Remark** A property like the one that was stated for AIC in Theorem 8.2.8 is not true for RIC. Let for this the statement 8.2.8 a)

$$(Sol_{SC}\wedge Sol_{RIC}^{\mu'_r,\delta'_r,\mu'_f,\delta'_f})\circ(Sol_{SC}\wedge Sol_{RIC}^{\mu_r,\delta_r,\mu_f,\delta_f})=$$

$$=(Sol_{SC}\circ(Sol_{SC}\wedge Sol_{RIC}^{\mu_r,\delta_r,\mu_f,\delta_f}))\wedge Sol_{RIC}^{\mu'_r,\delta'_r,\mu'_f,\delta'_f}\subset$$

$$\subset(Sol_{SC}\circ Sol_{SC})\wedge Sol_{RIC}^{\mu''_r,\delta''_r,\mu''_f,\delta''_f}\qquad(1)$$

where $\mu''_r=\mu'_r,\delta''_r=\delta'_r,\mu''_f=\mu'_f,\delta''_f=\delta'_f$ or, in any case, $\mu''_r,\delta''_r,\mu''_f,\delta''_f$ are fixed and depend on $\mu_r,\delta_r,\mu_f,\delta_f,\mu'_r,\delta'_r,\mu'_f,\delta'_f$ only. We take $u(t)=\chi_{[t_1,\infty)}(t),\ x(t)=1, y(t)=\chi_{[t_0,\infty)}(t),\ 0\le t_0,0\le t_1$ for which

$$y\in Sol_{SC}(x)\ and\ y\in Sol_{RIC}^{\mu'_r,\delta'_r,\mu'_f,\delta'_f}(x)\ and\ x\in Sol_{SC}(u)\ and\ x\in Sol_{RIC}^{\mu_r,\delta_r,\mu_f,\delta_f}(u)$$

but

$$y\in(Sol_{SC}\circ Sol_{SC})(u)\ and\ y\notin Sol_{RIC}^{\mu''_r,\delta''_r,\mu''_f,\delta''_f}(u)$$

if $t_1>t_0-\delta''_r$ and this shows the falsity of (1). In other words, inertia's inertia is not inertia, the inertia's paradox that we have mentioned in our introduction (Section 1).

The explanation of this paradox brings us from 8.2.8 to 6.8.6 a), where the proof for

$$(i\wedge U)\circ j=(i\circ j)\wedge U$$

was the next one: for any u

$$((i\wedge U)\circ j)(u)=\{y\,|\,\exists x, y\in i(x)\ and\ y\in U\ and\ x\in j(u)\}=((i\circ j)\wedge U)(u)$$

and this was true for $U=Sol_{AIC}^{\delta'_r,\delta'_f}$ at 8.2.8. If U is variable however $U=\varphi(\cdot)$ like here, with $\varphi(u)=Sol_{RIC}^{\mu'_r,\delta'_r,\mu'_f,\delta'_f}(u)$ the property 6.8.6 is false because the statements

$$((i\wedge\varphi)\circ j)(u)=\{y\,|\,\exists x, y\in i(x)\ and\ y\in\varphi(x)\ and\ x\in j(u)\}$$
$$((i\circ j)\wedge\varphi)(u)=\{y\,|\,\exists x, y\in i(x)\ and\ y\in\varphi(u)\ and\ x\in j(u)\}$$

are not equivalent. The first equality from (1) is false.

9.3 The Consistency Condition

9.3.1 Theorem The numbers $0 \le m_r \le d_r, 0 \le m_f \le d_f, 0 \le \mu_r \le \delta_r, 0 \le \mu_f \le \delta_f$ are given. The next system

$$\bigcap_{\xi\in[t-d_r,t-d_r+m_r]} u(\xi) \le x(t) \le \bigcup_{\xi\in[t-d_f,t-d_f+m_f]} u(\xi)$$

$$\overline{x(t-0)}\cdot x(t) \le \bigcap_{\xi\in[t-\delta_r,t-\delta_r+\mu_r]} u(\xi)$$

$$x(t-0)\cdot \overline{x(t)} \le \bigcap_{\xi\in[t-\delta_f,t-\delta_f+\mu_f]} \overline{u(\xi)}$$

where $u, x \in S$ has solutions for any u if and only if one of the next requests is satisfied:

a) $$d_f - m_f \le \delta_r \le d_r \le \delta_r - \mu_r + m_r$$
$$d_r - m_r \le \delta_f \le d_f \le \delta_f - \mu_f + m_f$$

b) $$d_r - m_r + \mu_r \le \delta_r \le d_f - m_f \le d_r$$
$$d_f - m_f + \mu_f \le \delta_f \le d_r - m_r \le d_f$$

c) $$d_f - m_f \le \delta_r \le d_r - m_r + \mu_r \le d_r$$
$$d_r - m_r \le \delta_f \le d_f - m_f + \mu_f \le d_f$$

d) $$\delta_r \le d_f - m_f \le \delta_r + m_r - \mu_r \le d_r$$
$$\delta_f \le d_r - m_r \le \delta_f + m_f - \mu_f \le d_f$$

Proof Solutions exist iff whenever x must have the value 1, respectively the value 0 in t ($\bigcap_{\xi\in[t-d_r,t-d_r+m_r]} u(\xi)$ switches in t from 0 to 1, respectively $\bigcup_{\xi\in[t-d_f,t-d_f+m_f]} u(\xi)$ switches in t from 1 to 0), RIC gives this possibility (t' exists so that $\bigcap_{\xi\in[t'-\delta_r,t'-\delta_r+\mu_r]} u(\xi) = 1$, respectively so that $\bigcap_{\xi\in[t'-\delta_f,t'-\delta_f+\mu_f]} \overline{u(\xi)} = 1$) in time ($t' \in [t - d_r + d_f - m_f, t]$, respectively $t' \in [t - d_f + d_r - m_r, t]$).

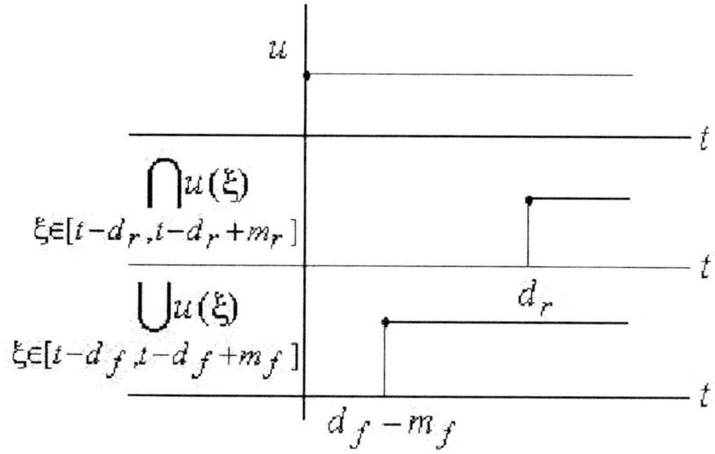

Fig 18

This happens for example in Fig 18 for $t = d_r$. We can write

$$\overline{u(t-d_r-0)}\cdot \bigcap_{\xi\in[t-d_r,t-d_r+m_r]} u(\xi) \le \bigcup_{t'\in[t-d_r+d_f-m_f,t]} \bigcap_{\xi\in[t'-\delta_r,t'-\delta_r+\mu_r]} u(\xi) \quad (1)$$

inequality that is true for any u [4]. The next statements are all equivalent with the previous one:

$$\forall u, \quad \bigcap_{\xi\in[t-d_r,t-d_r+m_r]} u(\xi) \le \bigcup_{t'\in[t-d_r+d_f-m_f,t]} \bigcap_{\xi\in[t'-\delta_r,t'-\delta_r+\mu_r]} u(\xi) \quad (2)$$

($(1)\Rightarrow(2)$: Let $0 \le t_0$ and u so that $\bigcap_{\xi\in[t_0,t_0+m_r]} u(\xi) = 1$ and we define $v(\xi) = \begin{cases} u(\xi), \xi \ge t_0 \\ 0, \xi < t_0 \end{cases}$. From (1) and from $v(t) \le u(t)$ we have $\overline{v(t_0-0)}\cdot \bigcap_{\xi\in[t_0,t_0+m_r]} v(\xi) = 1$ thus $\exists t' \in [t_0+d_f-m_f, t_0+d_r]$, $1 = \bigcap_{\xi\in[t'-\delta_r,t'-\delta_r+\mu_r]} v(\xi) \le \bigcap_{\xi\in[t'-\delta_r,t'-\delta_r+\mu_r]} u(\xi)$ thus (2) is truc. $(2)\Rightarrow(1)$:We have

$$\overline{u(t-d_r-0)}\cdot \bigcap_{\xi\in[t-d_r,t-d_r+m_r]} u(\xi)$$

$$\le \bigcap_{\xi\in[t-d_r,t-d_r+m_r]} u(\xi) \le \bigcup_{t'\in[t-d_r+d_f-m_f,t]} \bigcap_{\xi\in[t'-\delta_r,t'-\delta_r+\mu_r]} u(\xi) \;)$$

$$\exists t' \in [t-d_r+d_f-m_f,t], [t-d_r,t-d_r+m_r] \supset [t'-\delta_r, t'-\delta_r+\mu_r]$$

(3)

---

[4] The left term of this inequality represents $D_{01} \bigcap_{\xi\in[t-d_r,t-d_r+m_r]} u(\xi)$, see 4.2.2

$$\exists t',\begin{cases} t-d_r+d_f-m_f\le t' \\ t-d_r+\delta_r \le t'\end{cases} \text{and} \begin{cases} t'\le t \\ t'\le t-d_r+m_r+\delta_r-\mu_r\end{cases}$$

(4)

$$\max(t-d_r+d_f-m_f, t-d_r+\delta_r)\le \min(t, t-d_r+m_r+\delta_r-\mu_r)$$

(5)

one of the next possibilities is true:

(6)

j) $-d_r+d_f-m_f\le -d_r+\delta_r$

$0\le -d_r+m_r+\delta_r-\mu_r$

$-d_r+\delta_r\le 0$

jj) $-d_r+d_f-m_f\ge -d_r+\delta_r$

$0\le -d_r+m_r+\delta_r-\mu_r$

$-d_r+d_f-m_f\le 0$

jjj) $-d_r+d_f-m_f\le -d_r+\delta_r$

$0\ge -d_r+m_r+\delta_r-\mu_r$

$-d_r+\delta_r\le -d_r+m_r+\delta_r-\mu_r$

jv) $-d_r+d_f-m_f\ge -d_r+\delta_r$

$0\ge -d_r+m_r+\delta_r-\mu_r$

$-d_r+d_f-m_f\le -d_r+m_r+\delta_r-\mu_r$

It is shown that j), jj), jjj), jv) are equivalent with the first statements of a), b), c), d).

9.3.2 Definition The condition

9.3.1 a) *or* 9.3.1 b) *or* 9.3.1 c) *or* 9.3.1 d)

is called the *consistency condition* (of the bounded relative inertial delay condition) (CC_{BRIDC}).

9.3.3 Theorem

a) Any of 9.3.1 a),...,9.3.1 d) implies $d_f\ge d_r-m_r, d_r\ge d_f-m_f$ in other words CC_{BRIDC} in stronger than CC_{BDC}.

b) CC_{BRIDC} implies the next conditions (that are conditions of necessity for the existence of a solution of the system 9.3.1)

$$m_r\ge\mu_r, m_f\ge\mu_f$$

$$\delta_r\le d_r, \delta_f\le d_f$$

$$d_f-m_f\le\delta_r-\mu_r+m_r, d_r-m_r\le\delta_f-\mu_f+m_f$$

c) The next conditions (that are sufficient for the existence of a solution of the system 9.3.1)

$$d_f-m_f\le\delta_f-\mu_f\le\delta_r\le d_r$$

$$d_r - m_r \le \delta_r - \mu_r \le \delta_f \le d_f$$

imply CC_{BRIDC}.

Proof b) It is shown that any of 9.3.1 a),…,d) implies these inequalities..

c) It is shown that they imply 9.3.1 a).

9.3.4 Remarks (*Special cases of* CC_{BRIDC}) If in CC_{BRIDC} $\mu_r = m_r = \mu_f = m_f = 0$, then it takes the form $\delta_r = d_r = \delta_f = d_f = d$ and the system 9.3.1 degenerates in FDC. If $m_r = d_r, m_f = d_f$, $\mu_r = \delta_r$, $\mu_f = \delta_f$ then CC_{BRIDC} becomes $\delta_r \le d_r, \delta_f \le d_f$. If $d_r = \delta_r, d_f = \delta_f, m_r = \mu_r$, $m_f = \mu_f$, then CC_{BRIDC} becomes $d_f \ge d_r - m_r, d_r \ge d_f - m_f$, i.e. CC_{BDC}.

9.4 Bounded Relative Inertial Delays

9.4.1 Definition Let $u, x \in S$ and the numbers $0 \le m_r \le d_r, 0 \le m_f \le d_f$, $0 \le \mu_r \le \delta_r, 0 \le \mu_f \le \delta_f$ so that CC_{BRIDC} be satisfied. The system of inequalities

$$\bigcap_{\xi\in[t-d_r,t-d_r+m_r]} u(\xi) \le x(t) \le \bigcup_{\xi\in[t-d_f,t-d_f+m_f]} u(\xi)$$

$$\overline{x(t-0)} \cdot x(t) \le \bigcap_{\xi\in[t-\delta_r,t-\delta_r+\mu_r]} u(\xi)$$

$$x(t-0) \cdot \overline{x(t)} \le \bigcap_{\xi\in[t-\delta_f,t-\delta_f+\mu_f]} \overline{u(\xi)}$$

is called the *bounded relative inertial delay condition* (BRIDC); We say that the tuple $(u, m_r, d_r, m_f, d_f, \mu_r, \delta_r, \mu_f, \delta_f, x)$ satisfies BRIDC.

We call also bounded relative inertial delay condition the DC $Sol_{BDC}^{m_r,d_r,m_f,d_f} \wedge Sol_{RIC}^{\mu_r,\delta_r,\mu_f,\delta_f}$.

9.4.2 Remark BRIDC is obviously a DC, from Theorem 9.3.1. Its meaning results from Fig 19 representing the situation from 9.3.1 c), where we have supposed that $x(0-0) = 0, u(t) = \chi_{[0,\tau)}(t), \tau > m_r$. The functions $\bigcap_{\xi\in[t-d_r,t-d_r-m_r]} u(\xi)$, $\bigcup_{\xi\in[t-d_f,t-d_f+m_f]} u(\xi)$ from BDC give the possibility, respectively state the necessity of a value of x, while the functions $\bigcap_{\xi\in[t-\delta_r,t-\delta_r+\mu_r]} u(\xi)$, $\bigcap_{\xi\in[t-\delta_f,t-\delta_f+\mu_f]} \overline{u(\xi)}$ from RIC give the possibility that some switches of x happen.

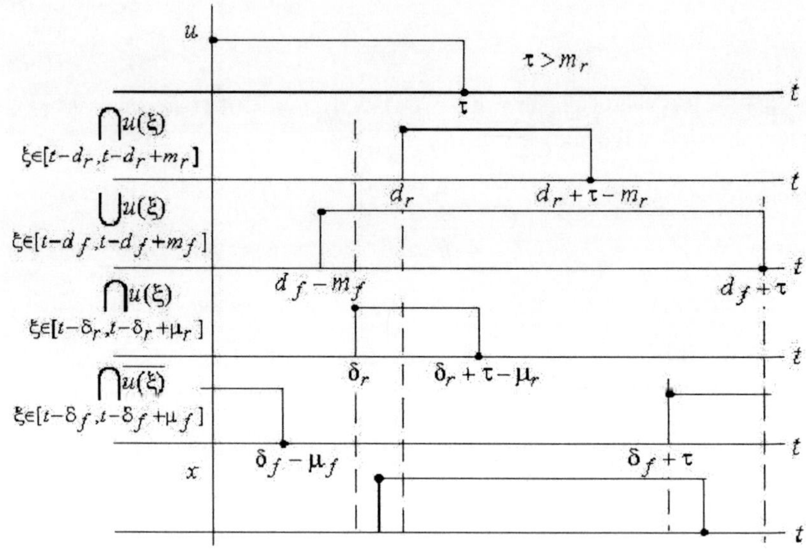

Fig 19

These interpretations may be done in other cases of CC_{BRIDC} (or violations of CC_{BRIDC}!), for example 9.3.1 a) from Fig 20, where $x(0-0)=0, u(t)=\chi_{[0,\tau)}(t), \tau > m_r$

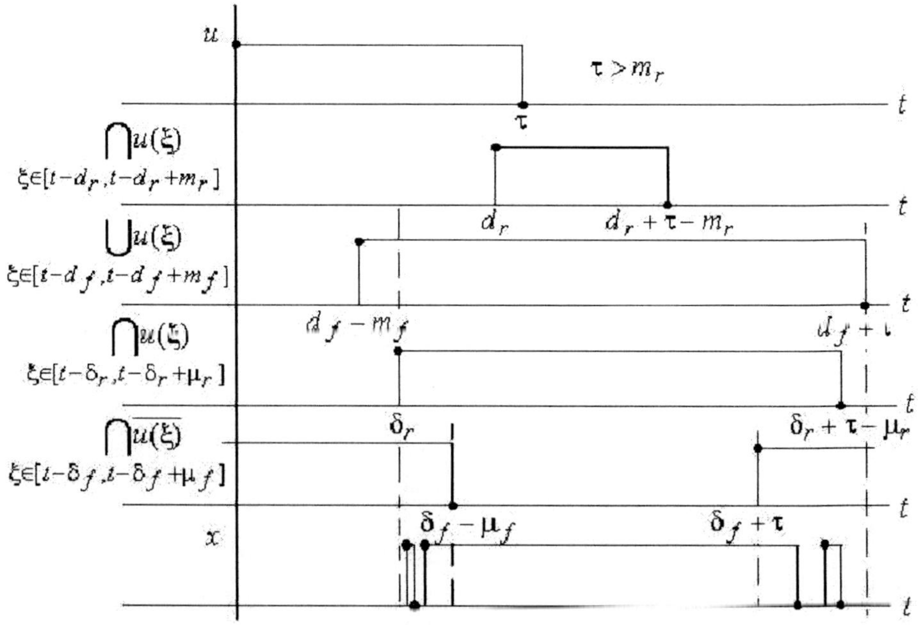

Fig 20

The intervals $[\delta_r, \delta_f - \mu_f]$ and $[\delta_f + \tau, \delta_r + \tau - \mu_r]$ are observed; if they are non-empty, then Zeno solutions of RIC exist.

We refer in Fig 21 to the requests 9.3.3 c); we suppose without loss that $x(0-0)=0, u(t)=\chi_{[0,\tau)}(t), \tau > m_r$ and we have the next time intervals when u has sufficiently long pulses (u is 1 strictly longer than m_r and then u is 0 strictly longer than m_f).

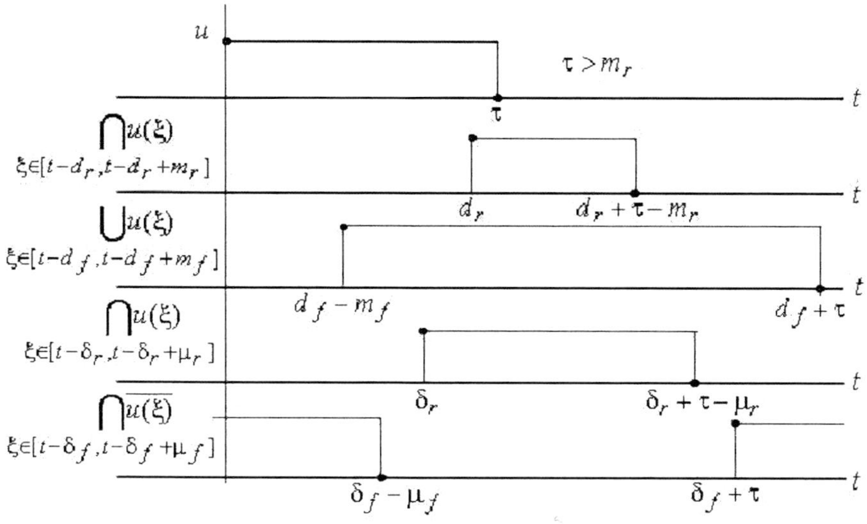

Fig 21

- $t \in (-\infty, d_f - m_f)$; $x(t)=0$ and the only possible switch -that does not happen- is from 1 to 0

- $t \in [d_f - m_f, \delta_f - \mu_f)$, $x(t)=0$;. $x(t)$ could be 1, but it is allowed to switch only from 1 to 0 and this does not happen

- $t \in [\delta_f - \mu_f, \delta_r)$, $x(t)=0$;. $x(t)$ could be 1, but no switch is allowed

- $t \in [\delta_r, d_r]$; $x(t)=0$ and $x(t)=1$ are both allowed, switching from 0 to 1 may happen and exactly one such switch takes place

- $t \in (d_r, d_r + \tau - m_r)$; $x(t)=1$ and the only possible switch -that does not happen- is from 0 to 1

- $t \in [d_r + \tau - m_r, \delta_r + \tau - \mu_r)$, $x(t)=1$; $x(t)$ could be 0, but it is allowed to switch only from 0 to 1 and this does not happen

- $t \in [\delta_r + \tau - \mu_r, \delta_f + \tau)$, $x(t)=1$; $x(t)$ could be 0, but no switches are possible in this time interval

- $t \in [\delta_f + \tau, d_f + \tau]$; $x(t)=1$ and $x(t)=0$ are both possible, switching from 1 to 0 is allowed and exactly one such switch takes place

- $t \in (d_f + \tau, \infty)$; $x(t)=0$ and the only possible switch -that does not happen- is from 1 to 0.

This succession of time intervals is repetitive if u is suitable chosen.

9.4.3 Theorem The next properties are equivalent in the sense that the arbitrary signals u,x satisfy one of them if and only if they satisfy the other one.

a) $m_r, d_r, m_f, d_f, \mu_r, \delta_r, \mu_f, \delta_f$ are given and the next inequalities are fulfilled (see also 9.3.3 c))

$$0 \le m_r \le d_r, 0 \le m_f \le d_f \tag{1}$$

$$0 \le \mu_r \le \delta_r, 0 \le \mu_f \le \delta_f \tag{2}$$

$$d_f - m_f \le \delta_f - \mu_f \le \delta_r \le d_r \tag{3}$$

$$d_r - m_r \le \delta_r - \mu_r \le \delta_f \le d_f \tag{4}$$

$$\bigcap_{\xi \in [t-d_r, t-d_r+m_r]} u(\xi) \le x(t) \le \bigcup_{\xi \in [t-d_f, t-d_f+m_f]} u(\xi) \tag{5}$$

$$\overline{x(t-0)} \cdot x(t) \le \bigcap_{\xi \in [t-\delta_r, t-\delta_r+\mu_r]} u(\xi) \tag{6}$$

$$x(t-0) \cdot \overline{x(t)} \le \bigcap_{\xi \in [t-\delta_f, t-\delta_f+\mu_f]} \overline{u(\xi)} \tag{7}$$

b) The numbers $m_{r,\min}, d_{r,\min}, m_{r,\max}, d_{r,\max}, m_{f,\min}, d_{f,\min}, m_{f,\max}, d_{f,\max}$ are given and we have

$$0 \le m_{r,\max} \le d_{r,\max}, 0 \le m_{f,\max} \le d_{f,\max} \tag{8}$$

$$0 \le m_{r,\min} \le d_{r,\min}, 0 \le m_{f,\min} \le d_{f,\min} \tag{9}$$

$$d_{f,\max} - m_{f,\max} \le d_{f,\min} - m_{f,\min} \le d_{r,\min} \le d_{r,\max} \tag{10}$$

$$d_{r,\max} - m_{r,\max} \le d_{r,\min} - m_{r,\min} \le d_{f,\min} \le d_{f,\max} \tag{11}$$

$$\overline{x(t-0)} \cdot \bigcap_{\xi \in [t-d_{r,\max}, t-d_{r,\max}+m_{r,\max}]} u(\xi) \le \overline{x(t-0)} \cdot x(t) \le \overline{x(t-0)} \cdot \bigcap_{\xi \in [t-d_{r,\min}, t-d_{r,\min}+m_{r,\min}]} u(\xi) \tag{12}$$

$$x(t-0) \cdot \bigcap_{\xi \in [t-d_{f,\max}, t-d_{f,\max}+m_{f,\max}]} \overline{u(\xi)} \le x(t-0) \cdot \overline{x(t)} \le x(t-0) \cdot \bigcap_{\xi \in [t-d_{f,\min}, t-d_{f,\min}+m_{f,\min}]} \overline{u(\xi)} \tag{13}$$

Proof The next equalities take place

$$m_{r,\min} = \mu_r, d_{r,\min} = \delta_r \tag{14}$$

$$m_{r,\max} = m_r, d_{r,\max} = d_r \tag{15}$$

$$m_{f,\min} = \mu_f, d_{f,\min} = \delta_f \tag{16}$$

$$m_{f,\max} = m_f, d_{f,\max} = d_f \tag{17}$$

under the form 'equal by definition with' in both directions $a) \Rightarrow b)$ and $b) \Rightarrow a)$ resulting that (1),...,(4) and (8),...,(11) coincide.

$a) \Rightarrow b)$ The left inequality of (5) multiplied with $\overline{x(t-0)}$ gives the left inequality of (12) and (6) multiplied with $\overline{x(t-0)}$ gives the right inequality of (12). The rest results by duality.

$b) \Rightarrow a)$ We suppose that $\bigcap_{\xi \in [t-d_r, t-d_r+m_r]} u(\xi) = 1$ and we have the next possibilities

i) $x(t-0) = 0$

Then the left inequality of (12) shows that $x(t) = 1$ and the left inequality of (5) is satisfied.

ii) $x(t-0) = 1$

and the right inequality of (13) becomes

$$\overline{x(t)} \le \bigcap_{\xi \in [t-\delta_f, t-\delta_f+\mu_f]} \overline{u(\xi)} \tag{18}$$

(10), (11) are written under the form (3), (4) and this implies

$$t - \delta_f + \mu_f \ge t - d_r \tag{19}$$

$$t - d_r + m_r \ge t - \delta_f \tag{20}$$

i.e.

$$[t-d_r, t-d_r+m_r] \wedge [t-\delta_f, t-\delta_f+\mu_f] \ne \varnothing \tag{21}$$

and thus $\bigcap_{\xi \in [t-\delta_f, t-\delta_f+\mu_f]} \overline{u(\xi)} = 0$. From (18) we get $x(t) = 1$ and the left inequality of (5) is satisfied in this case too.

On the other hand, the right inequality of (12) gives

$$\overline{x(t-0)} \cdot x(t) \le \overline{x(t-0)} \cdot \bigcap_{\xi \in [t-\delta_r, t-\delta_r+\mu_r]} u(\xi) \le \bigcap_{\xi \in [t-\delta_r, t-\delta_r+\mu_r]} u(\xi) \tag{22}$$

i.e. (6).

The other implications result by duality.

9.5 Deterministic Bounded Relative Inertial Delays

9.5.1 Theorem Let the real numbers $0 \le m_r \le d_r, 0 \le m_f \le d_f$ arbitrary with $d_r - m_r \le d_f$, $d_f - m_f \le d_r$. The next systems are equivalent, in the sense that if $u, x \in S$ satisfy one of them, then they also satisfy any other.

---

a) $$\bigcap_{\xi \in [t-d_r, t-d_r-m_r]} u(\xi) \le x(t) \le \bigcup_{\xi \in [t-d_f, t-d_f+m_f]} u(\xi) \tag{1}$$

$$\overline{x(t-0)} \cdot x(t) \leq \bigcap_{\xi \in [t-d_r, t-d_r+m_r]} u(\xi) \quad (2)$$

$$x(t-0) \cdot \overline{x(t)} \leq \bigcap_{\xi \in [t-d_f, t-d_f+m_f]} \overline{u(\xi)} \quad (3)$$

b) $$\overline{x(t-0)} \cdot x(t) = \overline{x(t-0)} \cdot \bigcap_{\xi \in [t-d_r, t-d_r+m_r]} u(\xi) \quad (4)$$

$$x(t-0) \cdot \overline{x(t)} = x(t-0) \cdot \bigcap_{\xi \in [t-d_f, t-d_f+m_f]} \overline{u(\xi)} \quad (5)$$

c) $$\bigcap_{\xi \in [t-d_r, t-d_r+m_r]} u(\xi) \leq x(t) \quad (6)$$

$$\bigcap_{\xi \in [t-d_f, t-d_f+m_f]} \overline{u(\xi)} \leq \overline{x(t)} \quad (7)$$

$$\overline{\bigcap_{\xi \in [t-d_r, t-d_r+m_r]} u(\xi)} \cdot \overline{\bigcap_{\xi \in [t-d_f, t-d_f+m_f]} \overline{u(\xi)}} \leq$$

$$\leq \overline{x(t-0)} \cdot \overline{x(t)} \cup x(t-0) \cdot x(t) \quad (8)$$

d) $$x(t) = \begin{cases} 1, & \bigcap_{\xi \in [t-d_r, t-d_r+m_r]} u(\xi) = 1 \\ 0, & \bigcap_{\xi \in [t-d_f, t-d_f+m_f]} \overline{u(\xi)} = 1 \\ x(t-0), & otherwise \end{cases} \quad (9)$$

e) $$x(t) = \bigcap_{\xi \in [t-d_r, t-d_r+m_r]} u(\xi) \cup x(t-0) \cdot \bigcup_{\xi \in [t-d_f, t-d_f+m_f]} u(\xi) \quad (10)$$

f) $$Dx(t) = \overline{x(t-0)} \cdot \bigcap_{\xi \in [t-d_r, t-d_r+m_r]} u(\xi) \cup$$

$$\cup\, x(t-0) \cdot \bigcap_{\xi \in [t-d_f, t-d_f+m_f]} \overline{u(\xi)} \quad (11)$$

g) $$\overline{x(t-0)} \cdot x(t) \cdot \bigcap_{\xi \in [t-d_r, t-d_r+m_r]} u(\xi) \cup x(t-0) \cdot \overline{x(t)} \cdot \bigcap_{\xi \in [t-d_f, t-d_f+m_f]} \overline{u(\xi)} \cup$$

$$\cup\, \overline{x(t-0)} \cdot \overline{x(t)} \cdot \overline{\bigcap_{\xi \in [t-d_r, t-d_r+m_r]} u(\xi)} \cup$$

$$\cup\, x(t-0) \cdot x(t) \cdot \overline{\bigcap_{\xi \in [t-d_f, t-d_f+m_f]} \overline{u(\xi)}} = 1 \quad (12)$$

Proof In a),...,g) three possibilities exist, due to the satisfaction of CC_{BDC}:

i) $$\bigcap_{\xi\in[t-d_r,t-d_r+m_r]} u(\xi) = \bigcup_{\xi\in[t-d_f,t-d_f+m_f]} u(\xi) = 0$$

ii) $$\bigcap_{\xi\in[t-d_r,t-d_r+m_r]} u(\xi) = 0, \quad \bigcup_{\xi\in[t-d_f,t-d_f+m_f]} u(\xi) = 1$$

iii) $$\bigcap_{\xi\in[t-d_r,t-d_r+m_r]} u(\xi) = \bigcup_{\xi\in[t-d_f,t-d_f+m_f]} u(\xi) = 1$$

Case i) a) gives $0 \le x(t) \le 0$ from (1), thus $x(t)=0$. By taking into account the fact that $\overline{\bigcup_{\xi\in[t-d_f,t-d_f+m_f]} u(\xi)} = \bigcap_{\xi\in[t-d_f,t-d_f+m_f]} \overline{u(\xi)} = 1$, b) is

$$\overline{x(t-0)} \cdot x(t) = 0$$
$$x(t-0) \cdot \overline{x(t)} = x(t-0)$$

whose unique solution is $x(t)=0$. c) shows, from (7), that $1 \le \overline{x(t)}$, that is $x(t)=0$. d) and e) give $x(t)=0$ too. f) becomes $x(t-0) \oplus x(t) = x(t-0)$, in other words $x(t)=0$. Because $\overline{\bigcap_{\xi\in[t-d_r,t-d_r+m_r]} u(\xi)} = 1$, g) is in this case

$$x(t-0)\cdot\overline{x(t)} \cup \overline{x(t-0)}\cdot\overline{x(t)} = (x(t-0) \cup \overline{x(t-0)})\cdot\overline{x(t)} = \overline{x(t)} = 1$$

i.e. $x(t)=0$.

The other two cases are similar, with $x(t)=x(t-0)$ for ii) and $x(t)=1$ for iii).

9.5.2 Remarks In any of the equivalent conditions 9.5.1 a),...,9.5.1 g), CC_{BRIDC} and CC_{BDC} coincide, as we have mentioned at 9.3.4.

The implications of the violation of this condition in 9.5.1 a),...,9.5.1 g) are the following. Let u and t' so that

$$[t'-d_r,t'-d_r+m_r] \wedge [t'-d_f,t'-d_f+m_f] = \varnothing$$
$$\forall\xi\in[t'-d_r,t'-d_r+m_r], u(\xi)=1$$
$$\forall\xi\in[t'-d_f,t'-d_f+m_f], u(\xi)=0$$

Let us suppose, in order to make a choice, that $t'-d_r+m_r < t'-d_f$. From the last two equations and from the right continuity of u in $t'-d_r+m_r, t'-d_f+m_f$ we get the existence of $\varepsilon > 0$ so that $t'-d_r+m_r+\varepsilon < t'-d_f$ and

$$\forall\xi\in[t'-d_r,t'-d_r+m_r+\varepsilon], u(\xi)=1$$
$$\forall\xi\in[t'-d_f,t'-d_f+m_f+\varepsilon], u(\xi)=0$$

9.5.1 a) shows that $Sol_{BDC}^{m_r,d_r,m_f,d_f}(u) = \varnothing$

9.5.1 b) becomes for any $t \in [t', t'+\varepsilon]$

$$\overline{x(t-0)} \cdot x(t) = \overline{x(t-0)}$$
$$x(t-0) \cdot \overline{x(t)} = x(t-0)$$

and the system accepts two possibilities $x(t) = 0, x(t-0) = 1$ and $x(t) = 1$, $x(t-0) = 0$, meaning that x should continuously switch in this interval; no signal satisfies such requests. 9.5.1 c) has no solution either, because 9.5.1 (6), 9.5.1 (7) show that $x(t) = 0$ and $x(t) = 1$ are both true for $t \in [t', t'+\varepsilon]$ and this is the case of 9.5.1 d) also, where $x(t)$ is not a well defined function for $t \in [t', t'+\varepsilon]$. 9.5.1 e) gives $x(t) = 1,\ t \in [t', t'+\varepsilon]$. 9.5.1 f) and 9.5.1 g) become both

$$Dx(t) = 1, t \in [t', t'+\varepsilon]$$

and this equation represents a nonsense similar with the one from 9.5.1 b), because the set $\{t \mid t \in [t', t'+\varepsilon], Dx(t) = 1\}$ should be finite (x has resulted to be 'everywhere discontinuous' in $[t', t'+\varepsilon]$).

On the other hand, Theorem 8.2.5 characterizes, via 9.5.1 b), all of 9.5.1 a),…,9.5.1 g).

9.5.3 Definition For $u, x \in S$ and $0 \le m_r \le d_r, 0 \le m_f \le d_f$ so that CC_{BDC} is satisfied, any of the equivalent properties 9.5.1 a), ..., 9.5.1 g) is called the *deterministic bounded relative inertial delay condition* (DBRIDC). We say that the tuple $(u, m_r, d_r, m_f, d_f, x)$ satisfies DBRIDC.

We call also deterministic bounded relative inertial delay condition the function $Sol_{DBRIDC}^{m_r, d_r, m_f, d_f} : S \to P^*(S)$ defined by

$$Sol_{DBRIDC}^{m_r, d_r, m_f, d_f}(u) = Sol_{BDC}^{m_r, d_r, m_f, d_f}(u) \wedge Sol_{RIC}^{m_r, d_r, m_f, d_f}(u)$$

10 Alternative Definitions. Symmetrical Deterministic Upper Bounded, Lower Unbounded Relative Inertial Delays

10.1 Alternative Definitions

We just mention the possibility of replacing

- in BDC the functions $\bigcap_{\xi \in [t-d_r, t-d_r+m_r]} u(\xi)$, $\bigcup_{\xi \in [t-d_f, t-d_f+m_f]} u(\xi)$ with $\bigcap_{\xi \in [t-d_r, t)} u(\xi)$, $\bigcup_{\xi \in [t-d_f, t)} u(\xi)$; new notation BDC'

- in AIC the functions $\bigcap_{\xi\in[t,t+\delta_r]} x(\xi)$, $\bigcap_{\xi\in[t,t+\delta_f]} \overline{x(\xi)}$ with $\bigcap_{\xi\in[t,t+\delta_r)} x(\xi)$, $\bigcap_{\xi\in[t,t+\delta_f)} \overline{x(\xi)}$; new notation AIC'
- in RIC the functions $\bigcap_{\xi\in[t-\delta_r,t-\delta_r+\mu_r]} u(\xi)$, $\bigcap_{\xi\in[t-\delta_f,t-\delta_f+\mu_f]} \overline{u(\xi)}$ with $\bigcap_{\xi\in[t-\delta_r,t)} u(\xi)$, $\bigcap_{\xi\in[t-\delta_f,t)} \overline{u(\xi)}$; new notation RIC'.

In BDC' $d_r > 0, d_f > 0$ is a consistency condition, but in AIC' and RIC' any of δ_r, δ_f can be null, resulting trivial conditions. Such substitutions are natural, but BDC' and RIC' are suggested also by the 'common form of implementation...', from Convention 5.3.

None of the six new functions are signals, however, because they are not right continuous.

10.2 Symmetrical Deterministic Upper Bounded, Lower Unbounded Relative Inertial Delays

10.2.1 Lemma Let $d_r > 0, d_f > 0$ and $u \in S$. The next formulas are true:

$$\bigcap_{\xi\in[t-d_r,t)} u(\xi) = u(t-0)\cdot \overline{\bigcup_{\xi\in(t-d_r,t)} Du(\xi)}$$

$$\bigcap_{\xi\in[t-d_f,t)} \overline{u(\xi)} = \overline{u(t-0)}\cdot \overline{\bigcup_{\xi\in(t-d_f,t)} Du(\xi)}$$

Proof We prove the first of these two relations and let t arbitrary, fixed. We have:

$$\bigcap_{\xi\in[t-d_r,t)} u(\xi) = 1 \Leftrightarrow u(t-0) = 1 \; and \; u_{|[t-d_r,t)} \text{ is constant}$$

$$\Leftrightarrow u(t-0) = 1 \; and \; u_{|(t-d_r,t)} \text{ is constant}$$

(because u is right continuous in $t-d_r$)

$$\Leftrightarrow u(t-0) = 1 \; and \; \forall \xi \in (t-d_r,t), Du(\xi) = 0$$

$$\Leftrightarrow u(t-0)\cdot \overline{\bigcup_{\xi\in(t-d_r,t)} Du(\xi)} = 1$$

Because t was arbitrary, the equation is proved.

10.2.2 Remarks The idea from 10.1 has implications in the way of understanding 9.5.1, for example 9.5.1 f) can be thought under the form

$$Dx(t) = \overline{x(t-0)}\cdot \bigcap_{\xi\in[t-d_r,t)} u(\xi) \cup x(t-0)\cdot \bigcap_{\xi\in[t-d_f,t)} \overline{u(\xi)} \quad (1)$$

The natural notation of equation (1) following the previous patterns is DBRIDC'.

In the rising-falling symmetric version, when $d_r = d_f = d > 0$:

$$\overline{x(t-0)}\cdot\bigcap_{\xi\in[t-d,t)}u(\xi)\cup x(t-0)\cdot\bigcap_{\xi\in[t-d,t)}\overline{u(\xi)}=$$

$$=\overline{x(t-0)}\cdot u(t-0)\cdot\overline{\bigcup_{\xi\in(t-d,t)}Du(\xi)}\cup x(t-0)\cdot\overline{u(t-0)}\cdot\overline{\bigcup_{\xi\in(t-d,t)}Du(\xi)}= \quad \text{(from 10.2.1)}$$

$$=(\overline{x(t-0)}\cdot u(t-0)\cup x(t-0)\cdot\overline{u(t-0)})\cdot\overline{\bigcup_{\xi\in(t-d,t)}Du(\xi)}=$$

$$=(x(t-0)\oplus u(t-0))\cdot\overline{\bigcup_{\xi\in(t-d,t)}Du(\xi)}$$

and equation (1) becomes

$$Dx(t)=(x(t-0)\oplus u(t-0))\cdot\overline{\bigcup_{\xi\in(t-d,t)}Du(\xi)} \tag{2}$$

In [23], the equation of the inertial delay circuit with null initial conditions was written under the form

$$Dx(t)=(x(t-0)\oplus u(t-0))\cdot\overline{\bigcup_{\xi\in(t-d,t)}Du(\xi)}\cdot\chi_{[d,\infty)}(t) \tag{3}$$

The context from there demanded that the signals f satisfy by definition the non-restrictive request $supp\ f\subset[0,\infty)$, thus the general form of equation (3) is

$$Dx(t)=(x(t-0)\oplus u(t-0))\cdot\overline{\bigcup_{\xi\in(t-d,t)}Du(\xi)}\cdot\chi_{[d,\infty)}(t)\oplus x^{0}\cdot\chi_{\{0\}}(t) \tag{3'}$$

where the initial value $x^0\in\boldsymbol{B}$ stands for $x(0-0)$ in our present work.

In the next drawing

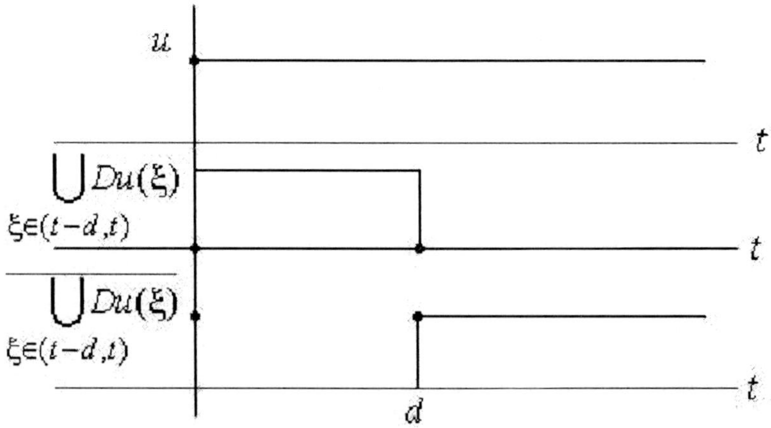

Fig 22

we have shown that, because $x(0-0)\oplus u(0-0)=0$ (a slightly modified version of Theorem 7.2.4 is valid here) both equations (2) and (3) satisfy $\forall u,\forall t<d, Dx(t)=0$ thus they are equivalent. The abbreviation is SDBRIDC'.

11. Other Examples and Applications

11.1 A Delay Line for the Falling Transitions Only

The proposed circuit that is reproduced from [11] has the gates and the wires governed by delays

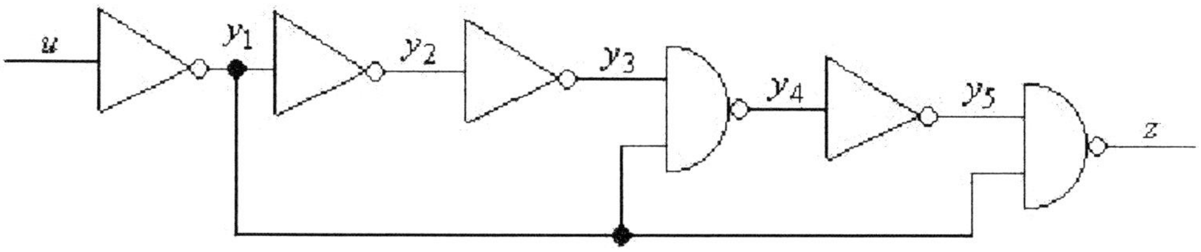

Fig 23

From the static point of view, $u, y_1,..., y_5, z \in \boldsymbol{B}$ and we observe that

$$z=\overline{y_1\cdot y_5}=\overline{y_1\cdot \overline{y_4}}=\overline{y_1\cdot (y_3\cdot y_1)}=\overline{y_1\cdot y_3}=\overline{y_1\cdot \overline{y_2}}=\overline{y_1\cdot y_1}=\overline{y_1}=u \quad (1)$$

i.e. the Boolean function that this circuit computes is the identity.

The model is offered by the next circuit

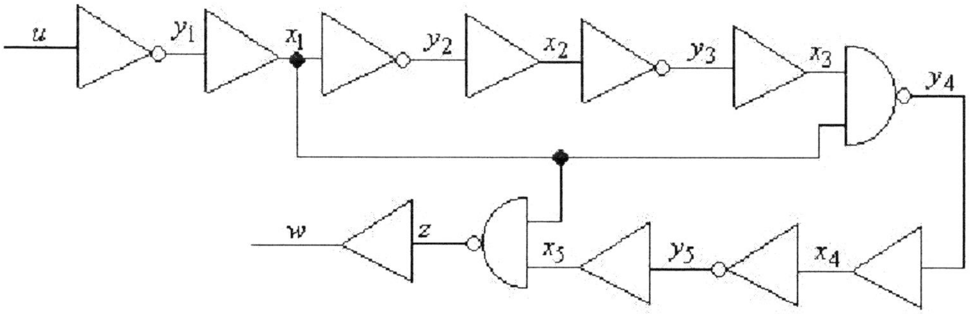

Fig 24

where all the variables that occur are signals, the gates and the wires have no delays and the delays are concentrated in the delay circuits. The system of equations and inequalities is:

$$y_1(t)=\overline{u(t)} \quad (2)$$

$$y_2(t)=\overline{x_1(t)} \quad (3)$$

$$y_3(t) = \overline{x_2(t)} \tag{4}$$

$$y_4(t) = \overline{x_3(t) \cdot x_1(t)} \tag{5}$$

$$y_5(t) = \overline{x_4(t)} \tag{6}$$

$$z(t) = \overline{x_5(t) \cdot x_1(t)} \tag{7}$$

$$\bigcap_{\xi \in [t-d_r, t)} y_i(\xi) \le x_i(t) \le \bigcup_{\xi \in [t-d_f, t)} y_i(\xi), i = \overline{1,5} \tag{8}$$

$$\bigcap_{\xi \in [t-d_r, t)} z(\xi) \le w(t) \le \bigcup_{\xi \in [t-d_f, t)} z(\xi) \tag{9}$$

thus we use BDC' with $d_r > 0, d_f > 0$ the parameters that characterize the six delay circuits.The compatibility with the initial conditions is supposed to be satisfied under the form

$$u(0-0) = \overline{y_1(0-0)} = x_1(0-0) = \overline{y_2(0-0)} = x_2(0-0) = \overline{y_3(0-0)} = \overline{x_3(0-0)} =$$
$$= y_4(0-0) = x_4(0-0) = \overline{y_5(0-0)} = \overline{x_5(0-0)} = z(0-0) = w(0-0)$$

that simplifies (2),…,(7). For example (5) was written in the next manner:

$$y_4(t) = y_4(0-0) \cdot \chi_{(-\infty,0)}(t) \oplus \overline{x_3(t) \cdot x_1(t)} \cdot \chi_{[0,\infty)}(t) =$$
$$= \overline{x_3(0-0) \cdot x_1(0-0)} \cdot \chi_{(-\infty,0)}(t) \oplus \overline{x_3(t) \cdot x_1(t)} \cdot \chi_{[0,\infty)}(t) = \overline{x_3(t) \cdot x_1(t)}$$

We have

$$\bigcap_{\xi \in [t-d_r, t)} y_1(\xi) \le x_1(t) \le \bigcup_{\xi \in [t-d_f, t)} y_1(\xi) \quad \text{(equation (8))} \tag{10}$$

$$\bigcap_{\xi \in [t-d_r, t)} \overline{u(\xi)} \le x_1(t) \le \bigcup_{\xi \in [t-d_f, t)} \overline{u(\xi)} \quad \text{(from (2) and (10))} \tag{11}$$

$$\bigcap_{\xi \in [t-d_r, t)} y_3(\xi) \le x_3(t) \le \bigcup_{\xi \in [t-d_f, t)} y_3(\xi) \quad \text{(equation (8))} \tag{12}$$

$$\bigcap_{\xi \in [t-d_r, t)} \overline{x_2(\xi)} \le x_3(t) \le \bigcup_{\xi \in [t-d_f, t)} \overline{x_2(\xi)} \quad \text{(from (4) and (12))} \tag{13}$$

$$\bigcap_{\xi \in [t-d_r, t)} y_2(\xi) \le x_2(t) \le \bigcup_{\xi \in [t-d_f, t)} y_2(\xi) \quad \text{(equation (8))} \tag{14}$$

$$\bigcap_{\xi \in [t-d_f, t)} \overline{y_2(\xi)} \le \overline{x_2(t)} \le \bigcup_{\xi \in [t-d_r, t)} \overline{y_2(\xi)} \quad \text{(from (14))} \tag{15}$$

$$\bigcap_{\xi \in [t-d_f, t)} x_1(\xi) \le \overline{x_2(t)} \le \bigcup_{\xi \in [t-d_r, t)} x_1(\xi) \quad \text{(from (3) and (15))} \tag{16}$$

$$\bigcap_{\xi \in [t-d_r-d_f, t)} x_1(\xi) \le x_3(t) \le \bigcup_{\xi \in [t-d_r-d_f, t)} x_1(\xi) \quad \text{(from (13) and (16))} \tag{17}$$

$$\bigcap_{\xi\in[t-2d_r-d_f,t)}\overline{u(\xi)} \le x_3(t) \le \bigcup_{\xi\in[t-d_r-2d_f,t)}\overline{u(\xi)} \qquad \text{(from (11) and (17))} \tag{18}$$

$$\overline{y_4(t)} = x_3(t)\cdot x_1(t) \qquad \text{(from (5))} \tag{19}$$

$$\bigcap_{\xi\in[t-2d_r-d_f,t)}\overline{u(\xi)} \cdot \bigcap_{\xi\in[t-d_r,t)}\overline{u(\xi)} \le \overline{y_4(t)} \le \bigcup_{\xi\in[t-d_r-2d_f,t)}\overline{u(\xi)} \cdot \bigcup_{\xi\in[t-d_f,t)}\overline{u(\xi)} \tag{20}$$

from (18), (11) and (19). But $[t-2d_r-d_f,t)\supset[t-d_r,t),[t-d_r-2d_f,t)\supset[t-d_f,t)$

imply $\bigcap_{\xi\in[t-2d_r-d_f,t)}\overline{u(\xi)} \le \bigcap_{\xi\in[t-d_r,t)}\overline{u(\xi)}, \quad \bigcup_{\xi\in[t-d_r-2d_f,t)}\overline{u(\xi)} \ge \bigcup_{\xi\in[t-d_f,t)}\overline{u(\xi)}$

$$\bigcap_{\xi\in[t-2d_r-d_f,t)}\overline{u(\xi)} \cdot \bigcap_{\xi\in[t-d_r,t)}\overline{u(\xi)} = \bigcap_{\xi\in[t-2d_r-d_f,t)}\overline{u(\xi)}$$

$$\bigcup_{\xi\in[t-d_r-2d_f,t)}\overline{u(\xi)} \cdot \bigcup_{\xi\in[t-d_f,t)}\overline{u(\xi)} = \bigcup_{\xi\in[t-d_f,t)}\overline{u(\xi)}$$

from where (20) becomes

$$\bigcap_{\xi\in[t-2d_r-d_f,t)}\overline{u(\xi)} \le \overline{y_4(t)} \le \bigcup_{\xi\in[t-d_f,t)}\overline{u(\xi)} \tag{21}$$

Furthermore

$$\bigcap_{\xi\in[t-d_r,t)} y_5(\xi) \le x_5(t) \le \bigcup_{\xi\in[t-d_f,t)} y_5(\xi) \qquad \text{(equation (8))} \tag{22}$$

$$\bigcap_{\xi\in[t-d_r,t)}\overline{x_4(\xi)} \le x_5(t) \le \bigcup_{\xi\in[t-d_f,t)}\overline{x_4(\xi)} \qquad \text{(from (6) and (22))} \tag{23}$$

$$\bigcap_{\xi\in[t-d_f,t)}\overline{y_4(\xi)} \le \overline{x_4(t)} \le \bigcup_{\xi\in[t-d_r,t)}\overline{y_4(\xi)} \qquad \text{(similar with (15))} \tag{24}$$

$$\bigcap_{\xi\in[t-d_r-d_f,t)}\overline{y_4(\xi)} \le x_5(t) \le \bigcup_{\xi\in[t-d_r-d_f,t)}\overline{y_4(\xi)} \qquad \text{(from (23) and (24))} \tag{25}$$

$$\bigcap_{\xi\in[t-3d_r-2d_f,t)}\overline{u(\xi)} \le x_5(t) \le \bigcup_{\xi\in[t-d_r-2d_f,t)}\overline{u(\xi)} \qquad \text{(from (21) and (25))} \tag{26}$$

$$\overline{z(t)} = x_5(t)\cdot x_1(t) \qquad \text{(from (7))} \tag{27}$$

$$\bigcap_{\xi\in[t-3d_r-2d_f,t)}\overline{u(\xi)} \cdot \bigcap_{\xi\in[t-d_r,t)}\overline{u(\xi)} \le \overline{z(t)} \le \bigcup_{\xi\in[t-d_r-2d_f,t)}\overline{u(\xi)} \cdot \bigcup_{\xi\in[t-d_f,t)}\overline{u(\xi)} \tag{28}$$

from (27), (26) and (11). With arguments like those around (20) we infer from (28)

$$\bigcap_{\xi\in[t-3d_r-2d_f,t)}\overline{u(\xi)} \le \overline{z(t)} \le \bigcup_{\xi\in[t-d_f,t)}\overline{u(\xi)} \tag{29}$$

$$\bigcap_{\xi\in[t-d_f,t)} u(\xi) \le z(t) \le \bigcup_{\xi\in[t-3d_r-2d_f,t)} u(\xi) \tag{30}$$

From (9) and (30) we get

$$\bigcap_{\xi\in[t-d_r-d_f,t)} u(\xi) \le w(t) \le \bigcup_{\xi\in[t-3d_r-3d_f,t)} u(\xi) \tag{31}$$

The conclusion expressed by (31) is that the circuit increases the one gate rising delay from d_r to $d_r + d_f$ and respectively the one gate falling delay from d_f to $3d_r + 3d_f$, i.e. the growth of the falling delay is bigger than the growth of the rising delay. This justifies the title of the paragraph.

11.2 Example of Circuit with Tranzient Oscillations

We reproduce in Fig 25 an example of circuit from [3].

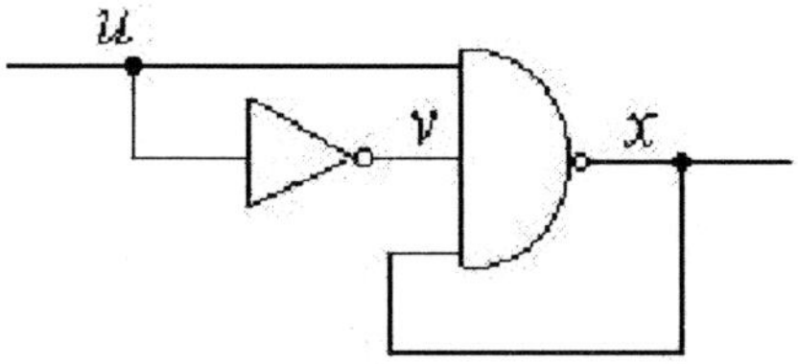

Fig 25

Even if the static analyzis, when $u, v, x \in \boldsymbol{B}$ of such a circuit is not appropriate due to the feedback loop we remark that the proposed circuit computes the 1 Boolean function because

$$x = \overline{u \cdot v \cdot x} = \overline{u \cdot \overline{u} \cdot x} = \overline{0} = 1$$

Modeling is done like in the next drawing

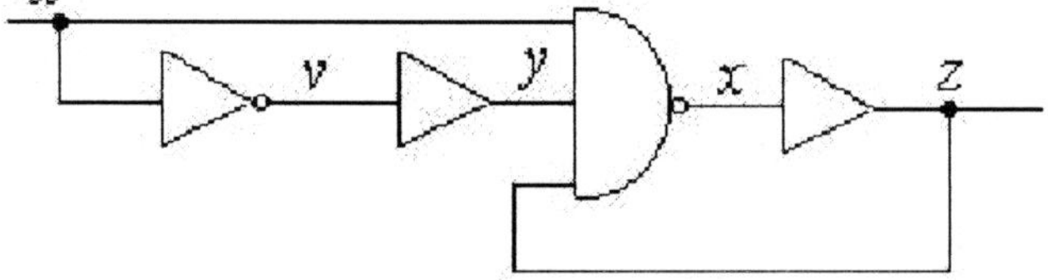

Fig 26

where $u, v, x, y, z \in S$ and after solving the system we must obtain $\lim_{t\to\infty} z(t) = 1$ independent on the type of DC's that we choose. The delays of the gates and of the wires from the original circuit have been concentrated in the two delay circuits from Fig 26, where the gates and the wires have no delays. We choose that the delays associated to the two logical gates be FDC's. The equations are:

$$v(t) = v(0-0)\cdot\chi_{(-\infty,0)}(t)\oplus\overline{u(t)}\cdot\chi_{[0,\infty)}(t) \qquad (1)$$

$$y(t) = v(t-d) \qquad (2)$$

$$x(t) = x(0-0)\cdot\chi_{(-\infty,0)}(t)\oplus\overline{u(t)\cdot y(t)\cdot z(t)}\cdot\chi_{[0,\infty)}(t) \qquad (3)$$

$$z(t) = x(t-d') \qquad (4)$$

resulting

$$y(t) = v(0-0)\cdot\chi_{(-\infty,0)}(t-d)\oplus\overline{u(t-d)}\cdot\chi_{[0,\infty)}(t-d)$$

$$= v(0-0)\cdot\chi_{(-\infty,d)}(t)\oplus\overline{u(t-d)}\cdot\chi_{[d,\infty)}(t) \quad \text{(from (1), (2))} \qquad (5)$$

$$x(t) = x(0-0)\cdot\chi_{(-\infty,0)}(t)\oplus \quad \text{(from (3), (4), (5))} \qquad (6)$$

$$\oplus\overline{u(t)\cdot(v(0-0)\cdot\chi_{(-\infty,d)}(t)\oplus\overline{u(t-d)}\cdot\chi_{[d,\infty)}(t))\cdot x(t-d')}\cdot\chi_{[0,\infty)}(t)$$

We solve (6) in the special case when $x(0-0) = v(0-0) = 1$ and $u(t) = 1$, when it becomes

$$x(t) = \chi_{(-\infty,0)}(t)\oplus\overline{\chi_{(-\infty,d)}(t)\cdot x(t-d')}\cdot\chi_{[0,\infty)}(t) \qquad (7)$$

The solution of (7) is the following

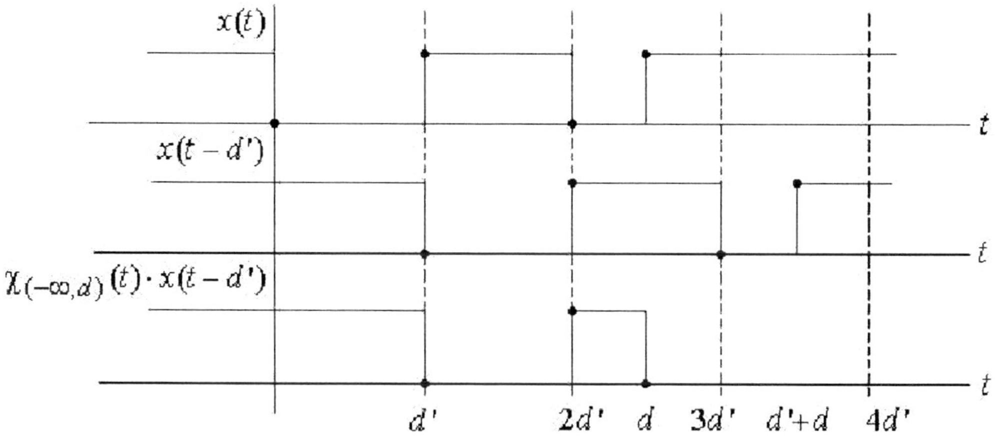

Fig 27

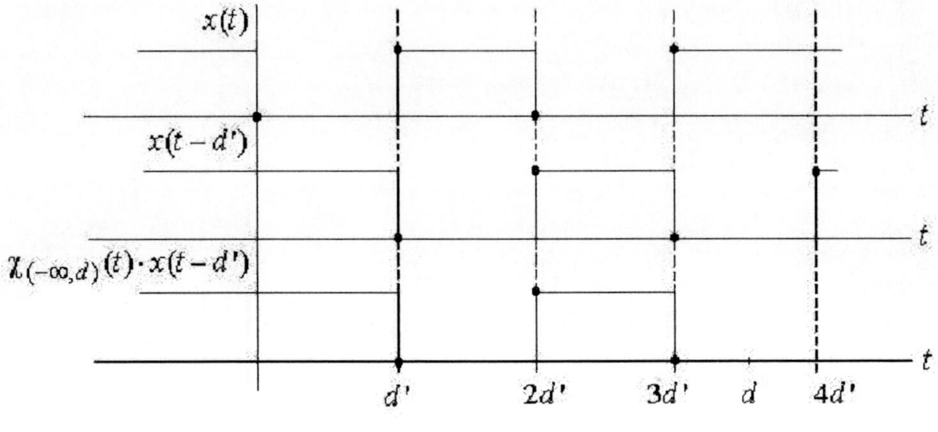

Fig 28

$2kd' < d \le (2k+1)d'$ implies

$$x(t)=\begin{cases}\chi_{(-\infty,0)}(t)\oplus\chi_{[d',2d')}(t)\oplus\ldots\oplus\chi_{[(2k-1)d',2kd')}(t)\oplus\chi_{[d,\infty)}(t), k\ge 1\\ \chi_{(-\infty,0)}(t)\oplus\chi_{[d,\infty)}(t), k=0\end{cases}$$

$(2k+1)d' < d \le (2k+2)d'$ implies

$$x(t)=\begin{cases}\chi_{(-\infty,0)}(t)\oplus\chi_{[d',2d')}(t)\oplus\ldots\oplus\chi_{[(2k-1)d',2kd')}(t)\oplus\chi_{[(2k+1)d',\infty)}(t), k\ge 1\\ \chi_{(-\infty,0)}(t)\oplus\chi_{[d',\infty)}(t), k=0\end{cases}$$

where $k=0,1,2,...$ We have represented in Fig 27 and Fig 28 these two formulas for $k=1$.

The output $z(t)$ of the circuit is obtained from (4).

The idea of solving the equation (6) in other cases as well as the behavior of the circuit from Fig 25 are obvious now.

11.3 Example of C Gate. Generalization

The circuit from Fig 29 where the gates and the wires have delays is modeled like in Fig 30

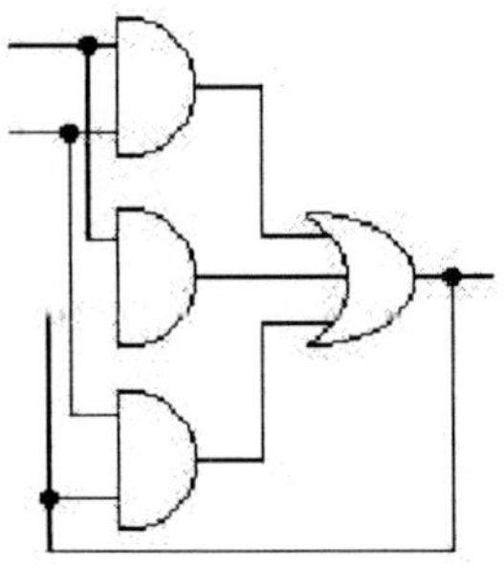

Fig 29

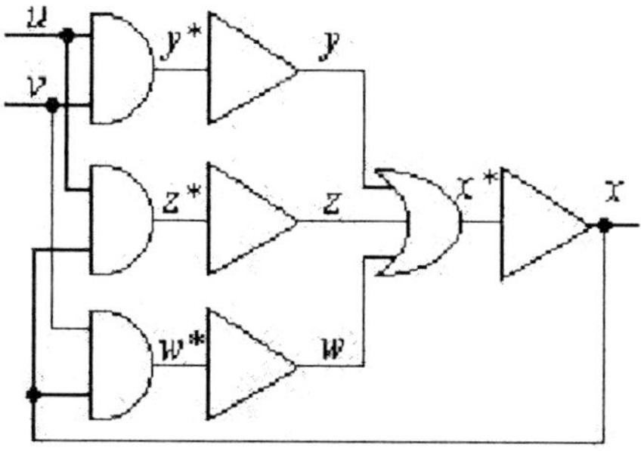

Fig 30

where the Boolean functions are computed instantaneously:

$$y^*(t) = u(t) \cdot v(t) \tag{1}$$

$$z^*(t) = u(t) \cdot x(t) \tag{2}$$

$$w^*(t) = v(t) \cdot x(t) \tag{3}$$

$$x^*(t) = y(t) \cup z(t) \cup w(t) \tag{4}$$

and the delays on gates and wires are localized in the four delay circuits. We have supposed for simplicity that all the signals have the same initial values $u(0-0) = v(0-0) = ... = x(0-0)$ and for example equation (1) has resulted in the next way:

$$y^*(t) = y^*(0-0) \cdot \chi_{(-\infty,0)}(t) \oplus u(t) \cdot v(t) \cdot \chi_{[0,\infty)}(t) =$$
$$= u(0-0) \cdot v(0-0) \cdot \chi_{(-\infty,0)}(t) \oplus u(t) \cdot v(t) \cdot \chi_{[0,\infty)}(t) = u(t) \cdot v(t)$$

a) The bounded delay model

$$\bigcap_{\xi \in [t-d_r, t-d_r+m_r]} y^*(\xi) \le y(t) \le \bigcup_{\xi \in [t-d_f, t-d_f+m_f]} y^*(\xi) \tag{5}$$

$$\bigcap_{\xi \in [t-d_r, t-d_r+m_r]} z^*(\xi) \le z(t) \le \bigcup_{\xi \in [t-d_f, t-d_f+m_f]} z^*(\xi) \tag{6}$$

$$\bigcap_{\xi \in [t-d_r, t-d_r+m_r]} w^*(\xi) \le w(t) \le \bigcup_{\xi \in [t-d_r, t-d_r+m_r]} w^*(\xi) \tag{7}$$

$$\bigcap_{\xi \in [t-D_r, t-D_r+M_r]} x^*(\xi) \le x(t) \le \bigcup_{\xi \in [t-D_f, t-D_f+M_f]} x^*(\xi) \tag{8}$$

with $0 \le m_r \le d_r$, $0 \le m_f \le d_f$, $0 \le M_r \le D_r$, $0 \le M_f \le D_f$ and the consistency conditions are fulfilled under the form: $d_r \ge d_f - m_f$, $d_f \ge d_r - m_r$ respectively $D_r \ge D_f - M_f$, $D_f \ge D_r - M_r$. We have considered that the three AND gates are identical. We eliminate the intermediary variables $y^*, z^*, w^*, y, z, w, x^*$:

$$x(t)\overset{(4),(8)}{\geq}\bigcap_{\xi\in[t-D_r,t-D_r+M_r]}(y(\xi)\cup z(\xi)\cup w(\xi))\geq\bigcap_{\xi\in[t-D_r,t-D_r+M_r]}y(\xi)\geq$$

$$\overset{(5)}{\geq}\bigcap_{\xi\in[t-D_r,t-D_r+M_r]}\ \bigcap_{\omega\in[\xi-d_r,\xi-d_r+m_r]}y^*(\omega)=\bigcap_{\xi\in[t-d_r-D_r,t-d_r-D_r+m_r+M_r]}y^*(\xi)=$$

$$\overset{(1)}{=}\bigcap_{\xi\in[t-d_r-D_r,t-d_r-D_r+m_r+M_r]}(u(\xi)\cdot v(\xi)) \qquad (9)$$

$$x(t)\overset{(4),(8)}{\leq}\bigcup_{\xi\in[t-D_f,t-D_f+M_f]}(y(\xi)\cup z(\xi)\cup w(\xi))=$$

$$=\bigcup_{\xi\in[t-D_f,t-D_f+M_f]}y(\xi)\cup\bigcup_{\xi\in[t-D_f,t-D_f+M_f]}z(\xi)\cup\bigcup_{\xi\in[t-D_f,t-D_f+M_f]}w(\xi)\leq$$

$$\overset{(5),(6),(7)}{\leq}\bigcup_{\xi\in[t-D_f,t-D_f+M_f]}\ \bigcup_{\omega\in[\xi-d_f,\xi-d_f+m_f]}y^*(\omega)\cup$$

$$\cup\bigcup_{\xi\in[t-D_f,t-D_f+M_f]}\ \bigcup_{\omega\in[\xi-d_f,\xi-d_f+m_f]}z^*(\omega)\cup$$

$$\bigcup_{\xi\in[t-D_f,t-D_f+M_f]}\ \bigcup_{\omega\in[\xi-d_f,\xi-d_f+m_f]}w^*(\omega)=$$

$$=\bigcup_{\xi\in[t-d_f-D_f,t-d_f-D_f+m_f+M_f]}y^*(\xi)\cup\bigcup_{\xi\in[t-d_f-D_f,t-d_f-D_f+m_f+M_f]}z^*(\xi)\cup$$

$$\cup\bigcup_{\xi\in[t-d_f-D_f,t-d_f-D_f+m_f+M_f]}w^*(\xi)=$$

$$\overset{(1),(2),(3)}{=}\bigcup_{\xi\in[t-d_f-D_f,t-d_f-D_f+m_f+M_f]}u(\xi)\cdot v(\xi)\cup\bigcup_{\xi\in[t-d_f-D_f,t-d_f-D_f+m_f+M_f]}u(\xi)\cdot x(\xi)\cup$$

$$\cup\bigcup_{\xi\in[t-d_f-D_f,t-d_f-D_f+m_f+M_f]}v(\xi)\cdot x(\xi)=$$

$$=\bigcup_{\xi\in[t-d_f-D_f,t-d_f-D_f+m_f+M_f]}(u(\xi)\cdot v(\xi)\cup(u(\xi)\cup v(\xi))\cdot x(\xi))$$

$$\leq\bigcup_{\xi\in[t-d_f-D_f,t-d_f-D_f+m_f+M_f]}(u(\xi)\cdot v(\xi)\cup u(\xi)\cup v(\xi))=$$

$$=\bigcup_{\xi\in[t-d_f-D_f,t-d_f-D_f+m_f+M_f]}(u(\xi)\cup v(\xi)) \qquad (10)$$

thus, by cumulating (9), (10)

$$\bigcap_{\xi\in[t-d_r-D_r,t-d_r-D_r+m_r+M_r]}(u(\xi)\cdot v(\xi)) \leq x(t) \leq \bigcup_{\xi\in[t-d_f-D_f,t-d_f-D_f+m_f+M_f]}(u(\xi)\cup v(\xi))$$

we have obtained a system that is very much similar with BDC.

b) The deterministic model

We ask that (9), (10) be fulfilled together with

$$\overline{x(t-0)}\cdot x(t) \leq \bigcap_{\xi\in[t-d_r-D_r,t-d_r-D_r+m_r+M_r]}(u(\xi)\cdot v(\xi)) \tag{11}$$

$$x(t-0)\cdot \overline{x(t)} \leq \bigcap_{\xi\in[t-d_f-D_f,t-d_f-D_f+m_f+M_f]}\overline{u(\xi)}\cdot \overline{v(\xi)} \tag{12}$$

The system (9), (10), (11), (12) represents a deterministic model, similar with 9.5.1 a) and it is equivalent with the next one, that is similar with 9.5.1 b):

$$\overline{x(t-0)}\cdot x(t) = \overline{x(t-0)}\cdot \bigcap_{\xi\in[t-d_r-D_r,t-d_r-D_r+m_r+M_r]}(u(\xi)\cdot v(\xi))$$

$$x(t-0)\cdot \overline{x(t)} = x(t-0)\cdot \bigcap_{\xi\in[t-d_f-D_f,t-d_f-D_f+m_f+M_f]}\overline{u(\xi)}\cdot \overline{v(\xi)}$$

etc. The C gate, also called Muller C element generalizes the delay circuit, in the sense that when the two inputs are equal, it becomes a delay circuit. In the same manner, the systems that we have obtained generalize our systems BDC, respectively DBRIDC and may be called 2-delays: 2-BDC, respectively 2-DBRIDC. The general case of n-BDC and n-DBRIDC is obvious now.

References

[1] E. Asarin, O. Maler, A. Pnueli, On Discretization of Delays in Timed Automata and Digital Circuits, in R. de Simone and D. Sangiorgi (Eds), *Proc. Concur '98*, 470-484, LNCS 1466, Springer, 1998

[2] M. Bozga, Hou Jianmin, O. Maler, S. Yovine, *Verification of Asynchronous Circuits using Timed Automata*, Rejected from ASCD'01

[3] J. A. Brzozowski, C-J. H. Seger, Advances in Asynchronous Circuit Theory, Part I: Gate and Unbounded Inertial Delay Models, *Bulletin of the European Association for Theoretical Computer Science*, Number 42, pp. 198-249, February 1990

[4] J. A. Brzozowski, C-J. H. Seger, Advances in Asynchronous Circuit Theory, Part II: Bounded Inertial Delay Models, MOS Circuits, Design Techniques, *Bulletin of the European Association for Theoretical Computer Science*, Number 43, pp. 199-263, February 1991

[5] Supratik Chakraborty, *Polynomial-Time Techniques for Approximate Timing Analysis of Asynchronous Systems*, PhD Thesis, August, 1998

[6] Graham Clark, George Taylor, The Verification of Asynchronous Circuits Using CCS, *Technical Report ECS-LCFS-97-369*, Department of Computer Science, University of Edinburgh, October 23, 1997

[7] Al Davis, Steven Mark Nowick, *An Introduction to Asynchronous Circuit Design*, UUCS-97-013, 1997

[8] Anton Dumitriu, *The Logical Mechanism of Mathematics* (in Romanian), Editura Academiei Republicii Socialiste Romania, Bucuresti, 1968

[9] Michael Kishinevsky, Luciano Lavagno, P. Vanbekbergen, *The Systematic Design of Asynchronous Circuits*, ICCAD '95, Tutorial

[10] William Kwei-Cheung Lam, *Algebraic Methods for Timing Analysis and Testing in the High Performance Designs*, PhD Thesis, Univ. of California at Berkeley, 1993

[11] Luciano Lavagno, *Synthesis and Testing of Bounded Wire Delay Asynchronous Circuits from Signal Transition Graphs*, PhD Thesis, Electrical Engineering and Computer Sciences, Univ. of California at Berkeley, 1992

[12] M. J. Liebelt, Progress Report on Research on the Testing of Asynchronous Circuits, The University of Adelaide, Department of Electrical and Electric Engineering, *Internal report HPCA-ECS-95/03*, 29 December 1995

[13] Michael Liebelt, A Proposal for Research on the Testability of Asynchronous Circuits, The University of Adelaide, Department of Electrical and Electric Engineering, *Internal Report HPCA-ECS-96/01*, August 1998

[14] O. Maler, A. Pnueli, Timing Analysis of Asynchronous Circuits Using Timed Automata, in P. E. Camurati, H. Eveking (Eds), *Proc. CHARME'95*, 189-205, LNCS 987, Springer, 1995

[15] Steven Mark Nowick, Automatic Synthesis of Burst-Mode Asynchronous Controllers, *Technical Report CSL-TR-95-686*, 1995 (revised version of PhD dissertation, March 1993)

[16] Alexander Rabinovich, *Automata over Continuous Time*, Dept. of Computer Science, Tel-Aviv University, June 26, 1997

[17] Polly Sara Kay Siegel, *Automatic Technology Mapping for Asynchronous Designs*, Department of Electrical Engineering, Stanford University, PhD Thesis, 1995

[18] Serdar Tasiran, Rajeev Alur, Robert P. Kurshan, Robert K. Brayton, Verifying Abstractions of Timed Systems, In *Proc. of 7th International Conference on Concurrency Theory*, CONCUR '96, LNCS 1119, Pisa, Italy, 1996, pp. 546-562.

[19] Serdar Tasiran, Yuji Kukimoto, Robert K. Brayton, Computing Delay with Coupling Using Timed Automata, In *Proc. of IEEE/ACM Intl. Workshop on Timing Issues in the Specification and Synthesis of Digital Systems*, TAU '97, Austin, TX, 1997.

[20] Serdar Tasiran, *Compositional and Hierarchical Techniques for the Formal Verification of Real-Time Systems*, PhD Thesis, Univ. of California at Berkeley, 1998

[21] S. Tasiran, S.P.Khatri, S. Yovine, R.K. Brayton, A. Sangiovanni-Vincentelli, A Timed Automaton-Based Method for Accurate Computation of Circuit Delay in the Presence of Cross-Talk, In *Proc. of the* 2nd *Intl. Conf. on Formal Methods in Computer-aided Design*, FMCAD '98, LNCS 1522, Palo Alto, CA, 1998, pp. 149-166.

[22] Serban E. Vlad $\boldsymbol{R} \rightarrow \boldsymbol{B}$ *Differentiable Functions*, Analele Universitatii din Oradea, Fasciclola Matematica, TOM V, 1995-1996

[23] Serban E. Vlad, *Selected Topics in Asynchronous Automata*, Analele Universitatii din Oradea, Fascicola matematica, Tom VII, 1999

[24] Serban E. Vlad, On Timed Automata: the Inertial Delay Buffer, *the 9-th Symposium of Mathematics and Its Applications*, Timisoara-Romania, November 1-4, 2001

[25] Serban E. Vlad, *Towards a Mathematical Theory of the Delays of the Asynchronous Circuits*, Analele Universitatii din Oradea, Fascicola matematica, Tom IX, 2002

In: New Developments in Computer Science Research
Editor: Susan Shannon, pp. 91-125
ISBN 1-59454-256-2

Chapter 2

Approximate Computation of Reach Sets in Hybrid Systems

D. Ravi and R. K. Shyamasundar *

School of Technology and Computer Science
Tata Institute of Fundamental Research
Homi Bhabha Road, Colaba, Mumbai 400 005, India

Abstract

One of the most important problems of hybrid systems is the *reachability problem*. As this problem has been shown to be undecidable even for certain classes of linear hybrid systems, the main focus of the hybrid systems literature appears to be to find *effective* semi-decision procedures for this problem. Such an algorithmic approach involves finding methods of computation and representation of reach sets of the continuous variables within a discrete state of a hybrid system. In this paper, after presenting a brief introduction to hybrid systems and reachability problem, we propose a computational method for obtaining the reach sets of continuous variables in a hybrid system. In addition to this, we also describe a new algorithm to over-approximate with polyhedra the reach sets of the continuous variables with linear dynamics and polyhedral initial set. We illustrate these algorithms with some simple and interesting examples.

1 Introduction

Hybrid systems combine discrete and continuous dynamics. The dynamics of the continuous variables within a discrete state are specified by differential equations or differential inclusions. An important problem in the analysis and sysnthesis of such systems is the so called *reachability problem*, which asks, for two sets of configurations, where a configuration consists of discrete and continuous components, of a given hybrid system, say $\mathcal{X}_1$ and $\mathcal{X}_2$, whether or not there is a hybrid trajectory with the inital configuration in $\mathcal{X}_1$ and the final configuration in $\mathcal{X}_2$. A hybrid trajectory may be described as a trajectory of configurations consisting of discrete state jumps and smooth arcs, where each arc evolves according to the continuous dynamics of a discrete state, with the starting and end points of each arc satisfying the jump conditions of discrete transitions. A more precise definition is presented

*Corresponding author. E-mail: shyam@tcs.tifr.res.in

in Sec. 2, which provides a concise introduction to hybrid systems and the reachability problem.

The reachability problem is undecidable for certain classes of linear hybrid systems (i.e., hybrid systems having linear trajectories within each discrete state and linear or constant reset maps, also called *constant slope hybrid systems*) [1, 2], although in some cases decidability results have been obtained [3, 4] (see also [2]). Therefore, for a general hybrid system, a reasonable alternative appears to be to find semi-decision procedures for the reachability problem [5, 6, 7]. A computational approach to this problem also requires finding the set of states reached by the continuous variables evolving according to the dynamics of a discrete state. In this paper, we consider the problem of computing and representing the reach sets of the continuous variables within a discrete state when the dynamics of the continuous variables are specified by differential equations with initial conditions belonging to a specified initial set.

In this context, various methods have been proposed in the literature for finding reach sets of continuous variables [8, 9, 10]. In Sec. 3, we describe a method for computing the reach sets based on the idea that a subset of the boundary of the initial set may be found, such that it is sufficient to compute the solutions with the initial points lying in that set. This method is similar to that in [8] (and also to some extent to that described in [9]). In particular, we present a schematic algorithm, which is somewhat more general in its scope than that in [8] and simpler compared to that in [9].

Besides these algorithms for reach set computation, an equally important issue the representation of the reach sets for manipulating the sets efficiently. This requires representation of the reach sets in terms of more convenient sets such as, for example polyhedral or subalgebraic sets, that are simple to represent and easy to handle for practical purposes. However, since the representing class of sets may not contain a member that exactly equals the reach set, we may have to find approximations to the reach sets by those that belong to the representing class. (See, for example, [10, 12] for approximation with polyhedra, and [11] for approximation using ellipsoids). Typically, over-approximations may be used for verifying whether a safety requirement may potentially be violated by any of the behaviours starting from a given initial set, while under-approximations are needed for characterizing a set of states from which a desirable property is always achievable. We describe in Sec. 4 a method for over-approximating the reach sets by polyhedra when the dynamics are specified by linear differential equations and the initial set is a polyhedron. These algorithms are illustrated with some simple examples in Sec. 5, while Sec. 6 concludes the paper.

2 A Brief Introductin to Hybrid Systems

In this section, we present a brief introduction to hybrid systems, and provide motivation for the remaining sections.

2.1 Preliminary Definitions

We begin with a somewhat detailed but general definition of hybrid systems.

DEFINITION 1 *A* hybrid system *is a tuple* $H = (Q, X, \Sigma, G, E, Init, f)$, *where*

1. *Q is a finite set of discrete* states *(also called* locations*).*

2. $X = \mathbb{R}^n$, $n \geq 1$, *is the set of continuous states, where* $\mathbb{R}$ *denotes the set of real numbers. We demote the continuous state variable by* $\mathbf{x}$.

3. Σ *is a finite set of discrete events or environment actions. Some events in* Σ *are controllable, while others not. Hence, it is convenient to assume that* $\Sigma = \Sigma_c \bigcup \Sigma_d$, *where* Σ_c *is the set of controllable events, and* Σ_d *is the set of uncontrollable or disturbance events.*

4. $G \subseteq Q \times X$ *is a set of state invariance conditions. When the system is in state* q, *the continuous variables belong to* $G(q) = \{\mathbf{x} \in X \; : \; (q, \mathbf{x}) \in G\}$.

5. $E \subseteq Q \times \mathcal{P}(\mathbb{R}^n) \times \Sigma \times \{\mathbb{R}^n \to \mathbb{R}^n\} \times Q$ *is the set of transition edges. An edge* $e \in E$, *where* $e = (q_e, X_e, \sigma_e, r_e, q'_e)$, *is interpreted as follows:*

   - *If the continuous state is in* X_e *and the event* σ_e *occurs, then transition edge* e *is enabled in state* q_e. *Thus* X_e *is the set of switching points of the continuous variables from state* q_e *to* q'_e. *The set* X_e *is specified by a predicate, and is also called a* guard. *In case there are many transition edges simultaneously enabled, then the system may select one of the edges nondeterministically.*
   - *If a transition edge* e *is selected by the system, then the continuous state is reset using the function* r_e *when the system enters state* q'_e. *The reset values obey the state invariance condition,* $r_e(X_e) \subseteq G(q'_e)$.

6. $Init \subseteq G$ *is a set of initial conditions.*

7. f *is an* n*-dimensional vector field with real-valued components governing the dynamics of the continuous state* $\mathbf{x}$. *The domain of definition of the function* f *is a set* $\mathcal{D}$, *where* $\mathcal{D} = Q \times X$ *(if there are no continuous control variables) or* $\mathcal{D} = Q \times X \times U$ *(if* $U \subseteq \mathbb{R}^m$, $m \geq 1$, *is the range of the continuous control variable, which is a function* $\mathbf{u} : [0, T_q) \to U$, *where* $T_q > 0$ *is as large as may be necessary, depending on the discrete state* $q \in Q$*). When in state* q, *the continuous variables evolve according to the dynamical law*

$$\frac{d\mathbf{x}}{dt} = f(q, \mathbf{x})$$

   or according to the dynamical law

$$\frac{d\mathbf{x}}{dt} = f(q, \mathbf{x}, \mathbf{u})$$

   depending on the presence or absence of the continuous control variables.[1]

   The initial conditions of the continuous evolution are specified either by the reset maps when the system takes a discrete transition and reaches the state q, *or by the (nondeterministic) initial conditions of the system given as the set* $Init$.

---

[1]Another possibility is to specify the system dynamics of the continuous variables in terms of differential inclusions. In this case, $f(q, \mathbf{x})$ is a set, and the continuous variables evolve according to

$$\frac{d\mathbf{x}}{dt} \in f(q, \mathbf{x}).$$

But we do not consider this case here.

If, in addition to the set of initial values, $Init$, the set of final or accepting values in $Q \times X$, denoted by $Final$, are also specified, then the hybrid system is called a hybrid automaton.

Referring to the system dynamics in the above definition, for our purposes, we assume that there are no continuous control variables. Therefore, in the sequel, we assume that the dynamics of the continuous variables are specified in the form

$$\frac{d\mathbf{x}}{dt} = f(q, \mathbf{x})$$

without any continuous control variables.

DEFINITION **2** *Let $H = (Q, X, \Sigma, G, E, Init, f)$ be a hybrid system. Each point $(q, \mathbf{x}) \in Q \times X$ is called a* configuration *of the hybrid system H.*

In Definitions 3 - 6, we introduce certain terminology, starting with the notion of a *step* of a hybrid system, leading upto the notions of *predecessors* and *successors* of a configuration $(q, \mathbf{x})$. But before that, we mention that predecessors and successors may be defined irrespective of initial conditions, whereas for defining the executions of a hybrid system, we require the specification of the initial set $Init$, as will be seen later (refer to Definitions 4, 5 and 6) .

DEFINITION **3** *Let $H = (Q, X, \Sigma, G, E, Init, f)$ be a hybrid system, and let $(q, \mathbf{x})$ and $(q', \mathbf{x}')$ be two configurations of H. Then, the pair of configurations $((q, \mathbf{x}), (q', \mathbf{x}'))$ is called*

1. *a* time-step, *if $q = q'$ and, for some $t \geq 0$, there is a function $\mathbf{y} : [0, t] \rightarrow X$, satisfying $\dot{\mathbf{y}}(s) = f(q, \mathbf{y}(s))$, $\mathbf{y}(s) \in G(q)$, for $s \in [0, t]$, $\mathbf{y}(0) = \mathbf{x}$ and $\mathbf{y}(t) = \mathbf{x}'$.*

2. *an* edge-step *if there is an edge $e = (q_e, X_e, \sigma_e, r_e, q'_e) \in E$, such that $q = q_e$, $q' = q'_e$, $\mathbf{x} \in X_e$ and $\mathbf{x}' = r_e(\mathbf{x})$.*

3. *a σ-step, where $\sigma \in \Sigma$, if there is an edge $\ell = (q_\ell, X_\ell, \sigma_\ell, r_\ell, q'_\ell) \in E$ with $\sigma = \sigma_\ell$, such that $q = q_\ell$, $q' = q'_\ell$, $\mathbf{x} \in X_\ell$ and $\mathbf{x}' = r_\ell(\mathbf{x})$.*

A step *of the hybrid system H is a pair of configurations $((q, \mathbf{x}), (q', \mathbf{x}'))$, such that $((q, \mathbf{x}), (q', \mathbf{x}'))$ is either a time-step for some $t \geq 0$, or an edge-step for some $e \in E$, or a σ-step for some $\sigma \in \Sigma$.*

Of course, every edge-step is a σ-step for some $\sigma \in \Sigma$, and conversely, every σ-step is an edge-step for some edge $e \in E$. Hence these definitions may seem redundant. However, the distinction between the two types of transitions would become obvious if there is a *discrete state controller*, defined as a function $C : Q \times X \rightarrow \Sigma_c$, that triggers discrete controllable events to enable a particular transition depending on the present configuration (see for instance [13] for the case of *timed automata*). But in this work, we shall not have occasion to discuss about discrete state controllers.

DEFINITION **4 (Trajectories and Executions of a Hybrid System)** *A* hybrid trajectory *or simply a* trajectory *of H is a (finite or infinite) sequence of configurations $(q_1, \mathbf{x}_1), (q_2, \mathbf{x}_2), (q_3, \mathbf{x}_3), \ldots$, such that*

1. *$((q_1, \mathbf{x}_1), (q_2, \mathbf{x}_2))$ is a step, and*

2. *for* $i \geq 2$, *if* $((q_{i-1}, \mathbf{x}_{i-1}), (q_i, \mathbf{x}_i))$ *is a time-step then* $((q_i, \mathbf{x}_i), (q_{i+1}, \mathbf{x}_{i+1}))$ *is an edge-step or a* σ*-step, and if* $((q_{i-1}, \mathbf{x}_{i-1}), (q_i, \mathbf{x}_i))$ *is an edge-step or a* σ*-step then* $((q_i, \mathbf{x}_i), (q_{i+1}, \mathbf{x}_{i+1}))$ *is a step.*

A trajectory is

1. *finite, if the number of steps is finite;*
2. *an* execution*, if* $(q_1, \mathbf{x}_1) \in Init$*, where* $(q_1, \mathbf{x}_1)$ *is the initial configuration; and*
3. *a* finite execution*, if it is both.*

We now define, for each $\sigma \in \Sigma$, the set-valued successor function, $Post_\sigma : Q \times X \rightarrow 2^Q \times 2^X$. As will be briefly mentioned later (after Definition 6), our definitions lead in a natural way to extract a *labeled transition system* (see [14]) from a hybrid system.

DEFINITION **5** **(σ-Successors of a Configuration)**
Let $H = (Q, X, \Sigma, G, E, Init, f)$ *be a hybrid system,* $\sigma \in \Sigma$ *and* $(q, \mathbf{x}) \in Q \times X$*. Then, we define* $Post_\sigma(q, \mathbf{x})$ *to be the union of the two sets* $S_1, S_2^\sigma \subseteq Q \times X$*, where*

1. $S_1 = \{(q', \mathbf{x}') : ((q, \mathbf{x}), (q', \mathbf{x}'))$ *is a time-step for some* $t \geq 0\}$*; and*
2. $S_2^\sigma = \{(q'', \mathbf{x}'') : ((q', \mathbf{x}'), (q'', \mathbf{x}''))$ *is a* σ*-step for some* $(q', \mathbf{x}') \in S_1 \}$.

Further, if $(q_s, \mathbf{x}_s) \in Post_\sigma(q, \mathbf{x})$*, then* $(q_s, \mathbf{x}_s)$ *is called a* σ-successor *of* $(q, \mathbf{x})$.

The set S_1, as in the first part of this definition, is of main interest to us in the later sections of this paper. Specifically, we will deal with the set $Reach_q^G(X_0)$, where $q \in Q$ and $X_0 \subseteq G(q)$, defined as

$$Reach_q^G(X_0) = \{\mathbf{x} : ((q, \mathbf{x}_0), (q, \mathbf{x})) \text{ is a time-step for some } t \geq 0 \text{ and } \mathbf{x}_0 \in X_0 \}. \quad (1)$$

In the subsequent sections, we will be concerned more with this and a related set. But for now, we shall proceed with our discussion with the following definition:

DEFINITION **6** **(σ-Predecessors of a Configuration)**
Let $H = (Q, X, \Sigma, G, E, Init, f)$ *be a hybrid system,* $\sigma \in \Sigma$ *and* $(q, \mathbf{x}) \in Q \times X$*. Then, we define* $Pre_\sigma(q, \mathbf{x})$ *to be the union of the two sets* $P_1, P_2^\sigma \subseteq Q \times X$*, where*

1. $P_1 = \{(q', \mathbf{x}') : ((q', \mathbf{x}'), (q, \mathbf{x}))$ *is a time-step for some* $t \geq 0\}$*; and*
2. $P_2^\sigma = \{(q'', \mathbf{x}'') : ((q'', \mathbf{x}''), (q', \mathbf{x}'))$ *is a* σ*-step for some* $(q', \mathbf{x}') \in P_1 \}$.

Further, if $(q_p, \mathbf{x}_p) \in Pre_\sigma(q, \mathbf{x})$*, then* $(q_p, \mathbf{x}_p)$ *is called a* σ-predecessor *of* $(q, \mathbf{x})$.

Note that the notion of σ-successor generalizes the notion of σ-step by including time-steps. The set valued function $Post_\sigma(q, \mathbf{x})$ defines, in a natural way, a transition relation, $\xrightarrow{\sigma} \subseteq (Q \times X) \times (Q \times X)$, as follows: $(q, \mathbf{x}) \xrightarrow{\sigma} (q', \mathbf{x}')$, if $(q', \mathbf{x}') \in Post_\sigma(q, \mathbf{x})$. The transition relation $\xrightarrow{\sigma}$ is also called σ*-transition* relation. Similarly, the set valued function $Pre_\sigma(q, \mathbf{x})$ defines another transition relation, $\xleftarrow{\sigma} \subseteq (Q \times X) \times (Q \times X)$, as follows: $(q, \mathbf{x}) \xleftarrow{\sigma} (q', \mathbf{x}')$, if $(q, \mathbf{x}) \in Pre_\sigma(q', \mathbf{x}')$.

For two configurations $(q_1, \mathbf{x}_1)$ and $(q_2, \mathbf{x}_2)$, if $((q_1, \mathbf{x}_1), (q_2, \mathbf{x}_2))$ is a σ-step, then $(q_2, \mathbf{x}_2) \in Post(q_1, \mathbf{x}_1)$ and $(q_1, \mathbf{x}_1) \in Pre(q_2, \mathbf{x}_2)$; hence, in this case, we have $(q_1, \mathbf{x}_1) \overset{\sigma}{\longrightarrow} (q_2, \mathbf{x}_2)$ and $(q_1, \mathbf{x}_1) \overset{\sigma}{\longleftarrow} (q_2, \mathbf{x}_2)$. This may mislead us to get the false impression that $\overset{\sigma}{\longrightarrow}$ and $\overset{\sigma}{\longleftarrow}$ are the same; and to avoid any such possible confusion, we emphasize that, in general, it is not true that $(q_1, \mathbf{x}_1) \overset{\sigma}{\longrightarrow} (q_2, \mathbf{x}_2)$ implies $(q_1, \mathbf{x}_1) \overset{\sigma}{\longleftarrow} (q_2, \mathbf{x}_2)$; and the same with the converse statement. Hence, the two relations $\overset{\sigma}{\longrightarrow}$ and $\overset{\sigma}{\longleftarrow}$ are not the same.

The definitions of $Post_\sigma$ and Pre_σ can be extended straightforwardly to subsets of $Q \times X$, as follows: for $S \subseteq Q \times X$, define

$$Post_\sigma(S) = \bigcup_{(q,\mathbf{x}) \in S} Post_\sigma(q, \mathbf{x}), \quad \text{and} \quad Pre_\sigma(S) = \bigcup_{(q,\mathbf{x}) \in S} Pre_\sigma(q, \mathbf{x}).$$

Finally, define

$$Post(S) = \bigcup_{\sigma \in \Sigma} Post_\sigma(S), \quad \text{and} \quad Pre(S) = \bigcup_{\sigma \in \Sigma} Pre_\sigma(S).$$

We sometimes refer to $Post$ and Pre as the *1-step* transition functions[2]. More generally, the *k-step* transition functions $Post^k$ and Pre^k are defined inductively as follows: For $S \subseteq Q \times X$,

$$Post^1(S) = Post(S), \quad \text{and for } k \geq 2, \ Post^k(S) = Post(Post^{k-1}(S)).$$

Similarly,

$$Pre^1(S) = Pre(S), \quad \text{and for } k \geq 2, \ Pre^k(S) = Pre(Pre^{k-1}(S)).$$

Finally, define $Post^*$ and Pre^* as

$$Post^*(S) = \bigcup_{k \geq 1} Post^k(S), \quad \text{and} \quad Pre^*(S) = \bigcup_{k \geq 1} Pre^k(S).$$

2.2 Reachability Problem for Hybrid Systems

In the notation just discussed, the *reachability problem* for a hybrid system $H = (Q, X, \Sigma, G, E, Ir$ where $Init$ is not necessarily specified in advance, may be posed as follows:

> **ReachProblem1:** For two subsets S_1 and S_2 of $Q \times X$, is there a finite trajectory, $(q_1, \mathbf{x}_1), (q_2, \mathbf{x}_2), \ldots, (q_N, \mathbf{x}_N)$, for some $N \geq 1$, such that $(q_1, \mathbf{x}_1) \in S_1$ and $(q_N, \mathbf{x}_N) \in S_2$?

This may also be rephrased as

> **ReachProblem2:** For two subsets S_1 and S_2 of $Q \times X$,
> whether $Post^*(S_1) \bigcap S_2 \neq \emptyset$?
> *equivalently:* whether $S_1 \bigcap Pre^*(S_2) \neq \emptyset$?

If the initial set $Init$ is specified in advance, then, with $S_1 = Init$, the reachability problem **ReachProblem1** becomes

[2]This should not be confused with the notion of *step* as defined in Definition 3.

ReachProblem3:	For a subset S of $Q \times X$, is there a finite execution of H with the final configuration in S ?

There is a counterpart to the reachability problem, called the *avoidance problem*, which may be posed as follows:

AvoidProblem:	For two subsets S_1 and S_2 of $Q \times X$,
	whether $Post^*(S_1) \bigcap S_2 = \emptyset$?
	equivalently: whether $S_1 \bigcap Pre^*(S_2) = \emptyset$?

In the sequel, we restrict our attention to **ReachProblem1** or **ReachProblem2**. We observe that the answers to these questions depend, in general, not only on the hybrid system H, but also on the class $\mathcal{C}$ of subsets of $Q \times X$ that are under consideration. Informally, the class $\mathcal{C}$ is required to

1. include a specified class of sets $\mathcal{S}$, where $\mathcal{S}$ may consist of the initial set, sets defined by state invariance conditions, those defined by guard conditions, and domains and ranges of reset maps of edges (and also final sets, if specified),

2. be closed under the boolean set operations of union and complimentation, and under the functions $Post_\sigma$ and Pre_σ, and

3. have an effective decision procedure for answering questions such as, for two sets $S_1, S_2 \in \mathcal{C}$, whether $S_1 = S_2$ or not.

A formal presentation of these notions is beyond the scope of this work, although a brief discussion may be found in Appendix A. For more details, the interested reader may refer to the references on Model Theory, such as [19, 20, 21, 22]. But, for our purposes, we will be content with the following (somewhat informal) definition:

DEFINITION **7** *An algorithm for the reachability problem is said to be*

1. a decision procedure, *if the algorithm stops after a finite number of steps with the correct answer, where the answer can be either* yes *or* no.

2. a semi-decision procedure, *if the algorithm*

   (a) never stops with an incorrect answer, and

   (b) always stops after a finite number of steps with the correct answer, whenever the answer is yes.

A hybrid system H is decidable, *if there is a decision procedure for the reachability problem for H.*

Obviously, for a hybrid system H, if there are semi-decision procedures for both reachability problem and avoidance problem, then H is decidable.

We describe below a schematic semi-decision procedure for the reachability problem of a hybrid system:

Semi-Decision Procedure for **ReachProblem2**

Input : Sets S_1 and S_2
Output : "yes", if there is a trajectory from S_1 to S_2

Initialization $S := S_1$

while $S \bigcap S_2 = \emptyset$ **do**
$S := Post(S)$
end while

return "yes"

In the later part of this section, we shall be mainly concerned with the computational aspects of the *Post*-operator appearing in the while-loop of the above schematic.

2.3 Computation of the *Post*-operator

We describe here a computational approach to finding $Post(S)$, $S \subseteq Q \times \mathbb{R}^n$, as in the semi-decision procedure for **ReachProblem2** discussed in Sec. 2.2. Recall that, within a discrete state $q \in Q$, the continuous dynamics of $\mathbf{x}$ are specified by

$$\frac{d\mathbf{x}}{dt} = f(q, \mathbf{x}) \tag{2}$$

with the initial conditions $\mathbf{x}(0) = \mathbf{x}_0 \in X_0 \subseteq X = \mathbb{R}^n$. We begin our discussion with the following definition.

DEFINITION **8** *Let $\mathbb{R}^+$ denote the set of nonnegative real numbers. Then, for each discrete state $q \in Q$, the* flow *associated with equation (5) is a function $\phi_q : \mathbb{R}^n \times \mathbb{R}^+ \to \mathbb{R}^n$, defined as $\phi_q(\mathbf{x}, t) = \gamma_{\mathbf{x}}(t)$, $t \geq 0$ and $\mathbf{x} \in \mathbb{R}^n$, where the function $\gamma_{\mathbf{x}} : \mathbb{R}^+ \to \mathbb{R}^n$ satisfies*

$$\frac{d\gamma_{\mathbf{x}}(t)}{dt} = f(q, \gamma_{\mathbf{x}}(t)),$$

with the initial condition $\gamma_{\mathbf{x}}(0) = \mathbf{x}$.

Recall the set of reachable phases $Reach_q^G$ as defined in (1). In the following definition, the same is defined in terms of the flow function ϕ_q:

DEFINITION **9** *Let $q \in Q$ and $X_0 \subset \mathbb{R}^n$. Then, the set of reachable continuous phases in the state q, is the set $Reach_q^G(X_0)$ defined as*

$$\begin{aligned} Reach_q^G(X_0) &= \{\mathbf{x} \in \mathbb{R}^n : \exists \mathbf{x}_0 \in X_0 \; \exists t \geq 0 \; \mathbf{x} = \phi_q(\mathbf{x}_0, t) \text{ and} \\ & \qquad \forall s \; 0 \leq s \leq t \Rightarrow \phi_q(\mathbf{x}_0, s) \in G(q)\} \end{aligned} \tag{3}$$

We now define another operator, called the *projection* operators, as follows:

DEFINITION **10** *Let $S \subseteq Q \times X$. Then, define the* projection of S *on Q to be the set $\pi_Q(S) = \{q \in Q : (q, \mathbf{x}) \in S$ for some $\mathbf{x} \in X\}$. Further, for each $q \in Q$ define a projection operator $\pi_{(q,X)}$ as follows:*

$$\pi_{(q,X)}(S) = \{\mathbf{x} \in X : (q, \mathbf{x}) \in S\}.$$

Let $S \subseteq Q \times X$. Then, in terms of the operators π_Q, $\pi_{(q,X)}$ and $Reach_q^G$, the operator *Post* may be rewritten as

$$
\begin{aligned}
Post(S) \;=\; & \bigcup_{q \in \pi_Q(S)} \{q\} \times [Reach_q^G \circ \pi_{(q,X)}(S)] \; \bigcup \\
& \bigcup_{\substack{e=(q_e, X_e, \sigma_e, r_e, q_e') \in E \\ q_e \in \pi_Q(S)}} \{q_e'\} \times [r_e \circ Reach_{q_e}^G \circ \pi_{(q_e,X)}(S)],
\end{aligned} \tag{4}
$$

where, for two operators g and h, $g \circ h$ is the composition of the two operators. With regard to computational issues, the set operators π_X and r_e may not pose difficulties (provided r_e is suitably specified). Hence the problem reduces to that of computation of $Reach_q^G$, and effectively representing the resulting set. Referring to the definition of $Reach_q^G$ as in (3), the significant and challenging task is the elimination of quantifiers, whenever possible. But, as shown in [23], not all theories of the real number system may admit quantifier elimination (see also the discussion presented in [15] and in Appendix A). This fact provides a motivation for the study of alternative methods (without requiring quantifier elimination method) for computating the set $Reach_q^G(X_0)$.

Specifically, in the remaining part of the work, we shall be concerned with computation of the operator $Reach_q^G$ and with representation of the resulting sets. Below is a concise description of the questions that we shall be interested in and of the organization of the rest of the paper:

1. How to effectively compute the set operator $Reach_q^G$, at least when the global invariance condition is not imposed but a time bound is specified? In this case, we are interested in the set $Reach_q(X_0, [0, \tau])$, $\tau \geq 0$, $X_0 \subset \mathbb{R}^n$, defined as

   $$Reach_q(X_0, [0, \tau]) = \{\mathbf{x} \in \mathbb{R}^n : \exists \mathbf{x}_0 \in X_0 \; \exists t \; 0 \leq t \leq \tau \text{ and } \mathbf{x} = \phi_q(\mathbf{x}_0, t)\}.$$

   In Sec. 3, we present a schematic algorithm for computing $Reach_q(X_0, [0, \tau])$. This algorithm is based on a generalization of the method described in [8].

2. How to compute – either exactly or approximately – the set operator $Reach_q^G$ when the global invariance condition is imposed (without time bound). In this case, we have to deal with the set operator $Reach_q^G$ as defined in (3), and obviously, it would be best to find an algorithm based on quantifier elimination. But, as mentioned earlier, we do not assume that quantifier elimination method is feasible, hence we may have to find an algorithm that computes an approximation to $Reach_q^G$. In Sec. 3, we indicate how to extend the algorithm for computing $Reach_q(X_0, [0, \tau])$, as mentioned above, to compute an under-approximation or an over-approximation (depending on which one is preferred) to the set $Reach_q^G(X_0)$.

3. Finally, how to represent the reach sets obtained by the operators $Reach_q$ and $Reach_q^G$, i.e. the sets $Reach_q(X_0, [0, \tau])$ or $Reach_q^G(X_0)$ as the case may be, such that boolean set operations such as union and complementation can be performed efficiently. This requires represention of the reach sets in terms of sets that are simple and easy to handle, such as polyhedral sets and subalgebraic sets. In [12], an algorithm algorithm for over-approximating the reach sets using polyhedral sets is presented. In Sec. 4,

we describe another algorithm for over-approximating the reach sets with polyhedral sets. The algorithm presented in this paper differs from that of [12], but if these two methods – that described in Sec. 4 and that of [12] – are used together, then better results of over-approximation may be obtained.

The remaining part of the paper is orgainized as follows. In Sec. 3 and Sec. 4, we restrict our attention to these issues. We illustrate these algorithms with simple examples in Sec. 5, while Sec. 6 summarizes the paper.

3 Computational Approaches for Finding Reach Sets

3.1 Preliminary Discussion on Reach Sets

Let $H = (Q, X, \Sigma, G, E, Init, f)$ be a hybrid system. For $q \in Q$, consider the equation

$$\frac{d\mathbf{x}}{dt} = f(q, \mathbf{x}) \tag{5}$$

with the initial conditions $\mathbf{x}(0) = \mathbf{x}_0 \in X_0 \subset X = \mathbb{R}^n$. It is customary to assume that $f(q, \cdot)$ is Lipschitz continuous in the second variable, in order to ensure existence and uniqueness of solutions to the system of differential equations in (5). Further, we assume that the initial set X_0 is closed. Let, as before, the flow (refer to Defintion 8) associated with (5) be $\phi_q(\mathbf{x}, t)$ and let $Reach_q(X_0, t) = \{\phi_q(\mathbf{x}_0, t) : \mathbf{x}_0 \in X_0\}$ be the set of phases reached at time $t \geq 0$ in state q with initial conditions in X_0. Further, let

$$\begin{aligned} Reach_q(X_0, [0, \tau]) &= \bigcup_{0 \leq t \leq \tau} Reach_q(X_0, t), \qquad \tau \geq 0, \\ Reach_q(X_0, [0, \infty)) &= \bigcup_{\tau > 0} Reach_q(X_0, [0, \tau]). \end{aligned}$$

We shall now define, for a set X_q, such that $X_0 \subseteq X_q \subseteq \mathbb{R}^n$, another set $Reach'_q(X_0, X_q, [0, \infty))$. For this purpose, we first define, for each $\mathbf{x} \in X_0$, a number $\tau_{\mathbf{x}}$ as follows:

$$\tau_{\mathbf{x}} = \inf\{t > 0 : \phi_q(\mathbf{x}, t) \notin X_q\}, \tag{6}$$

where we assume that if $\tau_{\mathbf{x}} = \infty$, then $\phi_q(\mathbf{x}, \infty)$ denotes the set of all ω-limit points (see, for instance, [17]) of $\phi_q(\mathbf{x}, t)$, for $t \geq 0$, and

$$\{\phi_q(\mathbf{x}, t) : 0 \leq t \leq \infty\} = \{\phi_q(\mathbf{x}, t) : 0 \leq t < \infty\} \bigcup \phi(\mathbf{x}, \infty).$$

Further, let $\Theta_q(\mathbf{x}, X_q) \subseteq \mathbb{R}^n$ be defined as follows:

$$\Theta_q(\mathbf{x}, X_q) = \begin{cases} \{\phi_q(\mathbf{x}, t) \ : 0 \leq t \leq \tau_{\mathbf{x}}\}, & \text{if } \tau_{\mathbf{x}} < \infty \text{ and } \phi(\mathbf{x}, \tau_{\mathbf{x}}) \in X_q, \\ \{\phi_q(\mathbf{x}, t) \ : 0 \leq t < \tau_{\mathbf{x}}\}, & \text{otherwise.} \end{cases}$$

Then the set $Reach'_q(X_0, X_q, [0, \infty))$ is defined as

$$Reach'_q(X_0, X_q, [0, \infty)) = \bigcup_{\mathbf{x} \in X_0} \Theta_q(\mathbf{x}, X_q).$$

Now, by taking $X_q = G(q)$ in the above definition, we have

$$Reach_q^G(X_0) = Reach'_q(X_0, X_q, [0, \infty)),$$

where $Reach_q^G(X_0)$ is defined as in (3), reproduced below for convenience:

$$\begin{aligned} Reach_q^G(X_0) &= \{\mathbf{x} \in \mathbb{R}^n : \exists \mathbf{x}_0 \in X_0 \ \exists t \geq 0 \ \mathbf{x} = \phi_q(\mathbf{x}_0, t) \text{ and} \\ &\quad \forall s \ 0 \leq s \leq t \Rightarrow \phi_q(\mathbf{x}_0, s) \in G(q)\} \end{aligned}$$

Throughout the rest of the discussion, we fix a state q, and consider the problem of computing the sets $Reach_q(X_0, [0, \tau])$ and $Reach'_q(X_0, X_q, [0, \infty))$.

3.2 A Computational Method: Generalized Face-Lifting Algorithm

When X_0 is suitably specified (such as, for example, a rectangle), this problem may be solved by finding the solutions to (5) with $\mathbf{x}(0)$ on the boundary of X_0. This results in evolving the boundary of X_0. More precisely, let S_0 be the boundary of X_0, and $X(\tau) = X_0 \bigcup_{0 \leq t \leq \tau} \{\phi_q(\mathbf{x}_0, t) : \mathbf{x}_0 \in S_0\}$. Then $X(\tau) = Reach_q(X_0, [0, \tau])$ (see Appendix A for a proof). This is the idea underlying the computational approach, called *face lifting* method, described in [8]. In this section, we shall study this in considerably more general setting, and describe an algorithm, called *generalized face lifting* method. It may be noted that the method described in [8] does not assume that a global invarience requirement is imposed; hence the algorithm of [8] computes only $Reach_q(X_0, [0, \tau])$. However, we shall extend our method for computing $Reach_q(X_0, [0, \tau])$ for computing an approximation to the set $Reach_q^G(X_0)$, where the approximation can chosen to be either under-approximation or over-approximation.

Further, let $S_0^+ \subseteq S_0$ be the set of those boundary points of X_0, such that the solution with initial point in S_0^+ extends into $X_0^c \triangleq \mathbb{R}^n \backslash X_0$, i.e.,

$$S_0^+ = \{\mathbf{x}_0 \in S_0 : \exists \epsilon = \epsilon(\mathbf{x}_0) > 0 \text{ such that } \phi_q(\mathbf{x}_0, t) \in X_0^c, \ \forall t \in (0, \epsilon)\}, \tag{7}$$

and define $X^+(\tau) = X_0 \bigcup_{0 \leq t \leq \tau} \{\phi_q(\mathbf{x}_0, t) : \mathbf{x}_0 \in S_0^+\}$. It turns out that $X^+(\tau) = X(\tau) = Reach_q(X_0, [0, \tau])$ (see Appendix A). Therefore, in order to find $Reach_q(X_0, [0, \tau])$, we have to find only those solutions for which the initial conditions are in S_0^+.

If S_0^+ can be found explicitly (by inspection of $\mathbf{f}$ and S_0), then the problem reduces justifiably to finding the solutions with initial conditions in S_0^+. Otherwise, we may have to find a means of obtaining an outer approximation to S_0^+, i.e., a set S_1^+ satisfying $S_0^+ \subseteq S_1^+ \subseteq S_0$. We suggest a way to find such a set. For this purpose, we assume that X_0 is specified as follows: there is a continuously differentiable function, $\ell : \mathbb{R}^n \to \mathbb{R}$, such that if $\mathbf{x} \in \overset{\circ}{X}_0$ then $\ell(\mathbf{x}) < 0$ (where $\overset{\circ}{X}_0$ denotes the interior of X_0, i.e., the largest open set contained in X_0), and if $\mathbf{x} \in X_0^c$ then $\ell(\mathbf{x}) > 0$. Hence $\ell(\mathbf{x}) = 0$ on S_0. Define

$$S_1^+ = \{\mathbf{x} \in S_0 : \nabla \ell(\mathbf{x}) \cdot f(q, \mathbf{x}) \geq 0\}.$$

It may be easily shown that $S_0^+ \subseteq S_1^+$ (see Appendix A). Futher, we observe that the set of points for which $\nabla \ell(\mathbf{x}) \cdot f(q, \mathbf{x}) > 0$, constitutes an inner approximation to S_0^+. The method of finding an S_1^+ as described above can be extended easily to the situation where X_0 is specified as the set of intersection of finitely many sets of the form $\ell_i(\mathbf{x}) \leq 0$, with the strict inequality in $\overset{\circ}{X}_0$.

With this notation, we proceed to describe a schematic algorithm for finding $X^+(\tau)$ for $\tau \geq 0$. In order to exploit the semigroup property of the reach set, i.e., $Reach_q(X_0, [0,t]) = Reach_q(Reach_q(X_0, [0,s]), [0, t-s])$, for any t and s, with $0 \leq s \leq t$, we consider a sequence of time intervals $[0, \tau_1]$, $[\tau_1, \tau_2]$, $[\tau_2, \tau_3]$, etc., where $0 < \tau_1 < \tau_2 < \tau_3 < \ldots$, and $\tau_i \to \infty$, as $i \to \infty$. It may be convenient to choose for some $\tau > 0$, $\tau_i = i\tau$, $i = 0, 1, 2, \ldots$, although we do not require such an assumption in the algorithm.

```
Procedure for Reach_q (X_0, [0, τ])

initialize: X^+(0) := X_0, F_0 := S_1^+ and i := 0
while τ > τ_i and F_i ≠ ∅ do
  if τ < τ_{i+1} then Δ_i := τ − τ_i else Δ_i := τ_{i+1} − τ_i end if
  T_i := {φ_q(x, t) : t ∈ [0, Δ_i], x ∈ F_i}
      /* this computational step requires special attention! */
  X^+(τ_i + Δ_i) := X^+(τ_i) ⋃ T_i
  F_{i+1} := {φ(x, Δ_i) : x ∈ F_i}\X^+(τ_i)
  i := i + 1
end while
```

In the above schematic, the initialization step "$F_0 := S_1^+$" could be replaced with "$F_0 := S_0^+$", as it is not necessary to initialize F_0 to S_1^+. However, before proceeding further, it must be mentioned that with reference to this algorithm, we assume that the computational steps "$T_i := \{\phi_q(\mathbf{x}, t) \,:\, t \in [0, \Delta_i],\ \mathbf{x} \in F_i\}$" and "$F_{i+1} := \{\phi(\mathbf{x}, \Delta_i) \,:\, \mathbf{x} \in F_i\} \backslash X^+(\tau_i)$" can be performed effectively.

We now describe a method for extending this procedure to another procedure that computes an approximation to $Reach'_q(X_0, X_q, [0, \infty))$. But since $Reach_q^G(X_0) = Reach'(X_0, G(q), [0$ the procedure to be described below finds an approximation to $Reach_q^G(X_0)$, when $X_q = G(q)$. The approximation can be chosen to be either under-approximation or over-approximation, depeding on a flag "*under_approximate*", passed as input to the algorithm (refer to the schematic algorithm described below).

To facilitate the discussion, we consider the flow $\psi_q(\mathbf{x}, t)$, $t \geq 0$, $\mathbf{x} \in X = \mathbb{R}^n$, corresponding to the differential equation

$$\frac{d\mathbf{x}}{dt} = -f(q, \mathbf{x}) \tag{8}$$

with the initial conditions $\mathbf{x}(0) = \mathbf{x}_0 \in X = \mathbb{R}^n$. Now since the flow ψ_q has the opposite direction to that of ϕ_q, for any $t \geq 0$ and two subsets X_1 and X_2 of $\mathbb{R}^n$, we have, $X_2 = \phi_q(X_1, t)$ if and only if $X_1 = \psi_q(X_2, t)$. The function ψ_q will be used in the procedure for computing an approximation to $Reach'(X_0, X_q, [0, \infty))$, for finding, in each iteration, the set of initial conditions in F_i corresponding to which the solutions for the time interval $[0, \Delta_i]$ may violate the global invariance requirement. With this, we present the schematic algorithm as follows:

Procedure for $Reach'_q\,(X_0, X_q, [0,\infty))$

precondition: $X_0 \subseteq X_q$
boolean input flag: *under_approximate*
/* *under_approximate* = 1, if under-approximation is preferred */
/* by default, the procedure over-approximates the reach set */

initialize: $X^+(0) := X_0,\ F_0 := S_1^+$ and $i := 0$
while $F_i \neq \emptyset$ **do**
$\Delta_i := \tau_{i+1} - \tau_i$
$T_i := \{\phi_q(\mathbf{x}, t)\ :\ t \in [0, \Delta_i],\ \mathbf{x} \in F_i\}$

if $T_i \subseteq X_q$ **then** /* global invariance not violated */
$X^+(\tau_i + \Delta_i) := X^+(\tau_i) \bigcup T_i$
$F_{i+1} := \{\phi_q(\mathbf{x}, \Delta_i)\ :\ \mathbf{x} \in F_i\} \backslash X^+(\tau_i)$
else /* global invariance violated by at least one trajectory */
$U_i := T_i \backslash X_q$
$V_i := \{\psi_q(\mathbf{x}, t) : \ t \in [0, \Delta_i],\ \mathbf{x} \in U_i\}$
$F'_i = F_i \backslash V_i$

if *under_approximate* = 1 **then**
$T'_i := \{\phi_q(\mathbf{x}, t)\ :\ t \in [0, \Delta_i],\ \mathbf{x} \in F'_i\}$
$X^+(\tau_i + \Delta_i) := X^+(\tau_i) \bigcup T'_i$
else
$X^+(\tau_i + \Delta_i) := X^+(\tau_i) \bigcup (T_i \bigcap X_q)$
end if

$F_{i+1} := \{\phi_q(\mathbf{x}, \Delta_i)\ :\ \mathbf{x} \in F'_i\} \backslash X^+(\tau_i)$
end if

$i := i + 1$

end while

As with the previous algorithm, the initialization step "$F_0 := S_1^+$" could be replaced with "$F_0 := S_0^+$", depending on convenience. Termination of this procedure may be guaranteed, if certain assumptions are satisfied. The required assumptions are as follows:

1. the set $Y_q = \overline{X_q}$ is compact;
2. X_0 is closed in $\mathbb{R}^n$; and
3. for every $\mathbf{x}_0 \in X_0$, Y_q does not contain any ω-limit points of the trajectory of $\phi_q(\mathbf{x}_0, t)$, $t \geq 0$, more precisely,
$$\phi_q(\mathbf{x}_0, \infty) \bigcap Y_q = \emptyset, \quad \mathbf{x}_0 \in X_0.$$

Under these assumptions, it can be shown that (see Appendix C) there is a $\tau_{\max} > 0$, such that for every $\mathbf{x} \in X_0$, there is a $\tau(\mathbf{x}) > 0$ with $0 < \tau(\mathbf{x}) \leq \tau_{max}$ and $\phi_q(\mathbf{x}, \tau(\mathbf{x})) \notin X_q$. Obviously, with such a $\tau_{\max}$, we have $\tau_{\mathbf{x}} \leq \tau_{\max}$, for each $\mathbf{x} \in X_0$, where $\tau_{\mathbf{x}}$ is as in (6). Termination of the algorithm may be deduced from this as follows: Consider a sequence of sets $F_0^{(i)}$, $i \geq 0$, defined as $F_0^{(i)} = \{\mathbf{x} \in S_0 : \phi_q(\mathbf{x}, \tau_i) \in F_i\}$. It is easy to check that $F_0^{(i)}$ is a nonincreasing sequence of sets, i.e., $F_0^{(i+1)} \subseteq F_0^{(i)}$. Let $\mathbf{x} \in X_0$, and let k be a nonnegative integer such that $\tau_k \leq \tau_{\mathbf{x}} < \tau_{k+1}$. Now, during the k'th iteration of the while-loop, the global invariance condition (the condition that $T_k \subseteq X_q$) is violated, since $\phi_q(\mathbf{x}, t) \notin X_q$, for some t such that $\tau_{\mathbf{x}} \leq t < \tau_{k+1}$. Let $\tau'_{\mathbf{x}} \in [\tau_{\mathbf{x}}, \tau_{k+1})$ be a time instant such that $\phi_k(\mathbf{x}, \tau'_{\mathbf{x}}) \notin X_0$, and let $t_{\mathbf{x}} = \tau'_{\mathbf{x}} - \tau_k$. With this choice of $t_{\mathbf{x}}$, we have both $0 \leq t_{\mathbf{x}} < \Delta_k$ and $\phi_q(\mathbf{x}, \tau_k + t_{\mathbf{x}}) \notin X_q$. Thus, $\phi_q(\mathbf{x}, \tau_k + t_{\mathbf{x}}) \in U_k = T_k \backslash X_q$ (refer to the schematic above). Let $\mathbf{y} = \phi_q(\mathbf{x}, \tau_k + t_{\mathbf{x}})$, so $\phi_q(\mathbf{x}, \tau_k) = \psi_q(\mathbf{y}, t_{\mathbf{x}})$. But, since $\mathbf{y} \in U_k$, $\psi_q(\mathbf{y}, t_{\mathbf{x}}) \in V_k$ (refer to the schematic). Hence $\phi_q(\mathbf{x}, \tau_k) \in V_k$ and $\phi_q(\mathbf{x}, \tau_k) \notin F'_k = F_k \backslash V_k$. Therefore $\phi_q(\mathbf{x}, \tau_{k+1}) \notin F_{k+1}$, implying that $\mathbf{x} \notin F_0^{(k+1)}$. By the monotonicity of the sequence of sets $F_0^{(i)}$, we have $\mathbf{x} \notin F_0^{(i)}$, for any $i \geq k+1$. Finally, let $m \geq 0$ be an integer such that $\tau_m \leq \tau_{\max} < \tau_{m+1}$. Now since $\tau_{\mathbf{x}} \leq \tau_{\max}$, $\mathbf{x} \notin F_0^{(m+1)}$, for any $\mathbf{x} \in X_0$. Hence $F_0^{(m+1)} = \emptyset$, so $F_{m+1} = \emptyset$, satisfying the terminating condition of the while-loop of the algorithm, after at most m number of iterations.

In the rest of the paper, we discuss approximation of the set T_i appearing in the second line of the while-loop of the above schematic (see also the schematic for $Reach(X_0, [0, \tau])$), when $f(q, \mathbf{x})$ is of the form $f(q, \mathbf{x}) = A_q\mathbf{x}$, where A_q is a constant $n \times n$ matrix with real entries and the initial set X_0 is a polyhedron. For convenience, we drop the subscript q in A_q, and deal with the linear system

$$\frac{d\mathbf{x}(t)}{dt} = A\mathbf{x},$$

where A is a constant $n \times n$ matrix with real valued entries.

4 Representation of the Reach Sets

4.1 Preliminary Discussion

In this section, we discuss representation of the reach set $Reach_q(X_0, [0, \tau])$, such that boolean set operations such as union and complementation can be performed efficiently. The most convenient representation schemes appear to be representation in terms of the following classes of subsets of $\mathbb{R}^n$:

1. *Polyhedral Sets* : These are the sets which can be written as union of finitely many polyhedra. A polyhedron in $\mathbb{R}^n$ is a set which may be expressed as the intersection of finitely many closed half spaces [18], i.e., a finite intersection of sets of the form $\{\mathbf{x} \in \mathbb{R}^n : \mathbf{a}^T\mathbf{x} \leq b\}$, where $\mathbf{a} \in \mathbb{R}^n$ and $b \in \mathbb{R}$. It may be observed this class of sets corresponds to (and includes) the class of definable sets in the theory of linear inequalities of $\mathbb{R}$, i.e., the theory obtained when 0 and 1 are the constant elements, + and − are the (binary) function symbols, and < is the (binary) relation symbol (see Appendix A).

2. *Subalgebraic Sets* : These are the sets which can be written as union of finite number of sets defined by polynomial inequalities, i.e., sets that can be expressed as union of finitely many sets, each of which is the intersection of finitely many sets the form $\{\mathbf{x} \in \mathbb{R}^n : p(\mathbf{x}) \leq c\}$, where $p : \mathbb{R}^n \to \mathbb{R}$ is a polynomial function with real-valued coefficients and $c \in \mathbb{R}$. This class of sets corresponds to (and includes) the class of sets that are definable in the theory of $\mathbb{R}$ when viewed as an ordered field. The theory of ordered field of $\mathbb{R}$ is the theory obtained by extending the theory of linear inequalities of $\mathbb{R}$ by including a binary function symbol for representing the product of two real numbers, denoted by $\cdot$ (see Appendix A).

It may be observed that, for a general flow function ϕ_q, the reach set $Reach_q(X_0, [0, \tau])$ may not be exactly representable in any one of these classes, even if X_0 is. Hence, as an alternative, we may have to settle for an approximation of the reach set by sets that belong to the respective classes. In this context, we shall restrict our attention to over-approximation of the reach set with polyhedral sets.

Specifically, we describe an algorithm for reach set over-approximation with polyhedral sets, when the system dynamics (within a discrete state q) are specified as

$$\frac{d\mathbf{x}}{dt} = A\mathbf{x}, \quad \mathbf{x}(0) \in X_0, \tag{9}$$

where the initial set X_0 is a polyhedron and A is a constant real valued $n \times n$ matrix. Based on the discussion of the last section, we consider the problem of approximating the reach set of the solutions of the equation

$$\frac{d\mathbf{x}}{dt} = A\mathbf{x}, \quad \mathbf{x}(0) \in F_0, \tag{10}$$

where F_0 is a face of X_0.

The main references on approximate reach set computation using polyhedral sets appear to be [10] and [12]. In [10], the initial set is assumed to be convex (not necessarily a polyhedron), and for each time instance, each slice of the "reach tube" (i.e., for each $t \in [\tau_i, \tau_{i+1}]$, the set $\phi(F_i, t)$) is approximated by polyhedra. The method described in [12] assumes F_i to be a polyhedron, and approximates the tube for the time interval $[\tau_i, \tau_{i+1}]$, i.e., the set $T_i = \bigcup_{0 \leq t \leq \tau_{i+1} - \tau_i} \phi(F_i, t)$, by first constructing a polyhedral over-approximation of the reach tube for the time interval and further over-approximating the resulting polyhedron by a "griddy" polyhedron, i.e., a set that may be expressed as a union of unit hypercubes with integer left-most vertices [12].

Being a convex set, any polyhedron that over-approximates the reach set contains the convex hull of T_i. An algorithm based on this observation (as given in [12]) is to find a "bloated" convex hull of F_i and F_{i+1}. This method seems to be simple and straightforward, and gives reasonable approximations in a rather short time (refer to [12]). But we may note that those faces of the convex hull of F_i and F_{i+1}, for which the solution set T_i lies on one side, need not be bloated. By shrinking the convex hull, an under-approximation is obtained by the same method.

If the time steps are constant, i.e., $\tau_k = k\tau$, for some $\tau > 0$, as in [12], then we have to find approximation P_0 only for T_0, since symbolically, $T_k = e^{(A\tau)}T_{k-1}$, for $k \geq 1$, and therefore, $T_k = e^{(kA\tau)}T_0 = e^{(A\tau_k)}T_0$. Thus, $P_k = e^{(A\tau_k)}P_0$ is the required approximation, and if λ_j, $j = 1, 2, \ldots, N$, are the normals of the faces P_0, then the normals of the faces of P_k are given by $e^{(-A^T\tau_k)}\lambda_j$. From this, we may infer that in the subsequent iterations of the algorithm of [12], the convex hull of F_i and F_{i+1} need not be computed.

4.2 Over-approximating the Reach Set with Polyhedra

In this section, we consider the problem of over-approximating the reach sets, when the dynamics are specified as

$$\frac{d\mathbf{x}(t)}{dt} = A\mathbf{x}(t),\ t \geq 0,$$

with the initial conditions $\mathbf{x}(0) \in X_0$. The solution is given explicitly by $\mathbf{x}(t) = e^{(At)}\mathbf{x}(0)$. We assume that the initial set X_0 is a polyhedron, defined by

$$\lambda_i^T\mathbf{x} - h_i \leq 0, \quad i = 1, 2, \ldots, \kappa, \tag{11}$$

where κ is a fixed positive integer. We assume that $\lambda_i \in \mathbb{R}^n$, $|\lambda_i| = 1$ and $h_i \in \mathbb{R}$, for $1 \leq i \leq \kappa$. Then the boundary set of X_0 consists of sets C_j, $1 \leq j \leq \kappa$, of the form

$$\begin{aligned} \lambda_j^T\mathbf{x} - h_j &= 0, \quad \text{and} \\ \lambda_i^T\mathbf{x} - h_i &\leq 0, \quad \text{for } 1 \leq i \leq \kappa \text{ and } i \neq j\ . \end{aligned}$$

Further, we consider only those polyhedral initial sets X_0 and matrices A that satisfy the following assumptions:

($\mathcal{A}_1$) X_0 is compact.

($\mathcal{A}_2$) The set S_0^+, as defined in (7) corresponding to the flow function $\phi_q(\mathbf{x}, t) = e^{(At)}\mathbf{x}$, can be expressed as $S_0^+ = C_{j_1} \bigcup C_{j_2} \bigcup \ldots \bigcup C_{j_m}$, where $1 \leq j_1 < j_2 < \ldots < j_m \leq \kappa$, such that for each i with $1 \leq i \leq m$, $\lambda_{j_i}^T A\mathbf{x} - h_{j_i} \geq \delta_i > 0$, for every $\mathbf{x} \in C_{j_i}$.

Referring to these assumptions, it may be mentioned that the main limitation of this method appears to be the restriction imposed by assumption $\mathcal{A}_2$ on the initial set X_0 and the matrix A. In contrast, the method described in [12] does not require such an assumption. But for our purposes, we need this assumption.

Now, let j be an index such that $C_j \subseteq S_0^+$, as in assumption ($\mathcal{A}_2$). For simplicity and definiteness, let us assume that $j = \kappa$ and put $F_0 = C_\kappa$. Hence, F_0 is described by

$$\begin{aligned} \lambda_i^T\mathbf{x} - h_i &\leq 0, \quad 1 \leq i \leq \kappa - 1, \quad \text{and} \\ \lambda_\kappa^T\mathbf{x} - h_\kappa &= 0. \end{aligned}$$

After some manipulations and rearrangements, if necessary, the above system of linear constraints can be transformed into an equivalent system of linear constraints, which also describes F_0 but is of the following form:

$$\left.\begin{aligned} \mathbf{a}_i^T\mathbf{x} - b_i &\leq 0, \quad 1 \leq i \leq k - 1, \quad \text{and} \\ \mathbf{a}_k^T\mathbf{x} - b_k &= 0, \end{aligned}\right\} \tag{12}$$

where $k \leq \kappa$, $\mathbf{a}_k = \lambda_\kappa$, and for $1 \leq i < k$, $|\mathbf{a}_i| = 1$ and $\mathbf{a}_i^T\mathbf{a}_k = 0$. It may be observed that, since $|\lambda_k| = 1$ initially, we have $|\mathbf{a}_k| = 1$ as well. Also, by assumption ($\mathcal{A}_2$), there is a $\delta > 0$, such that for all the vectors $\mathbf{x} \in F_0$, $\mathbf{a}_k^T A\mathbf{x} \geq \delta$. Further, we assume that the system of linear constraints in (12) is consistent and that each of the constraints is linearly independent from the remaining constraints.

With this construction, our objective is to describe an algorithm to find a polyhedron P_0 as an over-approximation to the set

$$T_0 = \{e^{(At)}\mathbf{x}_0 \,:\, \mathbf{x}_0 \in F_0,\ t \in [0, \Delta]\}, \tag{13}$$

where Δ is a small positive number for which the the following condition holds:

(C_1) for some $\delta_0 > 0$, $\mathbf{a}_k^T A e^{(At)}\mathbf{x}_0 \geq \delta_0$, for all $\mathbf{x}_0 \in F_0$ and for all $t \in [-\Delta, \Delta]$.

The existence of such a Δ can be assured by our assumptions $(\mathcal{A}_1)$ and $(\mathcal{A}_2)$. Later, we shall derive an estimate for such a Δ, for any fixed $\delta_0 > 0$ such that $\delta_0 < \delta$. In comparison, the method of [12] does not impose any such restrictions on Δ. But, it may be mentioned that, in both cases, the accuracy of approximation of either method depends on how small a value is chosen for the parameter Δ. The two conditions (C_2) and (C_3) stated below follow from condition (C_1):

(C_2) $\mathbf{a}_k^T e^{(At)}\mathbf{x}_0 - b_k > 0$, for all $\mathbf{x}_0 \in F_0$ and for all t such that $0 < t \leq \Delta$; and

(C_3) $\mathbf{a}_k^T e^{(At)}\mathbf{x}_0 - b_k < 0$, for all $\mathbf{x}_0 \in F_0$ and for all t such that $-\Delta \leq t < 0$.

Before proceeding to describe our algorithm, we note that the set $F_\Delta = \{e^{(A\Delta)}\mathbf{x}_0 \,:\, \mathbf{x}_0 \in F_0\}$ may be described by the system of linear constraints

$$\begin{aligned} \mathbf{a}_i^T(\Delta)\mathbf{x} - b_i &\leq 0, \quad i = 1, 2, \ldots, k-1, \\ \mathbf{a}_k^T(\Delta)\mathbf{x} - b_k &= 0. \end{aligned}$$

where $\mathbf{a}_i(\Delta) = e^{(-A^T\Delta)}\mathbf{a}_i$, $1 \leq i \leq k$. Dividing throughout the last equation in the above system by $|\mathbf{a}_k(\Delta)|$, we get

$$\begin{aligned} \mathbf{a}_i^T(\Delta)\mathbf{x} - b_i &\leq 0, \quad i = 1, 2, \ldots, k-1, \\ \mathbf{b}_k^T\mathbf{x} - b'_k &= 0, \end{aligned}$$

where $\mathbf{b}_k = \frac{\mathbf{a}_k(\Delta)}{|\mathbf{a}_k(\Delta)|}$ and $b'_k = \frac{b_k}{|\mathbf{a}_k(\Delta)|}$. Now, we observe that, since $e^{(-A^T\Delta)}$ is invertible and $|\mathbf{a}_i| = 1$, each $\mathbf{a}_i(\Delta)$ is nonzero, and since $\mathbf{a}_k$ is orthogonal to $\mathbf{a}_i$, for $1 \leq i \leq k-1$, $\mathbf{a}_k(\Delta)$ and $\mathbf{a}_i(\Delta)$ are pair-wise independent. So, after subtracting from each of the inequalities of the above system an appropriate constant times the last equation, and after normalization, the above system of linear constraints can be transformed into the following system of linear constraints:

$$\left.\begin{aligned} \mathbf{b}_i^T\mathbf{x} - b'_i &\leq 0, \quad i = 1, 2, \ldots, k-1, \\ \mathbf{b}_k^T\mathbf{x} - b'_k &= 0, \end{aligned}\right\} \tag{14}$$

where, for $1 \leq i \leq k$, $|\mathbf{b}_i| = 1$, and for $1 \leq i \leq k-1$, $\mathbf{b}_i^T\mathbf{b}_k = 0$. Now, by the condition (C_3), for $0 \leq t < \Delta$ and $\mathbf{x}_0 \in F_0$, $\mathbf{a}_k^T(\Delta)e^{(At)} - b_k = \mathbf{a}_k^T e^{(A(t-\Delta))} - b_k < 0$. Hence, we also have, for $0 \leq t < \Delta$ and $\mathbf{x}_0 \in F_0$, $\mathbf{b}_k^T e^{(At)}\mathbf{x}_0 - b'_k < 0$.

In this notation, we now describe a schematic algorithm, the output of which is a set of $4k$ many parameters, consisting of pairs of vectors and constants, (μ_i, c_i) and (ν_i, d_i),

$i = 1, 2, \ldots, 2k$, where for each i, $\mu_i, \nu_i \in \mathbb{R}^n$ and $c_i, d_i \in \mathbb{R}$, such that the polyhedron P_0 of intersection of the $4k$ half-spaces defined by $L_i = \{\mathbf{x} \in \mathbb{R}^n : \mu_i^T \mathbf{x} - c_i \leq 0\}$ and $L'_i = \{\mathbf{x} \in \mathbb{R}^n : \nu_i^T \mathbf{x} - d_i \leq 0\}$ is an over-approximating polyhedron for the set T_0 as defined in (13).

Schematic Algorithm for Finding Over-approximating Polyhedron

Reach Set : $T_0 = \{e^{(At)}\mathbf{x}_0 : t \in [0, \Delta], \mathbf{x}_0 \in F_0\}$ (refer to (13))
Output : $4k$ vectors μ_i, ν_i and $4k$ real numbers c_i, d_i, $1 \leq i \leq 2k$

/* the $4k$ half-spaces are L_i and L'_i, $1 \leq i \leq 2k$, where */
/* $L_i = \{\mathbf{x} \in \mathbb{R}^n : \eta_i(\mathbf{x}) = \mu_i^T \mathbf{x} - c_i \leq 0\}$, and */
/* $L'_i = \{\mathbf{x} \in \mathbb{R}^n : \eta'_i(\mathbf{x}) = \nu_i^T \mathbf{x} - d_i \leq 0\}$ */

for $i = 1, 2, \ldots, k-1$, **do** /* to find (μ_i, c_i) and (ν_i, d_i) */
$l_i := \inf\{l : (\mathbf{a}_i^T \mathbf{x} - b_i) - l(\mathbf{a}_k^T \mathbf{x} - b_k) \leq 0, \forall \mathbf{x} \in T_0\}$;
$\mu_i := \mathbf{a}_i - l_i \mathbf{a}_k$; $c_i := b_i - l_i b_k$;

$l'_i := \inf\{l' : (\mathbf{b}_i^T \mathbf{x} - b'_i) + l'(\mathbf{b}_k^T \mathbf{x} - b'_k) \leq 0, \forall \mathbf{x} \in T_0\}$;
$\nu_i := \mathbf{b}_i + l'_i \mathbf{b}_k$; $d_i = b'_i + l'_i b'_k$;
end for
$\mu_k := -\mathbf{a}_k^T$; $c_k = -b_k$;
$\nu_k := \mathbf{b}_k^T$; $d_k = b'_k$;

$l_k := \inf\{l : (\mathbf{a}_k^T \mathbf{x} - b_k) - l \leq 0, \forall \mathbf{x} \in T_0\}$;
$\mu_k := \mathbf{a}_k$; $c_{k+1} := b_k + l_k$;

$l'_k := \inf\{l : -(\mathbf{b}_k^T \mathbf{x} - b'_k) - l \leq 0, \forall \mathbf{x} \in T_0\}$;
$\nu_k := -\mathbf{b}_k$; $d_{k+1} := -b'_k + l'_k$;

for $i = 1, 2, \ldots, k-1$, **do**
/* to find (μ_{i+k+1}, c_{i+k+1}) and (ν_{i+k+1}, d_{i+k+1}) */
$l_{i+k} = \inf\{l : (\mathbf{a}_i^T \mathbf{x} - b_i) - l \leq 0, \forall \mathbf{x} \in T_0\}$;
$\mu_{i+k} = \mathbf{a}_i$; $c_{i+k+1} = b_i + l_{i+k}$;

$l'_{i+k} = \inf\{l' : (\mathbf{b}_i^T \mathbf{x} - b'_i) - l' \leq 0, \forall \mathbf{x} \in F_0\}$;
$\nu_{i+k} = \mathbf{b}_i$; $d_{i+k+1} = b'_i + l'_{i+k}$;
end for

We first observe that both $l_i > -\infty$ and $l'_i > -\infty$. If $\mathbf{a}_k^T A\mathbf{x} \geq \delta > 0$, as in assumption $\mathcal{A}_2$, then both $l_i < \infty$ and $l'_i < \infty$, as we shall see in Sec. 4.3 below. If Δ is small, such that the set T_0 is nearly a polyhedron, then the above method gives reasonable results. Referring to Step 1 of the first for-loop of the above algorithm, the reason for choosing l_i to be the infimum over all l for which $(\mathbf{a}_i^T \mathbf{x} - b_i) - l(\mathbf{a}_k^T \mathbf{x} - b_k) \leq 0$, $\forall \mathbf{x} \in T_0$, is obvious: if P_1 and P_2 are two polyhedra such that P_1 is obtained by the above algorithm and P_2 is obtained by replacing a constraint $\mu_i^T \mathbf{x} - c_i \leq 0$, where μ_i and c_i are as in Step 2, with another constraint

$\lambda_i^T \mathbf{x} - h_i \leq 0$, where $\lambda_i = \mathbf{a}_i - l\,\mathbf{a}_k$ and $h_i = b_i - l\,b_k$, for some $l > l_i$, then $P_1 \subset P_2$.[3] (An analogous statement holds for each of the remaining parameters, l'_i, l_k, l'_k, l_{k+i} and l'_{k+i}, as in the algorithm.)

It can be shown that the polyhedron included in the $k+1$ half-spaces, specified by $L_1, L_2, \ldots, L_k, L_{k+1}$, is a bounded polyhedron (see Appendix D). We may also note that the hyperplanes $\mu_i^T \mathbf{x} - c_i = 0$ and $\nu_i^T \mathbf{x} - d_i = 0$, $1 \leq i \leq k-1$, are obtained by rotating the hyperplanes $\mathbf{a}_i^T \mathbf{x} - b_i = 0$ and $\mathbf{b}_i^T \mathbf{x} - b'_i = 0$ about their corresponding intersection with the hyperplanes $\mathbf{a}_k^T \mathbf{x} - b_k = 0$ and $\mathbf{b}_k^T \mathbf{x} - b'_k = 0$, respectively; whereas the hyperplanes $\mu_{k+1}^T \mathbf{x} - c_{k+1} = 0$ and $\nu_{k+1}^T \mathbf{x} - d_{k+1} = 0$ are obtained by translating the hyperplanes $\mathbf{a}_k^T \mathbf{x} - b_k = 0$ and $\mathbf{b}_k^T \mathbf{x} - b_k = 0$, respectively. Similarly, for $i = 1, 2, \ldots, k-1$, the hyperplanes $\mu_{k+i}^T \mathbf{x} - c_{k+i} = 0$ and $\nu_{k+i}^T \mathbf{x} - d_{k+i} = 0$ are translations of the hyperplanes $\mathbf{a}_i^T \mathbf{x} - b_i = 0$ and $\mathbf{b}_i^T \mathbf{x} - b'_i = 0$, respectively.

In remaining part of the section (in Sec. 4.3 below), we shall derive upper bounds for the numbers l_i and l'_i, $1 \leq i \leq 2k-1$, that are defined in the schematic. If all the l_i and l'_i are replaced with their corresponding upper bounds, $\hat{l}_i$ and $\hat{l}'_i$ respectively, then we obtain conservative estimates – $\hat{\mu}_i$, $\hat{c}_i$, $\hat{\nu}_i$ and $\hat{d}_i$ respectively – for μ_i, c_i, ν_i and d_i. After this replacement, we obtain a modified algorithm for over-approximation with polyhedra. It may be observed that these estimates overcome the difficulties in finding the infima required for obtaining l_i's and l'_i's. But unfortunately, the conservative upper bounds that we derive for l_i's and l'_i's (as in Sec. 4.3) may turn out to be very large. However, better accuracy may be obtained if the modified alogrithm is used in conjunction with that of [12] (see Fig. 5 in Sec. 5). More precisely, the intersection of the polyhedron obtained by the method described here with that obtained by the method of [12] gives a smaller over-approximating polyhedron, as will be discussed in Sec. 5, while illustrating these algorithms with simple examples.

4.3 Upper Bounds for l_i and l'_i

In this section, we derive upper bounds for the numbers l_i and l'_i appearing in the schematic algorithm. We begin with the following result:

Claim 1. For $i = 1, 2, \ldots, k$, with $\mathbf{a}_i$ and b_i as in (12) and $\mathbf{x}_0 \in F_0$ and $t \in (0, \Delta]$, we have

$$\left| \frac{(\mathbf{a}_i^T e^{(At)} \mathbf{x}_0 - \mathbf{a}_i^T \mathbf{x}_0)}{t} \right| \leq M_0 \|\mathbf{a}_i^T A\| e^{(\|A\|\Delta)},$$

where $M_0 = \max_{\mathbf{x}_0 \in F_0} \{\|\mathbf{x}_0\|\}$.

To prove the claim, we first note that $(\mathbf{a}_i^T e^{(At)} \mathbf{x}_0 - \mathbf{a}_i^T \mathbf{x}_0) = t \times \mathbf{a}_i^T A e^{(A\theta)} \mathbf{x}_0$, for some θ with $0 < \theta < t$, where θ may depend on t. Hence, we have

$$\begin{aligned} \left| \frac{(\mathbf{a}_i^T e e^{(At)} \mathbf{x}_0 - \mathbf{a}_i^T \mathbf{x}_0)}{t} \right| &= |\mathbf{a}_i^T A e^{(A\theta)} \mathbf{x}_0|, \quad \text{where } \theta \text{ is such that } 0 < \theta < t \\ &\leq |\mathbf{a}_i^T A e^{(A\theta)}| \times \|\mathbf{x}_0\| \\ &\leq M_0 \|\mathbf{a}_i^T A\| e^{(\|A\|\Delta)}. \end{aligned}$$

[3] This follows from the observation that if both $(\mathbf{a}_i^T \mathbf{x} - b_i) - l(\mathbf{a}_k^T \mathbf{x} - b_k) \leq 0$ and $-(\mathbf{a}_k^T \mathbf{x} - b_k) = \mu_k^T \mathbf{x} - c_k \leq 0$, where $l \in \mathbb{R}$ and $\mathbf{x} \in \mathbb{R}^n$, $\mathbf{x}$ not necessarily in T_0, then, for any $h > l$, $(\mathbf{a}_i^T \mathbf{x} - b_i) - h(\mathbf{a}_k^T \mathbf{x} - b_k) \leq 0$.

With $\mathbf{b}_i$ and b'_i, we have an analogous result, but with a slight modification, as in the following:

Claim 2. For $i = 1, 2, \ldots, k$, with $\mathbf{b}_i$ and b'_i as in (12) and $\mathbf{x}_0 \in F_0$ and $t \in [0, \Delta)$, we have

$$\left| \frac{(\mathbf{b}_i^T e^{(At)}\mathbf{x}_0 - \mathbf{b}_i^T e^{(A\Delta)}\mathbf{x}_0)}{(\Delta - t)} \right| \leq M_0 \|\mathbf{b}_i^T A\| e^{(\|A\|\Delta)},$$

where $M_0 = \max_{\mathbf{x}_0 \in F_0}\{\|\mathbf{x}_0\|\}$.

We have $(\mathbf{b}_i^T e^{(At)}\mathbf{x}_0 - \mathbf{b}_i^T e^{(A\Delta)}\mathbf{x}_0) = (t - \Delta) \times \mathbf{b}_i^T A e^{(A\theta)}\mathbf{x}_0$, for some θ with $t < \theta < \Delta$. Hence

$$\begin{aligned} \left| \frac{(\mathbf{b}_i^T e^{(At)}\mathbf{x}_0 - \mathbf{b}_i^T e^{(A\Delta)}\mathbf{x}_0)}{(\Delta - t)} \right| &= |\mathbf{b}_i A e^{(A\theta)}\mathbf{x}_0|, \quad \text{for some } \theta \text{ with } t < \theta < \Delta \\ &\leq \|\mathbf{b}_i^T A e^{(A\theta)}\| \times \|\mathbf{x}_0\| \\ &\leq M_0 \|\mathbf{b}_i^T A\| e^{(\|A\|\Delta)}. \end{aligned}$$

Finally, we shall make the following claim, before deriving upper bounds for l_i's and l'_i's:

Claim 3. Assume, for some $\delta > 0$, $\mathbf{a}_k^T A\mathbf{x}_0 \geq \delta$, for every $\mathbf{x}_0 \in F_0$, and let δ_0 be such that $0 < \delta_0 < \delta$. Then there is a $\Delta > 0$ such that $\mathbf{a}_k^T A e^{(At)}\mathbf{x}_0 \geq \delta_0$, for all $\mathbf{x}_0 \in F_0$ and for all $t \in [-\Delta, \Delta]$.

In order to prove the claim, we shall derive a conservative estimate for a $\Delta > 0$ for which the claim holds. Fix a δ_0 such that $0 < \delta_0 < \delta$. We have

$$\begin{aligned} \mathbf{a}_k^T A e^{(At)}\mathbf{x}_0 &= \mathbf{a}_k^T A\mathbf{x}_0 + \int_0^t \mathbf{a}_k^T A^2 e^{(As)}\mathbf{x}_0 \, ds, \quad \text{where } \mathbf{x}_0 \in F_0, \\ &\geq \mathbf{a}_k^T A\mathbf{x}_0 - \int_0^{|t|} \|\mathbf{a}_k^T\| \|A\|^2 e^{(\|A\|s)} \|\mathbf{x}_0\| \, ds \\ &\geq \mathbf{a}_k^T A\mathbf{x}_0 - M_0\|A\|(e^{\|A\||t|} - 1), \end{aligned}$$

where $M_0 = \max_{\mathbf{x}_0 \in F_0}\{\|\mathbf{x}_0\|\}$. Therefore, if Δ is such that

$$M_0\|A\|(e^{\|A\|\Delta} - 1) \leq \delta - \delta_0,$$

then the claim holds.

Upper Bounds for l_i and l'_i, $1 \leq i \leq k-1$. Recall that, for $1 \leq i \leq k-1$,

$$l_i = \inf\{l : (\mathbf{a}_i^T\mathbf{x} - b_i) - l(\mathbf{a}_k^T\mathbf{x} - b_k) \leq 0, \ \forall \mathbf{x} \in T_0\}. \tag{15}$$

Referring to the right hand side of (15), for every $\mathbf{x}_0 \in F_0$, since $\mathbf{a}_k^T\mathbf{x}_0 - b_k = 0$, for any real number l, we have $(\mathbf{a}_i^T\mathbf{x}_0 - b_i) - l(\mathbf{a}_k^T\mathbf{x}_0 - b_k) = (\mathbf{a}_i^T\mathbf{x}_0 - b_i) \leq 0$. Therefore, we may assume $\mathbf{x} \in T_0 \backslash F_0$, and $(\mathbf{a}_k^T\mathbf{x} - b_k) > 0$. Thus l_i has to be chosen such that

$$l_i = \sup_{\mathbf{x} \in T_0 \backslash F_0} \frac{(\mathbf{a}_i^T\mathbf{x} - b_i)}{(\mathbf{a}_k^T\mathbf{x} - b_k)}.$$

Rewriting the above, we have

$$l_i = \sup_{\substack{0<t\leq\Delta \\ \mathbf{x}_0\in F_0}} \frac{(\mathbf{a}_i^T e^{(At)}\mathbf{x}_0 - b_i)}{(\mathbf{a}_k^T e^{(At)}\mathbf{x}_0 - b_k)}.$$

Dividing the numerator and denominator by t, this may be written as

$$l_i = \sup_{\substack{0<t\leq\Delta \\ \mathbf{x}_0\in F_0}} \frac{\alpha_i(\mathbf{x}_0, t)}{\beta_i(\mathbf{x}_0, t)},$$

where $\alpha_i(\mathbf{x}_0, t)$ and $\beta_i(\mathbf{x}_0, t)$ are given by

$$\alpha_i(\mathbf{x}_0, t) = \frac{(\mathbf{a}_i^T e^{(At)}\mathbf{x}_0 - b_i)}{t} \quad \text{and} \quad \beta_i(\mathbf{x}_0, t) = \beta(\mathbf{x}_0, t) = \frac{(\mathbf{a}_k^T e^{(At)}\mathbf{x}_0 - b_k)}{t}.$$

But, since $\mathbf{a}_i^T\mathbf{x}_0 - b_i \leq 0$, for every $\mathbf{x}_0 \in F_0$, we have

$$\frac{(\mathbf{a}_i^T e^{(At)}\mathbf{x}_0 - b_i)}{t} \leq \frac{(\mathbf{a}_i^T e^{(At)}\mathbf{x}_0 - \mathbf{a}_i^T\mathbf{x}_0)}{t} \leq \left|\frac{(\mathbf{a}_i^T e^{(At)}\mathbf{x}_0 - \mathbf{a}_i^T\mathbf{x}_0)}{t}\right|.$$

By **Claim 1**, we have

$$\sup_{\substack{0<t\leq\Delta \\ \mathbf{x}_0\in F_0}} \alpha_i(\mathbf{x}_0, t) \leq M_0\|\mathbf{a}_i^T A\|e^{(\|A\|\Delta)}.$$

As to the denominator, since $\mathbf{a}_k^T\mathbf{x}_0 - b_k = 0$, for every $\mathbf{x}_0 \in F_0$, we have

$$\frac{(\mathbf{a}_k^T e^{(At)}\mathbf{x}_0 - b_k)}{t} = \frac{(\mathbf{a}_k^T e^{(At)}\mathbf{x}_0 - \mathbf{a}_k^T\mathbf{x}_0)}{t} = \mathbf{a}_k^T Ae^{(A\theta)}\mathbf{x}_0 \geq \delta_0,$$

where, θ is some number in the interval $(0, t)$, and the last inequality is due to **Claim 3**. Hence

$$\inf_{\substack{0<t\leq\Delta \\ \mathbf{x}_0\in F_0}} \beta(\mathbf{x}_0, t) \geq \delta_0 > 0.$$

Combining both inequalities, we have

$$l_i \leq \frac{\sup_{0<t\leq\Delta,\ \mathbf{x}_0\in F_0} \alpha_i(\mathbf{x}_0, t)}{\inf_{0<t\leq\Delta,\ \mathbf{x}_0\in F_0} \beta_i(\mathbf{x}_0, t)} \leq \hat{l}_i = \frac{M_0\|\mathbf{a}_i^T A\|e^{(\|A\|\Delta)}}{\delta_0}.$$

Likewise, l_i' must be chosen such that

$$l_i' = \sup_{\substack{0\leq t<\Delta \\ \mathbf{x}_0\in F_0}} \frac{\alpha_i'(\mathbf{x}_0, t)}{\beta_i'(\mathbf{x}_0, t)},$$

where $\alpha_i'(\mathbf{x}_0, t)$ and $\beta_i'(\mathbf{x}_0, t)$ are given by

$$\alpha_i'(\mathbf{x}_0, t) = \frac{(\mathbf{b}_i^T e^{(At)}\mathbf{x}_0 - b_i')}{(\Delta - t)} \quad \text{and} \quad \beta_i'(\mathbf{x}_0, t) = \beta'(\mathbf{x}_0, t) = \frac{(\mathbf{b}_k^T e^{(At)}\mathbf{x}_0 - b_k')}{(\Delta - t)}.$$

Now, since $\mathbf{b}_i^T e^{(A\Delta)}\mathbf{x}_0 - b_i' \leq 0$, for $\mathbf{x}_0 \in F_0$,

$$\begin{aligned}\frac{(\mathbf{b}_i^T e^{(At)}\mathbf{x}_0 - b_i')}{(\Delta - t)} &\leq \frac{(\mathbf{b}_i^T e^{(At)}\mathbf{x}_0 - \mathbf{b}_i^T e^{(A\Delta)}\mathbf{x}_0)}{(\Delta - t)} \\ &\leq \left|\frac{(\mathbf{b}_i^T e^{(At)}\mathbf{x}_0 - \mathbf{b}_i^T e^{(A\Delta)})}{(\Delta - t)}\right| \\ &\leq M_0\|\mathbf{b}_i^T A\| e^{(\|A\|\Delta)}, \quad \text{by } \textbf{Claim 2}.\end{aligned}$$

For the denominator function, since $\mathbf{b}_k^T e^{(A\Delta)}\mathbf{x}_0 - b_k' = 0$, for every $\mathbf{x}_0 \in F_0$, we have

$$\frac{(\mathbf{b}_k^T e^{(At)}\mathbf{x}_0 - b_k')}{(\Delta - t)} = \frac{(\mathbf{b}_k^T e^{(At)}\mathbf{x}_0 - \mathbf{b}_k^T e^{(A\Delta)}\mathbf{x}_0)}{(\Delta - t)} = -\mathbf{b}_k^T A e^{(A\theta)}\mathbf{x}_0,$$

where θ is some number in the interval (t, Δ). Now,

$$-\mathbf{b}_k^T A e^{(A\theta)}\mathbf{x}_0 = \frac{\mathbf{a}_k^T e^{(-A\Delta)} A e^{(A\theta)}\mathbf{x}_0}{\|\mathbf{a}_k^T e^{(-A\Delta)}\|} \geq \delta_1 = \frac{\delta_0}{\|\mathbf{a}_k^T e^{(-A\Delta)}\|}.$$

Hence, we have the following upper bound for l_i':

$$l_i' \leq \frac{\sup_{0<t\leq\Delta,\ \mathbf{x}_0\in F_0} \alpha_i'(\mathbf{x}_0, t)}{\inf_{0<t\leq\Delta,\ \mathbf{x}_0\in F_0} \beta_i'(\mathbf{x}_0, t)} \leq \hat{l}_i' = \frac{M_0\|\mathbf{a}_i^T A\| e^{(\|A\|\Delta)}}{\delta_1}.$$

Thus, we obtain the following upper bounds:

$$\begin{aligned} l_i &\leq \hat{l}_i = \frac{M_0\|\mathbf{a}_i^T A\| e^{(\|A\|\Delta)}}{\delta_0}, \quad 1 \leq i \leq k-1 \\ l_i' &\leq \hat{l}_i' = \frac{M_0\|\mathbf{a}_i^T A\| e^{(\|A\|\Delta)}}{\delta_1}, \quad 1 \leq i \leq k-1, \quad \text{where} \\ \delta_1 &= \frac{\delta_0}{\|\mathbf{a}_k^T e^{(-A\Delta)}\|}.\end{aligned}$$

Upper Bounds for l_k, l_k', l_{k+i} and l_{k+i}', $1 \leq i \leq k-1$. We have $l_{i+k} = \inf\{l : (\mathbf{a}_i^T\mathbf{x} - b_i) - l \leq 0,\ \forall \mathbf{x} \in T_0\}$, and $l_k = \inf\{l : (\mathbf{a}_k^T\mathbf{x} - b_k) - l \leq 0,\ \forall \mathbf{x} \in T_0\}$. Let $l_{2k} = l_k$, so we may consider l_{k+i}, for $1 \leq i \leq k$. We have to choose l_{k+i} such that

$$l_{k+i} = \sup_{\mathbf{x}\in T_0} (\mathbf{a}_i^T\mathbf{x} - b_i) = \sup_{\substack{0<t\leq\Delta \\ \mathbf{x}_0\in F_0}} (\mathbf{a}_i^T e^{(At)}\mathbf{x}_0 - b_i).$$

Now, since $(\mathbf{a}_i^T\mathbf{x}_0 - b_i) \leq 0$, for every $\mathbf{x}_0 \in F_0$, we have

$$\begin{aligned}\sup_{\substack{0<t\leq\Delta \\ \mathbf{x}_0\in F_0}} (\mathbf{a}_i^T e^{(At)}\mathbf{x}_0 - b_i) &\leq \sup_{\substack{0<t\leq\Delta \\ \mathbf{x}_0\in F_0}} (\mathbf{a}_i^T e^{(At)}\mathbf{x}_0 - \mathbf{a}_i^T\mathbf{x}_0) \\ &\leq \sup_{\substack{0<t\leq\Delta \\ \mathbf{x}_0\in F_0}} t \times \frac{(\mathbf{a}_i^T e^{(At)}\mathbf{x}_0 - \mathbf{a}_i^T\mathbf{x}_0)}{t} \\ &\leq \Delta \times \sup_{\substack{0<t\leq\Delta \\ \mathbf{x}_0\in F_0}} \left|\frac{(\mathbf{a}_i^T e^{(At)}\mathbf{x}_0 - \mathbf{a}_i^T\mathbf{x}_0)}{t}\right| \\ &\leq \Delta \times M_0\|\mathbf{a}_i^T A\| e^{(\|A\|\Delta)}.\end{aligned}$$

Similarly, for $1 \le i \le k-1$, we have to choose l'_{k+i} as follows

$$l'_{k+i} = \sup_{\mathbf{x}\in T_0} (\mathbf{b}_i^T \mathbf{x} \quad b'_i) - \sup_{\substack{0\le t<\Delta \\ \mathbf{x}_0\in F_0}} (\mathbf{b}_i^T e^{(At)}\mathbf{x}_0 - b'_i).$$

A calculation similar to the above shows

$$\sup_{\substack{0\le t<\Delta \\ \mathbf{x}_0\in F_0}} (\mathbf{b}_i^T e^{(At)}\mathbf{x}_0 - b'_i) \ \le\ \Delta \times M_0\|\mathbf{b}_i^T A\| e^{(\|A\|\Delta)}.$$

Finally, for l'_k, we have

$$l'_k = \sup_{\mathbf{x}\in T_0} [-(\mathbf{b}_k^T \mathbf{x} - b'_k)] = \sup_{\substack{0\le t<\Delta \\ \mathbf{x}_0\in F_0}} (\mathbf{b}_k^T e^{(A\Delta)}\mathbf{x}_0 - \mathbf{b}_k^T e^{(At)}\mathbf{x}_0)$$

Another sequence of similar calculations shows

$$\sup_{\substack{0\le t<\Delta \\ \mathbf{x}_0\in F_0}} (\mathbf{b}_k^T e^{(A\Delta)}\mathbf{x}_0 - \mathbf{b}_k^T e^{(At)}\mathbf{x}_0) \ \le\ \Delta \times M_0\|\mathbf{b}_k^T A\| e^{(\|A\|\Delta)}.$$

So, to collect all the estimates, we have

$$\begin{aligned} l_k &\le \hat{l}_k = M_0\Delta\|\mathbf{a}_k^T A\| e^{(\|A\|\Delta)} \\ l'_k &\le \hat{l}'_k = M_0\Delta\|\mathbf{b}_k^T A\| e^{(\|A\|\Delta)} \\ l_{k+i} &\le \hat{l}_{k+i} = M_0\Delta\|\mathbf{a}_i^T A\| e^{(\|A\|\Delta)}, \quad 1\le i\le k-1 \\ l'_{k+i} &\le \hat{l}'_{k+i} = M_0\Delta\|\mathbf{b}_i^T A\| e^{(\|A\|\Delta)}, \quad 1\le i\le k-1 \end{aligned}$$

5 Illustration

5.1 Example 1

We first illustrate the schematic algorithm presented in Sec. 3 with the help of an example taken from [8]. Let

$$\left.\begin{aligned} \dot{x} &= a \\ \dot{y} &= b \end{aligned}\right\} \quad a,\ b>0, \quad (x(0),y(0)) \in X_0 = [0,1]\times[0,1].$$

So, for $t \ge 0$, $x(t) = x(0) + at$ and $y(t) = y(0) + bt$. It is easy to check that $S_0^+ = \{1\}\times[0,1]\bigcup[0,1]\times\{1\}$. Therefore

$$X^+(\tau) = X_0 \bigcup_{0\le t\le\tau} \{(1+at, c+bt) \,:\, 0\le c\le 1\} \bigcup_{0\le t\le\tau} \{(c+at, 1+bt) \,:\, 0\le c\le 1\}.$$

This is illustrated in Fig. 1.

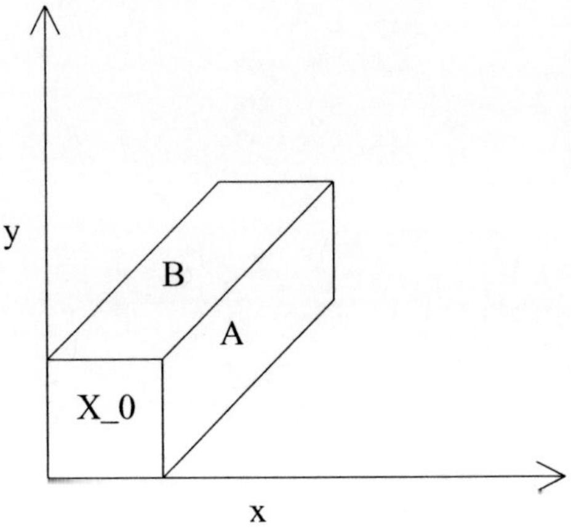

Figure 1: Illustration of the Generalized Face Lifting Method: $X^+(\tau) = X_0 \bigcup A \bigcup B$.

5.2 Example 2

In this example, we illustrate the over-approximation algorithm. Let $\mathbf{x}(t) = [x_1(t), x_2(t)]^T \in \mathbb{R}^2$ satisfy

$$\left.\begin{array}{rcl} \dot{x}_1 & = & -x_2 \\ \dot{x}_2 & = & x_1 \end{array}\right\} \quad (x_1(0), x_2(0)) \in F_0 = [1, \sqrt{2}] \times \{0\}.$$

The solution is given explicitly by

$$\begin{bmatrix} x_1(t) \\ x_2(t) \end{bmatrix} = \begin{bmatrix} \cos t & -\sin t \\ \sin t & \cos t \end{bmatrix} \begin{bmatrix} x_1(0) \\ x_2(0) \end{bmatrix}$$

With $\Delta = \pi/6$, for the time interval $[0, \pi/6]$, the solution set in a parametric form is $T_0 = \{(a\cos t, a\sin t) : a \in [1, \sqrt{2}],\ 0 \le t \le \pi/6\}$. For this example, in the notation of Sec. 4, we have

$$\mathbf{a}_1 = \begin{bmatrix} 1 \\ 0 \end{bmatrix}, \quad \mathbf{a}_2 = \begin{bmatrix} -1 \\ 0 \end{bmatrix}, \quad \mathbf{a}_3 = \begin{bmatrix} 0 \\ 1 \end{bmatrix}, \quad b_1 = \sqrt{2}, \quad b_2 = -1, \quad \text{and } b_3 = 0,$$

and

$$\mathbf{b}_1 = \begin{bmatrix} \frac{\sqrt{3}}{2} \\ 0.5 \end{bmatrix}, \quad \mathbf{b}_2 = \begin{bmatrix} -\frac{\sqrt{3}}{2} \\ -0.5 \end{bmatrix}, \quad \mathbf{b}_3 = \begin{bmatrix} -0.5 \\ \frac{\sqrt{3}}{2} \end{bmatrix}, \quad b_1' = \sqrt{2}, \ b_2' = -1, \quad \text{and } b_3' = 0.$$

The set T_0 and the result of the algorithm with l_i and l_i' exactly found as in the schematic of Sec. 4 are shown in Fig. 2, where the horizontal axis corresponds to x_1 and the vertical axis corresponds to x_2.

Now, recalling the notation of Sec. 4, we may take $\delta = 1$, $\delta_0 = \frac{\sqrt{3}}{2}$. It is easy to check that $M_0 = \sqrt{2}$ and $\|\mathbf{a}_i^T A\| = \|\mathbf{b}_i^T A\| = 1$, for $1 \le i \le 3$. Hence

$$l_i \le \hat{l} = \frac{\sqrt{2} \times 1 \times e^{\pi/6}}{\sqrt{3}/2} = \frac{2\sqrt{2} \times e^{\pi/6}}{\sqrt{3}} \approx 2.7566424$$

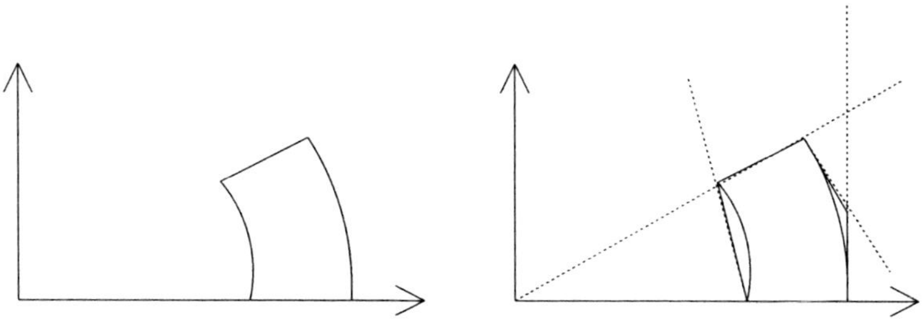

Figure 2: Illustration of over-approximation algorithm of Sec. 4 with Example 2. Left: The set T_0. Right: Result obtained by the schematic algorithm of Sec. 4, with exact values for l_i and l'_i. It may be observed that only 5 of the $4k = 4 \times 3 = 12$ hyperplanes that the the algorithm computes are required for this example, provided that l_i and l'_i can be found exactly.

and the same upper bound holds for l'_i, since $\delta_1 = \delta_0$ in this example. For l_k and l'_k we have the following bounds:

$$l_k = l'_k \leq \hat{l}_k = \sqrt{2} \times \frac{\pi}{6} \times e^{\pi/6} \approx 1.249999$$

In this example, the same upper bound, given by $\hat{l}_k$, holds for l_{k+i} and l'_{k+i}. Combining all this, the polyhedron is the intersection of the half-spaces given by $\eta_i(\mathbf{x}) \leq 0$ and $\eta'_i(\mathbf{x}) \leq 0$, $1 \leq i \leq 6$, where

$$\begin{aligned}
\eta_1(\mathbf{x}) &= x_1 - 2.7566424\, x_2 - \sqrt{2}, & \eta'_1(\mathbf{x}) &= -0.5122958\, x_1 + 2.8873223\, x_2 - \sqrt{2},\\
\eta_2(\mathbf{x}) &= -x_1 - 2.7566424\, x_2 + 1.0, & \eta'_2(\mathbf{x}) &= -2.2443466\, x_1 + 1.8873223\, x_2 + 1.0,\\
\eta_3(\mathbf{x}) &= -x_2, & \eta'_3(\mathbf{x}) &= -x_1 + \sqrt{3}x_2,\\
\eta_4(\mathbf{x}) &= x_2 - 1.249999, & \eta'_4(\mathbf{x}) &= 0.5\, x_1 - \frac{\sqrt{3}}{2} x_2 - 1.249999.\\
\eta_5(\mathbf{x}) &= x_1 - \sqrt{2} - 1.249999, & \eta'_5(\mathbf{x}) &= \frac{\sqrt{3}}{2} x_1 + 0.5\, x_2 - \sqrt{2} - 1.249999,\\
\eta_6(\mathbf{x}) &= -x_1 + 0.249999, & \eta'_6(\mathbf{x}) &= -\frac{\sqrt{3}}{2} x_1 - 0.5\, x_2 + 0.249999.
\end{aligned}$$

In this example, $\eta'_4(\mathbf{x}) \leq 0$, $\eta_6(\mathbf{x}) \leq 0$ and $\eta'_6(\mathbf{x}) \leq 0$, are redundant.

Fig. 3 illustrates the result of the algorithm with the first 8 half-spaces defined by $\eta_i(\mathbf{x}) \leq 0$ and $\eta'_i(\mathbf{x}) \leq 0$, $1 \leq i \leq 4$, where the dashed lines correspond to the lines $\eta_i(\mathbf{x}) = 0$ and $\eta'_i(\mathbf{x}) = 0$, and the polyhedron included in their intersection is shown in thick lines. The point of intersection of $\eta_1(\mathbf{x}) = 0$ and $\eta_4(\mathbf{x}) = 0$ is $(4.8600138, 1.249999)$, of $\eta_4(\mathbf{x}) = 0$ and $\eta'_1(\mathbf{x}) = 0$ is $(4.2845099, 1.249999)$, and of $\eta_2(\mathbf{x}) = 0$ and $\eta'_2(\mathbf{x}) = 0$ is $(0.575162, 0.154114)$. So the vertices in the counter-clockwise order are given by $(\sqrt{2}, 0)$, $(4.8600138, 1.249999)$, $(4.2845099, 1.249999)$, $(\sqrt{3}/\sqrt{2}, 1/\sqrt{2})$, $(\sqrt{3}/2, 0.5)$, $(0.575162, 0.154114)$ and $(1, 0)$.

Fig. 4 shows the result when the remaining two half-spaces defined by $\eta_5(\mathbf{x}) \leq 0$ and $\eta'_5(\mathbf{x}) \leq 0$ are also used. Finally, Fig. 5 shows the intersection of the polyhedron obtained by the method reported in this paper with that which may possibly be obtained by the method of [12], the latter being shown in dotted lines. The polyhedron corresponding to the method of [12] is obtained as follows: the convex hull of the sets $[1, \sqrt{2}] \times \{0\}$ and $\{(a \cos \frac{\pi}{6}, a \sin \frac{\pi}{6}) : a \in [1, \sqrt{2}]\}$ is the polygon with vertices in the counter-clockwise order $(\sqrt{2}, 0)$, $(\sqrt{3}/\sqrt{2}, 1/\sqrt{2})$, $(\sqrt{3}/2, 1/2)$ and $(1, 0)$. Therefore the polygon is the interesction of the half-spaces $\zeta_i(\mathbf{x}) \leq 0$ and $\zeta_i'(\mathbf{x}) \leq 0$, $i = 1, 2$, where

$$\zeta_1(\mathbf{x}) = -x_2, \ \zeta_1'(\mathbf{x}) = -x_1 + \sqrt{3}x_2, \quad \text{and}$$

$$\zeta_2(\mathbf{x}) = \frac{1}{\sqrt{2}}(x_1 - \sqrt{2}) - \left(\frac{\sqrt{3}}{\sqrt{2}} - \sqrt{2}\right) x_2, \ \zeta_2'(\mathbf{x}) = -\frac{1}{2}(x_1 - 1) + \left(\frac{\sqrt{3}}{2} - 1\right) x_2.$$

Now if $\hat{\epsilon}$ is an upper bound for the bloating parameter ϵ, then the half-spaces of the over-approximating polyhedron corresponding to the method of [12] are given by $\hat{\zeta}_i(\mathbf{x}) \leq 0$ and $\hat{\zeta}_i'(\mathbf{x}) \leq 0$, $i = 1, 2$, where

$$\begin{aligned}
\hat{\zeta}_1(\mathbf{x}) &= -x_2 + \hat{\epsilon}, \\
\hat{\zeta}_1'(\mathbf{x}) &= -x_1 + \sqrt{3}x_2 + \hat{\epsilon}, \\
\hat{\zeta}_2(\mathbf{x}) &= 0.70710678x_1 + 0.18946869x_2 - 1 + \hat{\epsilon}, \quad \text{and} \\
\hat{\zeta}_2'(\mathbf{x}) &= -0.70710678x_1 - 0.1339746x_2 + 0.70710678 + \hat{\epsilon}
\end{aligned}$$

The upper bound for the bloating parameter ϵ as given in [12] works out to be

$$\begin{aligned}
\epsilon &\leq M_0 \left(e^{(\|A\|\Delta)} - 1 - \|A\|\Delta - \frac{3}{8}\|A\|^2\Delta^2\right) \\
&= \sqrt{2} \times \left(e^{(\pi/6)} - 1 - \frac{\pi}{6} - \frac{3\pi^2}{8 \times 36}\right) \\
&= \sqrt{2} \times 0.06168464 \approx 0.087235255 < 0.09.
\end{aligned}$$

Fig. 5 shows the results when an upper bound for the bloating parameter is chosen to be $\hat{\epsilon} \approx 0.2$, where the dotted lines correspond to the line $\hat{\zeta}_1(\mathbf{x}) = 0$, $\hat{\zeta}_1'(\mathbf{x}) = 0$, $\hat{\zeta}_2(\mathbf{x}) = 0$ and $\hat{\zeta}_2'(\mathbf{x}) = 0$. As may be expected, the polyhedron of intersection of the two polyhedra – one polyhedron bounded by the dashed lines corresponding to the method described here and another bounded by the dotted lines corresponding to the method of [12] – gives better results of over-approximation.

6 Discussion and Conclusion

An important issue of hybrid systems appears to be computability of the reach sets of the continuous variables. From a computational point, both the problems of computation and efficient representation of the reach sets of the continuous variables are difficult, in general, owing to the limitatitons of quantifier elimination method. In this context, approximation of the reach sets by more convenient sets, such as polyhedra and subalgebraic sets, is discussed in the literature. In this paper, along with a method for finding the reach sets, an algorithm for over-approximation of the reach sets by polyhedra for the case when the dynamics of the continuous variables are specified by linear differential equations with polygonal initial sets is presented. A practical version of the over-approximation algorithm is also discussed

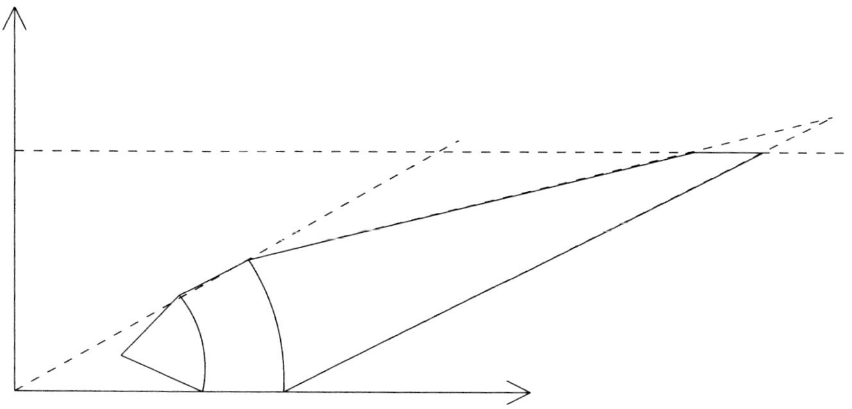

Figure 3: Illustration of polyhedral over-approximation for the soultion set T_0 of Example 2: without additional hyperplanes.

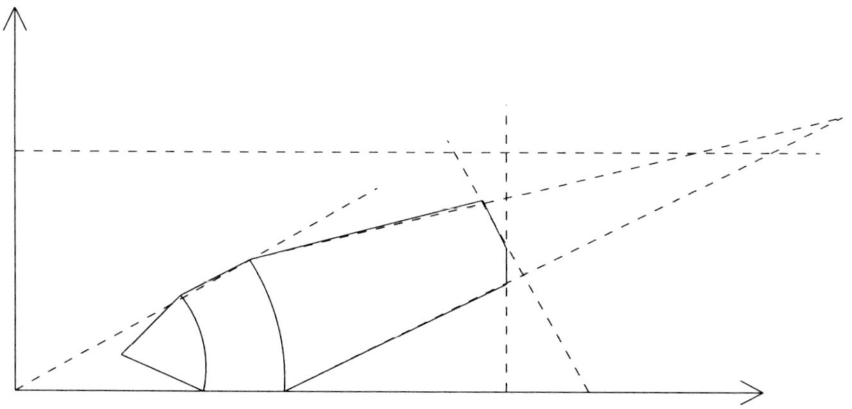

Figure 4: Illustration of polyhedral over-approximation for the reach set T_0 of Example 2: with additional hyperplanes.

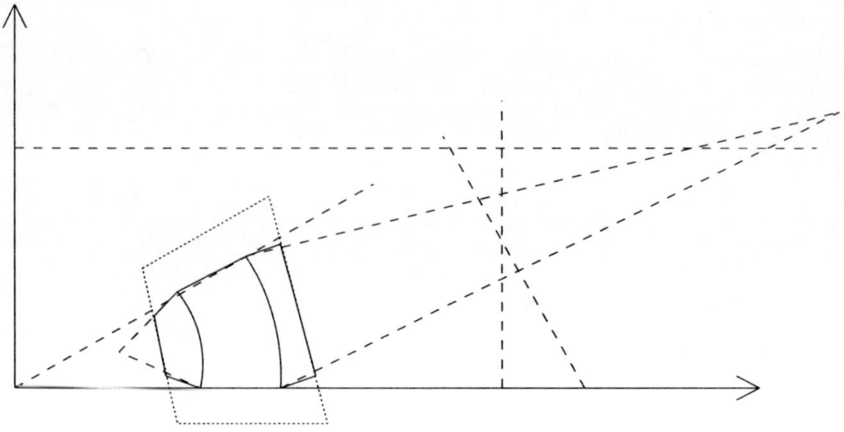

Figure 5: Illustration of polyhedral over-approximation for the solution set T_0 of Example 2: intersection of the polyhedron that may be obtained by the method of [12] with that obtained by the method reported here.

in this paper. However, it seems that better results of over-approximation may be obtained by taking the intersection of the polyhedron obtained by the method reported here with that obtained by the method given in [12]. It is hoped that the over-approximation method presented here may be extended to systems with more general dynamics and initial sets.

References

[1] R. Alur, C. Courcoubetis, N. Halbwachs, T. A. Henzinger, P.-H. Ho, X. Nicollin, A. Olivero, J. Sifakis and S. Yovine, "The algorithmic analysis of hybrid systems", *Theoretical Computer Science*, Vol 138, pp. 3-35, 1995.

[2] Y. Kesten, A. Pnueli, J. Sifakis, and S. Yovine, "Decidable Integration Graphs", *Information and Computation*, Vol. 150, No. 2, p. 209 - 243, 1999.

[3] G. Lafferriere, G. J. Pappas and S. Yovine, "A New Class of Decidable Hybrid Systems", *Lecture Notes in Computer Science*, Vol. 1569, pp. 137-151, 1999.

[4] G. Lafferriere, G. J. Pappas and S. Yovine, "Reachability Computation of Linear Hybrid Systems" *Proc. 14th IFAC World Congress*, Vol. E, pp. 7-12, Beijing, PRC, July 1999.

[5] T. A. Henzinger, P.-H. Ho, and H. Wong-Toi, "Algorithmic analysis of nonlinear hybrid systems", *IEEE Trans. Automatic Control*, Vol. 43, pp. 540-554, 1998.

[6] O. George J. Pappas, S. Sastry, "Semidecidable Controller Synthesis for Classes of Linear Hybrid Systems", *Proc. 39th IEEE Conf. on Decision and Control*, Sydney, Australia, Dec. 2000

[7] E. Asarin, O. Bournez, T. Dang, O. Maler, A. Pnueli, "Effective Synthesis of Switching Controllers for Linear Systems", *Proceedings of the IEEE*, Vol. 88, No. 7, pp. 1011-1025, 2000.

[8] T. Dang and O. Maler, "Reachability analysis via face lifting", T. A. Henzinger and S. Sastry (Eds.) *Hybrid Systems: Computation and Control*, LNCS 1386, pp. 96-109, Springer Verlag, New York, 1998.

[9] C. Tomlin, J. Lygeros, and S. Sastry, "Synthesizing controllers for nonlinear hybrid systems", in *Hybrid Systems: Computation and Control*, LNCS 1386, pp. 360–373, Springer Verlag, New York, 1998.

[10] P. Varaiya, "Reach set computation using optimal control", *Proc. KIT Workshop*, Verimag, Grenoble, 1998.

[11] A. B. Kurzhanski and P. Varaiya, "Ellipsoidal techniques for reachability analysis: internal approximation", *Systems & Control Letters*, Vol. 41, No. 3, Oct. 2000.

[12] E. Asarin, O. Bournez, T. Dang, and O. Maler, "Approximate reachability analysis of piece-wise linear dynamical systems", in *Hybrid Systems: Computation and Control*, March 2000, Pittsburgh, USA.

[13] O. Maler, A. Pnueli and J. Safakis, "On the Synthesis of Discrete Controllers for Timed Systems (An Extended Abstract)", *Proc. STACS '95*, LNCS 900, pp. 229-242, Springer, 1995.

[14] T. A. Henzinger, "Hybrid automata with finite bisimulations", *Proc. ICALP '95*, LNCS 944, pp. 324-33 Springer-Verlag, 1995.

[15] G. J. Pappas, "Hybrid Systems: Computation and Abstraction", Ph.D. Thesis, Electrical Engineering and Computer Sciences, *University of California at Berkeley.*

[16] J. H. Hubbard and B. H. West, *"Differential equations: a dynamical systems approach"*, Springer-Verlag, New York, 1995.

[17] M. W. Hirsch and S. Smale, *"Differential Equations, Dynamical Systems and Linear Algebra"*, Academic Press, New York, 1974.

[18] R. T. Rockafellar, "Convex Analysis", *Princeton University Press*, Princeton, New Jersey, 1970.

[19] W. Hodges, "A Shorter Model Theory", *Cambridge University Press*, 1997.

[20] D. Marker, "Model Theory and Exponentiation", *Notices of AMS*, Vol. 43, No. 7, pp. 753-759, 1996.

[21] D. van Dalen, "Logic and Structure", *Springer-Verlag*, Third Edition, 1994.

[22] A. Tarski, "A Decision Method for Elementary Algebra and Geometry", *University of California Press*, Second Edition, 1951.

[23] L. van Den Dries, "Remarks on Tarski's problem concerning $(\mathbb{R}, +, \cdot, exp)$", in G. Lolli, G. Longo and A. Marcja, editors, *Logic Colloquium '82*, pp. 97-121, Elsevier Science Publishers B.V., 1984.

Appendix A. Decidable Classes of Subsets of $Q \times \mathbb{R}^n$

We introduce here model theoretic concepts for formalizing the notion of decidable class $\mathcal{C}$ of subsets of $Q \times \mathbb{R}^n$ that we were interested in Sec. 2. Since Q is a finite set, for a decidable class $\mathcal{C}$ of subsets of $Q \times \mathbb{R}^n$, we may take, for each $q \in Q$, a decidable class of subsets of $\mathbb{R}^n$, $\mathcal{S}_q$, $q \in Q$, and choose $\mathcal{C}$ to be the product class $\bigcup_{q \in Q}\{\{q\} \times S_q : S_q \in \mathcal{S}_q\}$. Therefore, we restrict our attention to the discussion of classes of subsets of $\mathbb{R}^n$. Most parts of this section are taken from [3] (see also [15], which in turn cites the references [19, 20, 21]).

DEFINITION **11** *A* language *is a tuple of three sets, $\mathcal{L} = (L_r, L_f, L_c)$, where*

1. *L_r is a set of relations,*
2. *L_f is a set of functions, and*
3. *L_c are a set of constants.*

DEFINITION **12** *A* model *of a language $\mathcal{L} = (L_r, L_f, L_c)$ consists of a nonempty set $\mathcal{S}$, together with an interpretation of the relations, functions and constants.*

We denote a model by $(\mathcal{S}, L_r, L_f, L_c)$, where the interpretation is not made explicit. In the following, let $\mathcal{V} = \{x, y, z, x_0, x_2, \ldots\}$ denote a countable set of *variables*.

DEFINITION **13** *A* term *of a language, $\mathcal{L} = (L_r, L_f, L_c)$, is inductively defined as follows:*

1. *each variable $\theta \in \mathcal{V}$ is a term,*
2. *each constant $c \in L_c$ is a term, and*
3. *for an m-ary function $g \in L_f$, where $m \geq 1$, and m terms, $\theta_1, \theta_2, \ldots, \theta_m$, $g(\theta_1, \theta_2, \ldots, \theta_m)$ is a term.*

DEFINITION **14** *An* atomic formula *of a language $\mathcal{L}$ is either*

1. *$\theta_1 = \theta_2$, where θ_1 are θ_2 two terms of $\mathcal{L}$, or*
2. *$\rho(\theta_1, \ldots, \theta_n)$, where $n \geq 1$ and $\rho \in L_r$ is an n-ary relation.*

DEFINITION **15** *A* first order formula, *or simply a* formula, *of a language $\mathcal{L}$ is recursively defined as one of the following:*

1. *an atomic formula, or*
2. *$\neg\phi$, where ϕ is formula and $\neg$ is logical negation, or*
3. *$\phi_1 \wedge \phi_2$, where ϕ_1 and ϕ_2 are formulas and $\wedge$ is logical and, or*
4. *$\exists x : \phi$ or $\forall x : \phi$, where ϕ is a formula, x is a variable, and $\exists$ (there exists) and $\forall$ (for all) are quantifiers; in this case, each occurrence of the variable x in the formula ϕ is called a* bound *occurrence.*

DEFINITION **16** *The occurrence of a variable in a formula is* free, *if it is not* bound. *A* sentence *in a language $\mathcal{L}$ is a formula with no free variable. A* theory *of $\mathcal{L}$ is a subset of sentences.*

For a model $\mathcal{S}$ of the language $\mathcal{L}$, we shall be particularly interested in the theory defined by the set of all sentences that are true in $\mathcal{S}$. To emphasize this, we refer to this theory as *the theory of* $(\mathcal{S}, L_r, L_f, L_c)$.

DEFINITION **17** *Let* $\mathcal{L}$ *be a language and* $\mathcal{S}$ *be a model of* $\mathcal{L}$. *A set* $X \subset \mathcal{S}^n$ *is said to be* definable *in the language* $\mathcal{L}$, *if there is an n-ary formula* $\phi(x_1, \ldots, x_n)$ *such that* X *can be written as* $X = \{(x_1, \ldots, x_n) \in \mathcal{S}^n : \phi(x_1, \ldots, x_n)\}$.

DEFINITION **18** *Let* $\mathcal{L}$ *be a language,* $\mathcal{S}$ *be a model of* $\mathcal{L}$, *and* $\mathcal{C}$ *be the class of definable sets. Then* $\mathcal{C}$ *is said to be* decidable, *if the theory of* $(\mathcal{S}, L_r, L_f, L_c)$ *is decidable, i.e., there is a decision procedure that, given an* $\mathcal{L}$*-sentence* ϕ, *decides whether* ϕ *belongs to the theory of* $(\mathcal{S}, L_r, L_f, L_c)$ *or not.*

Examples

1. The theory $(\mathbb{R}, \{<\}, \{+, -\}, \{0, 1\})$ is the theory of linear constraints with integer coefficients, denoted by $Lin(\mathbb{R})$. The sets defined by these formulas are called *polyhedral sets*.

2. The theory $(\mathbb{R}, \{<\}, \{+, -, \cdot\}, \{0, 1\})$ is the theory of polynomial constraints with integer coefficients, denoted by $OF(\mathbb{R})$. The sets defined by these formulas are called *subalgebraic sets*.

The result stated below is due to A. Tarski [22]:

THEOREM **1** *The first order theory* $OF(\mathbb{R})$ *is decidable.*

DEFINITION **19** *Let* $\mathcal{L}$ *be a language and let* $\mathcal{S}$ *be a model of* $\mathcal{L}$. *We say the theory of* $(\mathcal{S}, L_r, L_f, L_c)$ *admits* quantifier elimination *if every first order formula of* $(\mathcal{S}, L_r, L_f, L_c)$ *is equivalent to a formula of* $(\mathcal{S}, L_r, L_f, L_c)$ *without quantifiers.*

Examples: Decidability and Quantifier Elimination

1. The theory $OF(\mathbb{R})$ consisting of $(\mathbb{R}, \{<\}, \{+, -, \cdot\}, \{0, 1\})$ admits quantifier elimination and is also decidable.

2. Let $OF_{exp}(\mathbb{R})$ be the theory consisting of $(\mathbb{R}, \{<\}, \{+, -, \cdot, exp\}, \{0, 1\})$, where exp, representing the exponential function, is a new function symbol. This theory does not admit quantifier elimination, and it is not known whether this theory is decidable. (See [15]).

Appendix B. $Reach_q(X_0, [0, \tau]) = X(\tau) = X^+(\tau)$

We assume that X_0 is closed and its boundary, denoted by S_0, consists of a finite union of smooth surfaces. Let

$$X(\tau) = X_0 \bigcup_{0 \le t \le \tau} \{\phi_q(\mathbf{x}_0, t) \ : \ \mathbf{x}_0 \in S_0\}.$$

Also let

$$S_0^+ = \{\mathbf{x} \in S_0 : \exists \epsilon = \epsilon(\mathbf{x}) > 0 \text{ such that } \phi(\mathbf{x}, t) \in X_0^c, \ \forall t \in (0, \epsilon)\}, \tag{16}$$

and $X^+(\tau) = X_0 \bigcup_{0 \le t \le \tau} \{\phi_q(\mathbf{x}_0, t) \ : \ \mathbf{x}_0 \in S_0^+\}$.

PROPOSITION **1** $X^+(\tau) = X(\tau) = Reach(X_0, [0, \tau])$.

Proof. Note that $X^+(\tau) \subset X(\tau) \subset Reach(X_0, [0, \tau])$. So we have to show that $Reach(X_0, [0, \tau]) \subset X^+(\tau)$. Let $\mathbf{z} \in Reach(X_0, t)$, $t > 0$. If $\mathbf{z} \in X_0$, then $\mathbf{z} \in X^+(\tau)$. Now suppose $\mathbf{z} \notin X_0$. So there is a $\mathbf{z}_0 \in X_0$ such that $\mathbf{z} = \phi(\mathbf{z}_0, s)$, for some s with $0 < s \leq \tau$. If $\mathbf{z}_0 \in S_0^+$, then $\mathbf{z} \in X^+(\tau)$. Otherwise let $\tau' = \sup\{t : t \leq s \text{ and } \phi(\mathbf{z}_0, t) \in X_0\}$, so $0 < \tau' < s \leq \tau$. Now $\mathbf{z}' = \phi(\mathbf{z}_0, \tau') \in S_0^+$. Therefore, $\mathbf{z} = \phi(\mathbf{z}', s - \tau') \in X^+(\tau)$.

Now suppose that X_0 is specified as $X_0 = \{\mathbf{x} \in \mathbb{R}^n : \ell(\mathbf{x}) \leq 0\}$, where $\ell : \mathbb{R}^n \to \mathbb{R}$ is continuously differentiable. Further, we assume that if $\mathbf{x} \in \overset{\circ}{X}_0$ then $\ell(\mathbf{x}) < 0$ (where $\overset{\circ}{X}_0$ denotes the interior of X_0, i.e., the largest open set contained in X_0) So, obviously, if $\mathbf{x} \in S_0$ then $\ell(\mathbf{x}) = 0$, and if $\mathbf{x} \in X_0^c$ then $\ell(\mathbf{x}) > 0$. Let $S_1^+ \subset S_0$ be defined as

$$S_1^+ = \{\mathbf{x} \in S_0 : \nabla\ell(\mathbf{x}) \cdot f(q, \mathbf{x}) \geq 0\}.$$

We now show that $S_0^+ \subset S_1^+$. To this end, we show that $S_0 \backslash S_1^+ \subset S_0 \backslash S_0^+$. Let $\mathbf{x} \in S_0 \backslash S_1^+$, so $\nabla\ell(\mathbf{x}) \cdot f(q, \mathbf{x}) < 0$. Now, since $\ell(\phi_q(\mathbf{x}, 0)) = \ell(\mathbf{x}) = 0$, and since at $t = 0$, $\frac{d\ell(\phi_q(\mathbf{x},t))}{dt} = \nabla\ell(\mathbf{x}) \cdot f(q, \mathbf{x}) < 0$, we have, for a sufficiently small $\epsilon > 0$, $\ell(\phi_q(\mathbf{x}, t)) < 0$, whenever $0 < t < \epsilon$, which happens only if $\phi_q(\mathbf{x}, t) \in \overset{\circ}{X}_0$, $\forall t \in (0, \epsilon)$, implying that $\mathbf{x} \notin S_0^+$; hence $\mathbf{x} \in S_0 \backslash S_0^+$. Thus $S_0 \backslash S_1^+ \subset S_0 \backslash S_0^+$, as required.

Appendix C. $Reach_q'(X_0, X_q, [0, \infty))$

Let $X_q \subset \mathbb{R}^n$ with compact closure, and let $Y_q = \overline{X_q}$. Let $\mathbf{f} : W \to \mathbb{R}^n$ be a continuous function defined on an open set W containing Y_q, satisfying a Lipschitz condition on W. Let X_0 be a closed subset of Y_q. We assume that for each $\mathbf{x} \in X_0$, a function $\gamma_\mathbf{x} : \mathbb{R}^+ \to \mathbb{R}^n$ exists and satisfies the differential equation

$$\frac{d\gamma_\mathbf{x}(t)}{dt} = \mathbf{f}(\gamma_\mathbf{x}), \quad t \geq 0, \tag{17}$$

with the initial condition $\gamma_\mathbf{x}(0) = \mathbf{x}$. Hence the flow $\phi(\mathbf{x}, t)$ associated with equation (17) is defined for all $t \geq 0$ and $\mathbf{x} \in X_0$. Further, assume that the ω-limit set of the flow $\phi(\mathbf{x}, t)$, $t \geq 0$, does not intersect Y_q for any point $\mathbf{x} \in X_0$. More precisely, we assume, for $\mathbf{x} \in X_0$,

$$L_\omega(\mathbf{x}) \bigcap Y_q = \emptyset, \tag{18}$$

where

$$L_\omega(\mathbf{x}) = \bigcap_{t \geq 0} \overline{\phi(\mathbf{x}, [t, \infty))}.$$

(See [16, 17].) In what follows, we show that if (18) holds for every $\mathbf{x} \in X_0$, then $\exists \tau_{\max} > 0$ (depending on X_0), such that for every $\mathbf{x} \in X_0$, there is a $\tau = \tau(\mathbf{x})$ with $0 < \tau(\mathbf{x}) \leq \tau_{max}$ and $\phi(\mathbf{x}, t(\mathbf{x})) \notin Y_q$. For this, let $0 < \tau_1 < \tau_2 < \ldots$ be an increasing sequence such that $\tau_k \to \infty$, as $k \to \infty$ (as in Sec. 3), and define the sets $A(\tau_k, \mathbf{x}) = \overline{\phi(\mathbf{x}, [\tau_k, \infty))}$. We first observe that $L_\omega(\mathbf{x}) = \bigcap_k A(\tau_k, \mathbf{x})$.

PROPOSITION **2** *Let* $\mathbf{x} \in X_0$. *If (18) holds, then* $\exists \tau = \tau(\mathbf{x}) > 0$ *such that* $\phi(\mathbf{x}, t) \notin Y_q$, $\forall t \geq \tau$.

Proof. We have $L_\omega(\mathbf{x})\bigcap Y_q = [\bigcap_k A(\tau_k,\mathbf{x})]\bigcap Y_q = \bigcap_k [A(\tau_k,\mathbf{x})\bigcap Y_q]$. Now let $E(\tau_k,\mathbf{x}) = A(\tau_k,\mathbf{x})\bigcap Y_q$. So, for a fixed $\mathbf{x} \in X_0$, the sets $E(\tau_k,\mathbf{x})$, $k = 1,2,3,\ldots$, is a decreasing sequence of closed subsets of Y_q. Since Y_q is compact, $\bigcap_k E(\tau_k,\mathbf{x}) = \emptyset$ implies $E(\tau_k,\mathbf{x}) = \emptyset$, for all but finitely many k. Therefore, for some $K \geq 1$, $\forall k \geq K$, $E(\tau_k,\mathbf{x}) = \emptyset$. Hence, $\phi(\mathbf{x},[t,\infty))\bigcap Y_q = \emptyset$, $\forall t \geq \tau_K$. Therefore, with $\tau = \tau_K$, $\phi(\mathbf{x},t) \notin Y_q$, $\forall t \geq \tau$.

We also need the following proposition:

PROPOSITION **3** *Let $\mathbf{x} \in X_0$ be a point for which there is a $\tau > 0$, such that $\phi(\mathbf{x},\tau) \notin Y_q$. Then there is a $\delta = \delta_{\mathbf{x}} > 0$, such that if $|\mathbf{x}-\mathbf{y}| < \delta_{\mathbf{x}}$ and $\mathbf{y} \in X_0$, then $\phi(\mathbf{y},\tau) \notin Y_q$.*

Proof. Let $|\mathbf{f}(\mathbf{x}) - \mathbf{f}(\mathbf{y})| \leq C|\mathbf{x}-\mathbf{y}|$. Then $|\phi(\mathbf{x},\tau) - \phi(\mathbf{y},\tau)| \leq |\mathbf{x}-\mathbf{y}|e^{C\tau}$ (see, for example, [17]), so for a fixed τ, $\phi(\cdot,\tau)$ is continuous in the first variable. Let $\mathbf{z} = \phi(\mathbf{x},\tau)$. Now since $W\backslash Y_q$ is open, there is an $\epsilon > 0$ such that $B(\mathbf{z},\epsilon) \subset W\backslash Y_q$. By the continuity of $\phi(\cdot,\tau)$ at $\mathbf{x}$, there is a $\delta > 0$, such that $|\phi(\mathbf{x},\tau) - \phi(\mathbf{y},\tau)| = |\mathbf{z} - \phi(\mathbf{y},\tau)| < \epsilon$, whenever $|\mathbf{y}-\mathbf{x}| < \delta$ and $\mathbf{y} \in X_0$. Therefore, $\phi(\mathbf{y},\tau) \in B(\mathbf{z},\epsilon) \subset W\backslash Y_q$.

From the previous two propositions, we get the following theorem:

THEOREM **2** *Let Y_q be compact, and $\mathbf{f}$ be a continuous function defined on an open set W containing Y_q satisfying a Lipschitz condition. Further assume condition (18) holds for every $\mathbf{x} \in X_0$. Then $\exists\tau_{\max} > 0$ independent of $\mathbf{x}$, such that for each $\mathbf{x} \in X_0$, there is a $\tau(\mathbf{x})$ with $0 < \tau(\mathbf{x}) \leq \tau_{max}$ and $\phi(\mathbf{x},\tau(\mathbf{x})) \notin Y_q$.*

Proof. Let $\mathbf{x} \in X_0$. By Proposition 2, there is a $\tau(\mathbf{x}) > 0$, such that $\phi(\mathbf{x},\tau(\mathbf{x})) \notin Y_q$. By Proposition 3, there is a $\delta_{\mathbf{x}} > 0$, such that for any $\mathbf{y} \in X_0$ with $|\mathbf{y}-\mathbf{x}| < \delta_{\mathbf{x}}$, $\phi(\mathbf{y},\tau(\mathbf{x})) \notin Y_q$. $\{B(\mathbf{x},\delta_{\mathbf{x}}) : \mathbf{x} \in X_0\}$ is an open cover of X_0, containing a finite subcover, say, $\{B(\mathbf{x}_1,\delta_{\mathbf{x}_1}),\ldots,B(\mathbf{x}_m,\delta_{\mathbf{x}_m})\}$. Let $\tau_{\max} = \max\{\tau(\mathbf{x}_1),\ldots,\tau(\mathbf{x}_m)\}$. To check wether this choice of τ_{max} is as in the theorem, let $\mathbf{y} \in X_0$ be an arbitrary point. Now $\mathbf{y} \in B(\mathbf{x}_i,\delta_{\mathbf{x}_i})$, for some i with $1 \leq i \leq m$, and by the choice of $\delta_{\mathbf{x}_i}$, $\phi(\mathbf{y},\tau(\mathbf{x}_i)) \notin Y_q$, concluding the proof.

Appendix D. Boundedness Results

In this section, we show that if the initial set F is bounded then the polyhedron, P, enclosing $F_{[0,\Delta]}$, as obtained by the algorithm described in Sec. 3 is bounded. We assume that F is nonempty. Recall that F is given as the set of points $\mathbf{x}$ in $\mathbb{R}^n$ which satisfy the following constraints:

$$\left.\begin{array}{rcl} \mathbf{a}_i^T\mathbf{x} - b_i & \leq & 0, \quad i = 1,2,\ldots,k-1, \\ \mathbf{a}_k^T\mathbf{x} - b_k & = & 0, \end{array}\right\} \tag{19}$$

and P is included in the set of points $\mathbf{x} \in \mathbb{R}^n$ satisfying

$$\left.\begin{array}{rcl} \mathbf{a}_i^T\mathbf{x} - b_i - l_i(\mathbf{a}_k^T\mathbf{x} - b_k) & \leq & 0, \quad i = 1,2,\ldots,k-1, \\ \mathbf{a}_k^T\mathbf{x} - b_k & \geq & 0, \quad \text{and} \\ \mathbf{a}_k^T\mathbf{x} - b_k - l_k & \leq & 0, \end{array}\right\} \tag{20}$$

where $l_i \in \mathbb{R}$ and $l_k > 0$. Looking at the constraints, one may visualize the set P_1 satisfying (20) as a prism or a truncated pyramid, with its bottom given by (19) and its top given by

$$\left.\begin{array}{rcl} \mathbf{a}_i^T\mathbf{x} - b_i - l_i(\mathbf{a}_k^T\mathbf{x} - b_k) & \leq & 0, \quad i = 1,2,\ldots,k-1, \\ \mathbf{a}_k^T\mathbf{x} - b_k - l_k & = & 0. \end{array}\right\} \tag{21}$$

We assume that F is nonempty, and wish to show that if F is bounded then so is the set P_1, defined as the set of points satisfying (20). We start with the following proposition:

PROPOSITION 4 *Assume that F is nonempty and P_1 is not bounded. Then there is a point $\mathbf{x}_0 \in F$ and a vector $\lambda \in \mathbb{R}^n$, with $|\lambda| = 1$, such that $\mathbf{x}_0 + t\lambda \in P_1$, for all $t \geq 0$.*

Proof. Fix a point $\mathbf{x}_0 \in F$, and suppose P_1 is not bounded. So for each positive integer k, there is a point $\mathbf{x}_k \in P_1$, such that $|\mathbf{x}_k - \mathbf{x}_0| \geq k$. Let $\lambda_k = \frac{(\mathbf{x}_k - \mathbf{x}_0)}{|\mathbf{x}_k - \mathbf{x}_0|}$. Now, since $F \subset P_1$, $\mathbf{x}_0 \in P_1$ and, by convexity, the entire line segment $\mathbf{x}_0 + t\lambda_k \in P_1$, for $0 \leq t \leq k$. In particular, the points on these line segments satisfy (20). Now, since for each k, $|\lambda_k| = 1$, and the closed unit ball in $\mathbb{R}^n$ is compact, there is a convergent subsequence of λ_k's – say, λ_{k_i}, $i = 1, 2, 3, \ldots$ – such that $\lambda_{k_i} \to \lambda \in \mathbb{R}^n$, as $i \to \infty$; since $|\lambda_{k_i}| = 1$, $|\lambda| = 1$. We show that $\mathbf{x}_0 + t\lambda \in P_1$ for $t \in [0, \infty)$. First note that for any positive integer m, and for all $i \geq m$, $\mathbf{x}_0 + t\lambda_{k_i}$ satisfies the constraints (20), for $t \in [0, k_m]$. Therefore, $\mathbf{x}_0 + t\lambda$ satisfies (20), for $t \in [0, k_m]$, and so $\mathbf{x}_0 + t\lambda \in P_1$, for $t \in [0, k_m]$. The proposition is concluded by letting $m \to \infty$.

We now show that such an λ, as in the previous proposition, must be parallel to the hyperplane passing through F, the normal of which is given by $\mathbf{a}_k$.

PROPOSITION 5 *If $\mathbf{x}_0 \in F$ and a unit vector $\lambda \in \mathbb{R}^n$ are such that $\mathbf{x}_0 + t\lambda \in P_1$, for all $t \in [0, \infty)$, then $\mathbf{a}_k^T \lambda = 0$.*

Proof. For a contradiction assume that $h = \mathbf{a}_k^T \lambda > 0$. Now since $\mathbf{x} + t\lambda$ satisfies (20), we must have

$$\mathbf{a}_k^T (\mathbf{x}_0 + t\lambda) - b_k - l_k \leq 0,$$

which holds only if $t \leq \frac{(b_k + l_k - \mathbf{a}_k^T \mathbf{x}_0)}{h}$, contrary to the hypothesis that, for all $t \in [0, \infty)$, $\mathbf{x}_0 + t\lambda \in P_1$. Similarly, if $h = \mathbf{a}_k^T \lambda < 0$, then the constraint

$$\mathbf{a}_k^T (\mathbf{x}_0 + t\lambda) - b_k \geq 0,$$

does not hold for $t > 0$. Therefore we must have $\mathbf{a}_k^T \lambda = 0$.

We now show that if F is bounded, then for any unit vector λ orthogonal to $\mathbf{a}_k$, there is an i with $1 \leq i \leq k - 1$, such that $h_i = \mathbf{a}_i^T \lambda > 0$.

PROPOSITION 6 *If F is nonempty and bounded, then for any unit vector $\lambda \in \mathbb{R}^n$, for which $\mathbf{a}_k^T \lambda = 0$, there is an i, with $1 \leq i \leq k - 1$, such that $\mathbf{a}_i^T \lambda > 0$.*

Proof. Let $\mathbf{x}_0 \in F$, and suppose that there is an $\lambda \in \mathbb{R}^n$, with $|\lambda| = 1$, $\mathbf{a}_k^T \lambda = 0$ and $\mathbf{a}_i^T \lambda \leq 0$, for $1 \leq i \leq k - 1$. Then for any $t > 0$, the vector $\mathbf{x}_0 + t\lambda$ satisfies the constraints (19), and so $\mathbf{x}_0 + t\lambda \in F$, contrary to the assumption that F is bounded.

We now combine all the previous propositions to get the following result:

THEOREM 3 *If F is nonempty and bounded, then P_1 is bounded.*

Proof. If P_1 is not bounded, then by Proposition 4, there is an $\mathbf{x}_0 \in F$ and a unit vector $\lambda \in \mathbb{R}^n$ such that $\mathbf{x}_0 + t\lambda \in P_1$, for any $t \geq 0$. By Proposition 5, $\mathbf{a}_k^T \lambda = 0$. Now, by the previous proposition, since F is bounded, there is an i, with $1 \leq i \leq k-1$, such that $h_i = \mathbf{a}_i^T \lambda > 0$. But then the constraint

$$\mathbf{a}_i^T (\mathbf{x}_0 + t\lambda) - b_i - l_i(\mathbf{a}_k^T (\mathbf{x}_0 + t\lambda) - b_k) \leq 0,$$

cannot hold for any t with

$$t > -\frac{\mathbf{a}_i^T \mathbf{x}_0 - b_i}{h_i},$$

contrary to the assumption that $\mathbf{x}_0 + t\lambda \in P_1$, for any $t \geq 0$. Hence P_1 is bounded.

In: New Developments in Computer Science Research
Editor: Susan Shannon, pp. 127-159
ISBN 1-59454-256-2

Chapter 3

Methods and Techniques for Defining Parameterized Types in Mathematics

Alina Andreica
ICT Department, Babeş-Bolyai University of Cluj-Napoca, Romania
e-mail: alina.andreica@euro.ubbcluj.ro

Abstract

Symbolic computation in algebraic categories enable the automatic modeling of modern algebra theories. On this theoretical background, we introduce constructive and algorithmic definitions for the basic concepts (category, domain, etc.) and for a number of algebraic structures. Adopting a parameterized and object oriented approach, the categories defined for the algebraic structures will be particularized in specific domains. The present paper reveals the utility of the parameterized categorical approach by deriving a multivariate polynomial category (over various coefficient domains), which is used by our Mathematica implementation of Buchberger's algorithms for determining the Gröbner basis. These implementations are designed according to domain and category parameterization principles and underline their advantages: operation protection, inheritance, generality, natural extendibility. In particular, such an extension of Mathematica, a widely used symbolic computation system, with a new type system has a certain practical importance.

1. Symbolic Computations in Algebraic Categories

The theme of symbolic computation in algebraic categories has become very important lately since it enables the automatic modeling of modern algebra theories. Based on the type theory concepts [San93], [San95], [San96], [Dav90], [Dav91], we define the algebraic structures by pursuing systematic, functional and algorithmic principles, which would facilitate their implementation into programming languages. A part of the algebraic structures' hierarchy is implemented as an extension of Mathematica system with a new type system.

Our package introduces new facilities, regarding the definition of abstract algebraic domains, into a SCS (symbolic computation system) that is widely used for performing computations in common mathematical domains. The approach has a good deal of advantages regarding the generality of symbolic computations which can be performed in the categories that are defined and in the domains derived from them.

The benefits of implementing symbolic computations by using parameterized definitions of categories and domains are very important for Mathematica users. The efficiency of the implementation we propose consists in its generality and in the fact that is easily extendable by defining new domains, which can be specified as parameters in the same category definition. A relevant example of this utility, described in sections 5 and 6, consists in deriving a multivariate polynomial category, whose parametrized definition is used in the construction of some specific polynomial domains, over various coefficient rings. These polynomial domains are used by the algorithms that implement Buchberger's method for computing the Gröbner basis and the reduced Gröbner basis for a given set of polynomials.

2. Defining the working frame and concepts

The *type theory in symbolic computation* lies between the mathematical category theory and the type theory from programming languages, extended with the inheritance concept, according to object oriented (OO) principles. The most important concepts within this theory are *domains* and *categories*, which are borrowed from algebra and correspond, in OO programming, to classes, respectively metaclasses. Therefore, the algebraic structures and the relationships between them will be modeled using classes, subclasses, instances and the inheritance concept. The necessity of adopting another approach than the theoretical algebraic one relies first of all in the constructive and algorithmic character of type theory, where new types, characterized by the same properties and methods, are introduced in a functional manner, using existing types [And98]. The types defined in this manner create general contexts of expressing algorithms, which can therefore be applied upon various types of data (similar to generic programming). These general structures are named categories and the more specific types generated by them are named domains.

Unifying the algebraic (see [Pur82] for specific concepts, i. e. category) and object oriented (see [FrePar94] for specific concepts, i. e. data type, instance, inheritance, etc.) points of view, we propose the following definitions for type theory concepts:

Definition 2.1. In symbolic computation, we define a ***category*** as a data type which describes an algebraic category.

Definition 2.2. In symbolic computation, we define a ***domain*** as a data type that instantiates (in OO sense) a category (see definition 1).

Definition 2.3. A ***package*** is a program unit which describes the behavior (specific processing algorithms) of a data type.

Definition 2.4. A ***parameterized*** data type is a data type that depends on one or more data types, given as parameters.

3. Constructive and Algorithmic Definitions for Algebraic Structures

Within this paragraph, we define the algebraic structures in a constructive, algorithmic and functional form (from the type theory point of view) [Dav90], in order to facilitate their implementation by using programming techniques. For each type of algebraic structure we introduce the characteristic operators (composition operator, equality operator, symmetric operator, or other operators that constructively describe certain mathematical properties). The operators are defined in a functional manner and can have additional axioms, such as associativity, commutativity or distributivity. Each type of algebraic structure inherits, from its ascendant, the corresponding operators; therefore, we shall supplementary specify only its specific operators and axioms.

According to these principles, we define the following algebraic types: set, semigroup, abelian semigroup, monoid, abelian monoid, left reduction monoid, right reduction monoid, reduction monoid, group, abelian group, ring, abelian ring, left ideal, right ideal, ideal, left module, right module, module, integrity domain, quotient field, Gcd (greatest common divisor) domain, unique factorization domain, Euclidean domain, principal ideal, field, abelian field. If an "ordered set category" is derived from the basic "set category", then the former can create the base for a new hierarchy, parallel with the above-described one, which supplementary introduces an order relation. These ordered categories can be used when it is necessary to define various sorting algorithms.

We further exemplify some of the definitions for the above mentioned structures.

Conventions. In order to simplify the definition syntax, we use the symbol $ for the current category / domain and we omit universal specifications for elements belonging to current structures in axioms: for example, we write shortly "a+b=b+a" instead of "$\forall$ a,b $\in$ $: a+b=b+a". The expression "y 'is a (type)' x" is used with its OO significance.

Definition 3.1. A ***Set*** is a data type that refers to a collection of elements of the same type, on which the equality operator is defined:

$$= : \$ \times \$ \rightarrow \text{Boolean}$$

Definition 3.2. The ***Semigroup*** category is a *Set* type (i. e. inherits directly the *Set* category) and supplementary introduces the binary operator

$$+ : \$ \times \$ \rightarrow \$$$

that satisfies the associativity axiom:

$$a+(b+c)=(a+b)+c.$$

Definition 3.3. The ***Abelian Semigroup*** category is a *Semigroup* category that supplementary satisfies the commutativity axiom:

$$a+b=b+a.$$

Definition 3.4. The *Monoid* category is a *Semigrup* category on which a null operator is defined

$$0 : \rightarrow \$$$

This operator satisfies the axioms

$$0+a=a,\ a+0=a.$$

Definition 3.5. The ***AbelianMonoid*** category is a type which directly inherits the *Monoid* and *AbelianSemigroup* categories, consequently acquiring their operators and axioms.

In order to obtain algebraic structures suitable for equation solving, the *LeftReductionMonoid*, *RightReductionMonoid* and *ReductionMonoid* are defined.

Definition 3.6. The ***LeftReductionMonoid*** category is a *Monoid* category that supplementary satisfies the axiom:

$$a+b=a+c \Rightarrow b=c$$

Definition 3.7. The ***RightReductionMonoid*** category is a *Monoid* category that supplementary satisfies the axiom:

$$b+a=c+a \Rightarrow b=c$$

Definition 3.8. The ***ReductionMonoid*** category is a type which directly inherits the *Monoid* and *AbelianSemigroup* categories.

Symmetrical elements are introduced within the *Group* category, by using a supplemental operator.

Definition 3.9. The ***Group*** category is a *ReductionMonoid* category that supplementary defines the unary operator:

$$- : \$ \rightarrow \$$$

which satisfies the axioms

$$a+(-a)=0 \text{ and } (-a)+a=0.$$

Practically, computations are simplified by the definition of a binary operator

$$- : \$ \times \$ \rightarrow \$$$

for which

$$a-b=a+(-b),$$

though it is logically redundant.

Within symbolic computation systems in which any user specified operator character can be used as a *Group* type operator, symmetrical elements can be introduced in a declarative way, by specifying pairs of symmetrical elements.

Definition 3.10. The ***AbelianGroup*** category is a *Group* category which supplementary introduces the commutativity axiom.

$$a+b=b+a.$$

Definition 3.11. The *Ring* category is an *AbelianGroup* category in which another operator and the distributivity axioms are supplementary introduced:

- the binary multiplicative operator:

$$* : \$ \times \$ \rightarrow \$$$

satisfying the associativity axiom

$$a*(b*c)=(a*b)*c$$

- the operator designating the neutral element for this operator:

$$1 : \to \$$$

with thc axioms

$$a*1=a \text{ and } 1*a=a$$

- the distributivity axioms (left and right) which connect the additive and multiplicative operators:

$$a*(b+c)=a*b+a*c \text{ and } (b+c)*a=b*a+c*a.$$

Our system, described in the following paragraph, allows the explicit declaration of the additive and multiplicative operators.

Scratchpad adopts another method than the one described above for defining the *Ring* category: the *Semigroup* and *Monoid* categories are defined [Dav90], including the multiplicative operator, and united into the *Ring* category.

If differentiations are required within the ring, the *PartialDifferentialRing / DifferentialRing* categories can be defined by introducing partial and total differential operators.

The Ring category generates important domains, such as the univariate or multivariate polynomial rings (dense or sparse) over a given coefficient ring, or the square matrices ring (with coefficients over a given ring). Within a type theory based symbolic computation system, this domains are implemented by pursuing the same constructive principles, applying the instantiation and inheritance concepts and expressing supplemental properties in a functional manner, by new operators and axioms, possibly conditioned by the attributes of the definition domains. In any specific domain, various symbolic computation algorithms can be applied.

Definition 3.12. The ***AbelianRing*** category is a *Ring* category which supplementary introduces the commutativity axiom for the multiplicative operator:

$$a*b=b*a.$$

In certain computations, ideal structures are necessary, as in Gröbner basis theory [Buc85].

Definition 3.13. The ***LeftIdeal*** category is defined over a *Ring* R (is parameterized with the ring R) with:

- the restriction on $ of the operator +

$$+ : \$ \times \$ \to \$$$

- the multiplicative operator

$$* : R \times \$ \to \$$$

(so $r*u \in \$$, for any $r \in R$, $u \in \$$)

Similarly, the *RightIdeal* type defines the multiplicative operator

$$* : \$ \times R \to \$$$

and the *Ideal* category inherits both *LeftIdeal* and *RightIdeal* categories.

Definition 3.14. The ***LeftModule*** category is a *AbelianGroup* category defined over a *Ring* R (is parameterized with the ring R) and supplementary introduces the multiplicative operator:

$$* : R \times \$ \to \$$$

with the axioms [Pur82]:

$$(a*b)*x=a*(b*x)$$
$$(a+b)*x=a*x+b*x$$
$$a*(x+y)=a*x+a*y$$

$$1*x=x.$$

where $a,b \in R$ and $x,y \in \$$.

The ***RightModule*** over a ring R is defined similarly, but the multiplicative operator is:

$$* : \$ \times R \rightarrow \$$$

with the axioms [Pur82]:

$$x*(a*b)=(x*a)*b$$
$$x*(a+b)=x*a+x*b$$
$$(x+y)*a=x*a+y*a$$
$$x*1=x.$$
$$(a,b \in R,\ x,y \in \$.)$$

The ***Module*** category inherits *LeftModule* and *RightModule* categories.

The remaining algebraic structures from those that were previously mentioned can be defined in the same constructive way – see [And00]; the entire hierarchy is shown, according to OO principles, in fig. 1.

4. Implementing Symbolic Computations within a Hierarchy of Algebraic Structures

Within this paragraph we pursue the goal of implementing symbolic computations in the following algebraic hierarchy: semigroup – monoid – abelian monoid – group – abelian group – ring – abelian ring, field – abelian field. In this respect, we designed specific methods of representing and simplifying expressions over the above-mentioned categories.

4.1. Representation and Simplification Methods

We shall represent an expression using a tree or a binary tree; initially, a given string-expression is converted into the corresponding binary tree. In Mathematica, the binary tree will be associated to a functional prefixed form that will retain its structure and information. In our implementation, processings corresponding to associativity, commutativity or distributivity axioms are performed using built-in attribute facilities [And97], which are however applied upon our own internal representations.

1) The ***transformation of a binary tree*** representing an expression ***with associative operators into the corresponding tree*** is performed by recursively transferring the subtrees related by the associative operator on the next ascending level. We distinguished the cases shown in figure 2, where "o" represents simultaneously a binary associative operator and its n-ary extension, Ss – a left subtree and Sd – a right subtree.

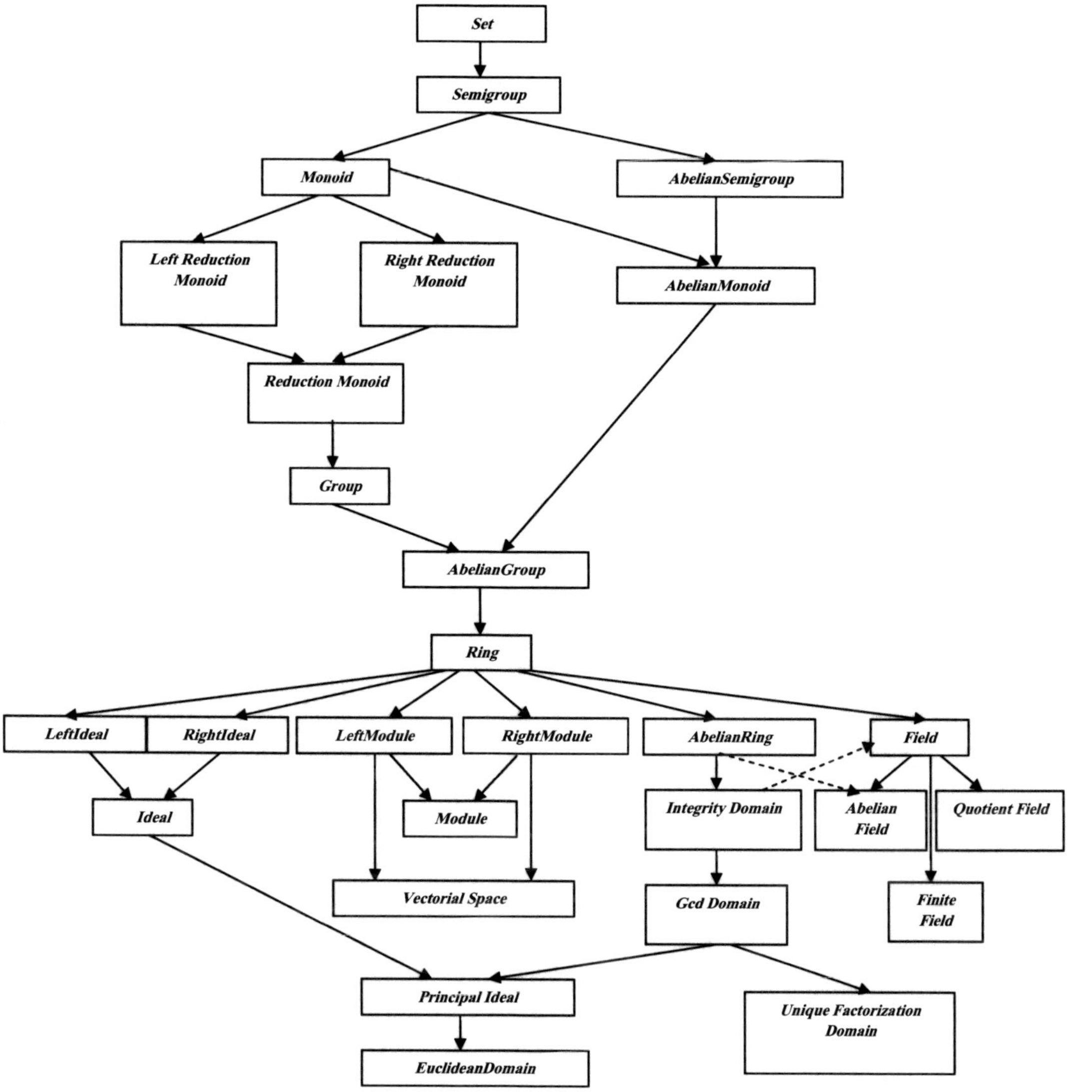

Fig.1: Hierarchy of algebraic structures

Fig.1: Hierarchy of algebraic structures

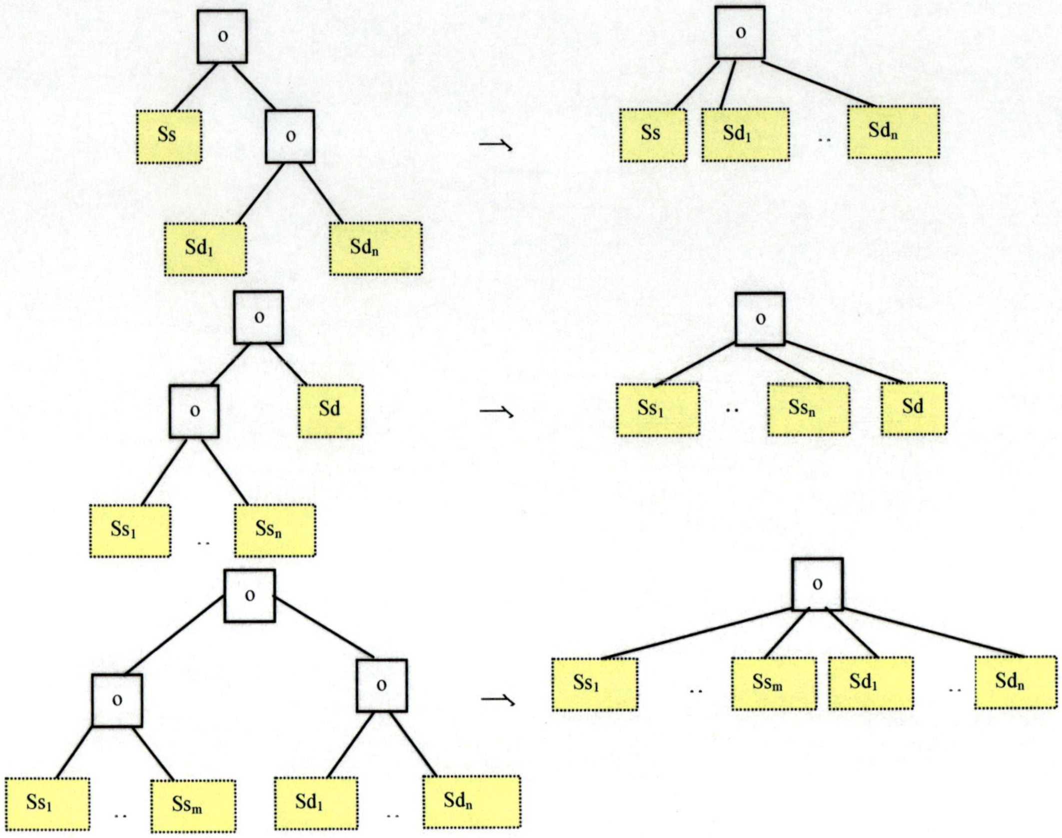

Fig. 2 – Applying associativity axiom on binary-tree representations

2) ***Reduction of neutral elements.*** For structures that admit a neutral element (at least monoid), simplification mechanisms are necessary. Neutral element reduction is simpler in the binary tree form, the problem being treated recursively on the two subtrees.

3) ***Reduction of symmetrical elements.*** In structures that are at least groups, this problem is treated similarly to the previous one, but in this case we also have to take into account the possibility of symmetrical elements appearing on successive binary levels.

4) ***Lexicographical ordering for commutative operators***. If the algebraic structure possesses an invertible and commutative operator, we generate a tree canonical form, in which the operands connected by the same commutative operator in a subexpression are lexicographically ordered. Moreover, we apply reductions of symmetrical and neutral elements. The problem of lexicographical sorting is not trivial, since operands may also be subexpressions; in this case, they will be added (as subtrees) after the elementary operands, which are lexicographically sorted, as well.

5) ***Applying the distributivity axiom***. For structures that are at least ring, it is simpler to apply distributivity on the binary tree representation, by recursively treating the cases of the additive operator appearing as root in the left subtree, right subtree, or in both descendant "roots" of a node that contains the multiplicative operator.

The above-described methods are used to construct the canonical form of expressions over various algebraic structures.

4.2. Mathematica Extension with a System of Algebraic Structures

Within the researches dedicated to the design of SCS able to process algebraic categories there appeared two directions: the creation of independent, exhaustive systems (represented by Axiom) and the extension of commonly used systems (Maple, Reduce). This latter approach, often preferred due to its flexibility, is adopted in designing an extension of Mathematica with a new type system, containing a hierarchy of algebraic categories. In this respect, we designed *HierMath* package, which implements symbolic computations within the following structures: semigroups, monoids, abelian monoids, groups, abelian groups, rings, fields, abelian rings and abelian fields. *HierMath* package enables the definition of different domains of the above-mentioned types, within which the user can perform various computations: assignments, symmetrical element declaration, expression evaluation (to a canonical form, according to current operator attributes and previously assigned symbols), equality and disequality test, explicitly applying or verifying certain properties.

The definition of an algebraic domain uses a functional and object oriented syntax and involves the following specifications: name, type, associated operator(s) and, if necessary, neutral element(s), for example *Semigrup[X, "*"]*. Operator characters can belong to a list of special characters. According to the same functional syntax principles, any operation within a previously defined domain will be pre-fixed with the domain name; for example, *X["*", expr1, expr2]* will generate the expression formed by applying the operator upon the two operands, in the domain *X*, and *X["=", expr1, expr2]* will test the equality of the two operands in the domain *X*. This working style enables the simultaneous use of many algebraic domains. Assignments use the common syntax and all value memorizations (including symmetrical pairs) use built-in symbolic facilities.

Since for expression evaluation we cannot apply built-in Mathematica facilities [Wol92], where operators have common mathematical properties or specific system semantics, we implemented our own representation and evaluation methods, which use, whenever possible, the host system's facilities. This internal representation is used for equality and disequality test, based on built-in pattern recognition mechanisms. The internal representation uses a pre-fixed functional syntax, corresponding to a binary tree (see 4.1).

The semigroup category is defined using a Mathematica module that describes valid operations within a semigroup. The semigroup category is the base of the entire hierarchy; therefore, each of the following structures will be defined by deriving it from the ascendant one, with the explicit call of the corresponding function, and by supplementary specifying additional operators and axioms (the latter – as Mathematica attributes). For each structure, according to its properties, we redefine the canonical form, and, consequently, the operator application, and the equality / disequality test.

In sections 5 and 6, we prove the practical utility of the categorical approach by deriving a multivariate polynomial category (over various coefficient domains), which is used by our

Mathematica implementation of Buchberger's algorithms for determining the Gröbner basis in [And02]. The parameterized implementations based on object oriented principles have significant advantages: generality, easy extendibility, operation protection, inheritance.

4.2.1. Internal Representations and Conversions

It is important that expressions represented within a symbolic computation system be extracted in a proper external format. In this respect, OForm[...] function generates the parentheses form of an expression by applying parentheses to the subexpressions for which the root contains a lower priority operand than the operator of the ascendant subtree. The user may access the string corresponding to the internal form of an expression by using FForm[] function, similar to Mathematica's FullForm[].

In order to obtain the binary internal form of an input expression, its string is processed. First of all we extract the operands, operators and priority arrays and afterwards, we apply a recursive constructive function, which looks for the minimum priority operator between two indexes of the operator array, and recursively introduces it as an expression header for the two arguments generated from the remaining subintervals.

In some cases, in order to obtain the internal form, it is more efficient to process Mathematica's internal form than the external string form, since the former implicitly applies some attributes associated to the operators (like *Flat* or *Orderless*). In order to transform the Mathematica internal form into our binary internal form we designed the function Tr which takes into account the characteristics of Mathematica internal form; therefore, its code is fairly complex. For example:

- *FullForm[a-b-c]* is *Plus[a, Times[-1,b], Times[-1,c]]* whereas its FForm is Ominus[a, Ominus[b,c]],
- *FullForm[a/b/c]* is *Times[a, Power[b,-1], Power[c,-1]]* whereas its FForm is Oslash[a, Oslash[b,c]],
- *FullForm[a#b#c]* is *Times[a, b, c, Power[Slot[1], 2]* whereas its FForm is Odiez[a, Odiez[b,c]].

The n-ary internal form, mainly used for equality tests, is obtained by applying to the internal binary form algorithms based on the principles described in 4.1. *Plus*'s and *Times*'s Mathematica attributes are deleted in order to prevent implicit applying of commutativity and associativity. Neutral elements are eliminated by applying the principles described in 4.1 - ElimUnit[] function.

Symmetrical elements are retained consequent to explicit user declarations with the syntax Sim[Domain, operator, identif] = identif-simetric, where Sim is a Mathematica table. Using the notations R for the root, Ss for the left subtree and Sd for the right subtree, symmetrical elements are reduced on our binary internal form (ElimSim[] function) by taking into account the following cases:

- if R(Ss) and R(Sd) are symmetrical, we return the neutral element
- if R(Ss(Sd)) and R(Sd(Sd)) are symmetrical, the function is recursively applied upon Ss
- if R(Ss) and R(Ss(Sd)) are symmetrical, the function is recursively applied upon Sd(Sd)
- if R(Ss(Ss)) and R(Sd(Ss)) are symmetrical, the function is recursively applied upon Sd
- if R(Sd(Ss)) and R(Sd) are symmetrical, the function is recursively applied upon Ss(Ss)
- otherwise, the function is recursively applied on the remaining subtrees Ss and Sd.

4.2.2. Implementing the Algebraic Structures

In order to define the algebraic structures, we use Mathematica blocks as working contexts which inherit characteristics from the larger context and supplementary define specific functions, i.e. functions for applying the operator, equality and disequality tests, etc. in each algebraic structure - semigroup, monoid, group, abelian group, ring, abelian ring, field, abelian field. Therefore, for executing these functions, the definitions from the appropriate working context will be used.

Notation conventions

For describing the algorithms implemented in Mathematica, we shall use an algorithmic pseudo-code, since understanding it does not require knowledge about Mathematica language. We shall refer our Mathematica functions which create workings contexts for defining new types by using the name **`Contextual_module`**. The **`Simbol`** type is used with the same significance as in Mathematica.

In the syntax used for describing the algorithms, we shall also borrow from symbolic computation systems, the pattern matching convention used for searching the functions to be applied in a certain context. For example, a definition

`Dom(arguments):= function_definition`

will enable us to define certain rules to be applied as functions named like the current domain `Dom` and having various parameters.

Notations like "`∀ expression x∈S`" or "`∀ expressions a,b∈S`" where S is a category (definition 2.1) introduce definitions dependant of the parameters `x`, `a` or `b`, which are expressions over S, temporarily fixed. We note that, according to definition 2.1, our category type, as a data type, also includes the expression objects over the algebraic definition set.

The module which defines a *semigroup* contains the definition for applying the operation upon two (not necessary elementary) operands, equality and disequality tests, the explicit applying of associativity upon FForm form and the "corect" operator, for closure tests (all operands belong to the list of identifiers defined in the current context). Supplementary, the domain operator is associated the appropriate attribute - *Flat*. The canonical form - Canonic function - of an expression over a semigroup is given by the internal representation - FForm function, where the operator appearing as a head is associative. For closure tests, we retained all the symbols used in a domain (D1,*) or (D2,+,*) in symbol lists assigned to a table (Simb) with symbolic indexes; its elements will be referred as Simb[D1,"*"] for one-operator domains or Simb[D2, "+", "*"] for two-operator domains. For ensuring proper use of name symbols, we also retained the names of the defined domains (LD list) and neutral elements for each domain.

Algorithm 4.2.2.1.

```
Contextual_module Semigrup(S:Simbol; op:String)
// defines the semigroup S with the operator op
  LD:=LD U {S}
  //S is added to the LD list of currently defined domains
  Prio(op):=1; //sets op's priority
```

```
  Set op's attributes;
  ∀ expression expr∈S, Canonic(expr):=FormaArb(FForm(expr));
    // canonical representation in S
  ∀ expressions a,b∈S,
S(op,a,b):=Function()
      Symbols from a and b are added to the list Simb(S,op) of
      symbols defined over the domain (S,op);
             Return OForm(op{FForm(a),FForm(b)});
      End Function
  ∀ expressions a,b∈S, S("=",a,b):= Canonic(a)=Canonic(b);
  ∀ expressions a,b∈S, S("<>",a,b):= Canonic(a)≠Canonic(b);
  ∀ expression ex∈S, S("corect",ex):=Function()
      If Simb(S,op) includes the symbols from ex
            then Return True
            else Return False
      End If
  End Function
  ∀ expression ex∈S, S("asoc",ex):=Function()
      // explicit applying of associativity
      Local variables:x:String; f,a,b,c:FormaArbB;//binary tree
      f:=FForm(ex); x:=Root(ex);
      If ex has 2 operands
      then Return ex
      else
        Case
          f of the form x{x{…,…},…} :
                  a:=LeftSubtree(LeftSubtree(f));
                  b:=RightSubtree(LeftSubtree(f));
                  c:=RightSubtree(f);
                  Return OForm(
              x{S("asoc",a),x{S("asoc",b),S("asoc",c)}})
          f of the form x{…,x{…,…}} :
                  a:=LeftSubtree(f);
                  b:=LeftSubtree(RightSubtree(f));
                  c:=RightSubtree(RightSubtree(f));
                  Return OForm(
                    x{x{S("asoc",a),S("asoc",b)},S("asoc",c)})
            End Case
      End If
    End Function
End Contextual_module
```

The implementation in Mathematica of this algorithm will contain a few peculiarities, mainly related to the specific pattern matching mechanisms. In order to reveal the characteristics of our Mathematica implementations, we give below the Mathematica code for algorithm 4.2.2.1.

```
Semigrup[S_,op_]:=Module[{f,ffa,ffb,i,x},
 If[Operator[op],
  LD=Append[LD,S]; TipDom[S,op]="Semigrup";
  Oper[S]=op; Simb[S,op]={}; f=NumeSimb[Nume[op]];
  prio[Evaluate[f]]=prio[Nume[op]]=1; prio[Symbol]=3;
  Canonic[expr__]:=FullForm[FForm[expr]][[1]];
  ClearAttributes[Evaluate[f],Temporary];
  If[Length[Attributes[Evaluate[f]]]==0,
   Attributes[Evaluate[f]]={Flat, Listable} ;(*Print[1] ,*)
   Attributes[Evaluate[f]]=Union[Attributes[Evaluate[f]],{Flat, Listable}]];
  S[op,a__,b__]:=Module[{x,y}, ffa=FForm[a]; ffb=FForm[b];
   Simb[S,op]=Union[Simb[S,op],Table[Sir[i],{i,dim}]]; x=FForm[a]; y=FForm[b];
 If[op=="$",OForm[x]<>" $ "<>OForm[y], OForm[Apply[Nume[op],List[x,y]]]]];
  S["=",a__,b__]:=SameQ[Canonic[a],Canonic[b]];
  S["<>",a__,b__]:=UnsameQ[Canonic[a],Canonic[b]];
  S["corect",ex__]:=ApDom1[ex,S,op]; S["asoc",expr__]:=Module[{f,x},
   f=FForm[expr]; x=Head[f];
   If[Depth[expr]<=2, Return[expr], Which[MatchQ[f,x[x[a__,b__],c__]],
          Return[x[S["asoc",a],x[S["asoc",b],S["asoc",c]]]],
        MatchQ[f,x[a__,x[b__,c__]]],
          Return[x[x[S["asoc",a],S["asoc",b]],S["asoc",c]]]]]],
  Fail]]
```

A semigroup X with the operator "*" will be defined with Semigrup[X,"*"] and an operation sequence over X might be:

m=X["*", a, b]
n=X["*", b, c]
X["=", m*c, a*n] will generate True.

From this point forward, each category will inherit the ascending one by the explicit call of the corresponding function and will supplementary define its specific operators and axioms. For monoids and groups, the neutral element can be specified as an argument when constructing the category, while for rings and fields, both operators (and both neutral elements) can be specified. If neutral elements are omitted in the declaration, they will be assigned the implicit values e - for one-operator domains and e, en - for two-operator domains.

For *monoids*, we redefine the operator function, the canonical form (also based on FForm), which reduces the neutral element, and the equality and disequality tests.

Algorithm 4.2.2.2.

```
Contextual_module Monoid(S:Simbol; op:String; eln:String="e")
//Defines the monoid S with the operator op and neutral
```

```
//element eln, which has the implicit value "e"
  Semigrup(S,op);  // creates the Semigrup working context
  ∀ expression expr∈S,
Canonic(expr):=FormaArb(ElimUnit(FForm(expr),op,eln));
       //the canonical form reduces neutral elements
  ∀ expressions a,b∈S, S(op,eln,a,b):=Function()
//redefined for reducing neutral elements
Add a and b to Simb(S,op) symbol list for (S,op) domain;
Local variables: ea,eb : FormaArbB; //binary tree
         ea:=ElimUnit(FForm(a),op,eln);
         eb:=ElimUnit(FForm(b),op,eln);
         If ea=eln // particular case important for op="$"
            then Return OForm(eb)
            else If eb=eln
              then Return OForm(ea)
              else Return OForm(ElimUnit(op{ea,eb},op,eln))
            End If
         End If
  End Function
  ∀ expressions a,b∈S, S(op,a,b):=S(op,e,a,b)
  ∀ expressions a,b∈S, S("=",a,b):=Canonic(a)=Canonic(b)
      // redefined for the new Canonic function
  ∀ expressions a,b∈S, S("<>",a,b):=Canonic(a)≠Canonic(b)
      // redefined for the new Canonic function
End Contextual_module
```

For implementing an *abelian monoid*, we create a monoid and add the commutativity attribute to the domain operator.

Algorithm 4.2.2.3.

```
Contextual_module MonoidCom(M:Simbol;op:String;eln:String="e")
//Defines the abelian monoid M with the operator op and //neutral
element eln, which has the implicit value "e"
  Add commutativity attribute to op;
  Monoid(M,op);  //the inherited context is explicitly called
End Contextual_module
```

For a *group*, the canonical form (`Canonic` function) supplementary reduces symmetrical elements in order to apply equality and disequality tests. For example, if we define a group Grup[G,"+"], with the implicit neutral element e, and we declare Sim[G,"+","a"] = "as", then G["+",c+as+a+e+d,e+f] will yield c+d+f, whereas G["=", (a+b)+c, a+(b+c)] will generate True (the operator is associative).

Algorithm 4.2.2.4.

```
Contextual_module Grup(G:Simbol; op:String; eln:String="e")
//Defines the group G with the operator op and neutral element
```

```
//eln, which has the implicit value "e"
  Monoid(G,op); //the inherited context is explicitly called
  ∀ expression expr∈G, Canonic(expr):= FormaArb(
  ElimUnit(ElimSim(FForm(expr),G,op,eln),op,eln));
    //the canonical form also reduces symmetrical elements
  ∀ expressions a,b∈G, G(op,a,b):=Function()
    //redefined for reducing neutral and symmetrical elements
    Local variables: fa,fb,aux:FormaArbB; //binary tree
    Add a and b to Simb(G,op) symbol list for (G,op) domain;
    fa:=ElimUnit(ElimSim(FForm(a),G,op,eln),op,eln);
    fb:=ElimUnit(ElimSim(FForm(b),G,op,eln),op,eln);
    If fa=eln  // particular case important for op="$"
      then Return OForm(fb)
      else If fb=eln
        then Return OForm(fa)
        else Return OForm(ElimUnit(ElimSim(op{fa,fb},G,op,eln),
                  op,eln))
      End If
    End If
  End Function
  ∀ expressions a,b∈S, S("=",a,b):=Canonic(a)=Canonic(b)
        // redefined for the new Canonic function
  ∀ expressions a,b∈S, S("<>",a,b):=Canonic(a)≠Canonic(b)
        // redefined for the new Canonic function
End Contextual_module
```

The function which defines abelian groups calls the one corresponding to groups and supplementary introduces the commutativity attribute (*Orderless*) for the head corresponding to the domain operator in the internal form (FForm). Therefore, expressions over abelian groups will be lexicographically ordered. The algorithm for defining an *abelian group* is similar to algorithm 4.2.2.2.

The *ring* category inherits the abelian group and monoid categories by calling the appropriate functions with the corresponding operators. The canonical form for ring categories (Canonic function) is obtained by reducing the neutral element for the multiplicative operator, followed by reducing symmetrical and neutral operators for the additive operator. In the definition of a ring (or field), we set the monoid operator with a higher priority than the group one, in order to ensure correct generation of external forms. The abelian ring supplementary introduces the commutativity attribute to the multiplicative operator.

Algorithm 4.2.2.5.

```
Contextual_module Inel(S:Simbol; plus,stea:String;
              el:String="e"; eln:String="en")
//Defines the ring S with the additive operator plus, stea
//multiplicative operator and neutral elements el, eln.
```

```
// el's implicit value is "e" while eln's - "en"
  GrupCom(S,plus,el);  Monoid(S,stea);
    // inherited contexts are explicitly called
  Prio(plus):=1;  Prio(stea):=2;  //set operator priorities
  Simb(S,plus,stea):=Simb(S,plus)∪Simb(S,stea);//S's symbol set
  ∀ expression expr∈S,
      S("simplif",expr):=S("+",S("*",expr,eln),el);
      //simplification: operator functions for monoid and group
// activate the appropriate simplification mechanisms
  ∀ expression ex∈S, S("corect",ex):=Function()
      If Simb(S,plus,stea) includes the symbols from ex
        then Return True; else Return False
      End If
  End Function
  ∀ expression expr∈S, S("distrib",expr):=explicit apply of distributivity
         //Mathematica built-in function will be used
  ∀ expression expr∈S, Canonic(expr):=Function()
  //canonical representation in the ring
Local variables: ex:FormaArbB; //binary tree
  ex:=ElimUnit(FForm(S("distrib",expr)),stea,eln);
  ex:=ElimUnit(ElimSim(ex,S,plus,el),plus,el);
  Return FormaArb(ex);
  End Function
  //For applying operators, functions from the group and
  //monoid will be used
  ∀ expressions a,b∈S, S("=",a,b):=Canonic(a)=Canonic(b)
  ∀ expressions a,b∈S, S("<>",a,b):=Canonic(a)≠Canonic(b)
End Contextual_module
```

Algorithm 4.2.2.6.

```
Contextual_module InelCom(S:Simbol; plus,stea:String;
             el:String="e"; eln:String="en")
//Defines the abelian ring S with the additive operator plus,
//multiplicative operator ori and neutral elements el, eln.
//el's implicit value is "e" while eln's - "en"
Add commutativity attribute to stea;
Inel(S,plus,stea,el,eln);
  //the inherited context is explicitly called
End Contextual_module
```

The *field* is derived from an abelian group and a group and supplementary introduces the reduction of symmetrical elements for the multiplicative operator; the *abelian field* also introduces the commutativity attribute for the multiplicative operator. The algorithm for defining a *field* category is similar to algorithm 4.2.2.5 for defining a ring category, but it applies the "`Grup`" context for the multiplicative operator.

The algorithm for defining an *abelian field* category is similar to algorithm 4.2.2.6 for defining an abelian ring category, but it applies the "`GrupCom`" context for the multiplicative operator.

The Mathematica package which implements these algorithms has many practical advantages, relying in its generality and possibility to efficiently derive new domains as working contexts for performing symbolic computations.

5. Parameterized Definitions of Polynomial Domains

Implementing symbolic computations from the category theory point of view brings in symbolic computations advantages that are similar to the ones introduced by object oriented (OO) principles in programming. Thus, there can be defined operations (methods) specific to certain working contexts, operations that will be protected to inconsistent access (similar to classes in OO programming). Moreover, the implementation of the category / domain hierarchy is simplified by using inheritance principles. The hierarchical and parameterized methods of definition have the advantage of easily extending the system of algebraic structures, on the same general definition principles.

We intend to exemplify these ideas by defining a multivariate polynomial category, which will be parameterized with various coefficient domains (, mod n, squared matrices). On the same parameterized principles [GruMon93], when a new coefficient domain will be defined, the same polynomial category will be used, by only modifying its parameter for the new coefficient domain.

5.1. Defining the Exponent Vector Domain

With the view to implementing the multivariate polynomial category, we define an auxiliary domain for processing monomials, naming it the *exponent vector domain* [Gru93]. For a given base of identifiers (for example, {x,y,z}), an exponent vector will be retained by the list of exponents corresponding to each variable. In operating upon exponent vectors, we use two types of representations: lists, respectively products of primes with the exponents in question. Thus, using the latter representation, the exponent vector $\{e_1, e_2, \ldots, e_n\}$ will be retained and processed with the number $p_1^{e_1} p_2^{e_2} \ldots p_n^{e_n}$ [Gru93], where $p_1, p_2, \ldots, p_n$ are prime numbers, for simplifying computations – the first prime numbers. In this representation, an exponent vector sum reduces to the corresponding prime numbers product, whereas the greatest common divisor (Gcd) and the least common multiple (Lcm) can be computed by similar operations upon prime products.

The exponent vector domain is an abelian monoid [And97] that introduces the following operations:

- computing neutral, minimum and maximum elements ("`0`", "`Max`", "`Min`");
- conversions between the list and number internal forms ("`ListaInVectorNr`", "`VectorNrInLista`");

- sum ("+"), greatest common divisor ("Gcd") and least common multiple ("Lcm") for two exponent vectors;
- positiveness test for an exponent vector ("Pozitiv");
- divisibility test for two exponent vectors ("|");
- relational operators ("<", ">", "=", "<=", ">=", "<>") between two exponent vectors – we shall consider the *lexicographical ordering* (corresponding relations are implemented by string[...] functions);
- conversions between external and internal forms ("Inp", "Out").

All operations within an exponent vector domain V, created by the function VectExp[V,lv], where lv is the variable list representing the base, will be prefixed with the domain name and will have as the first parameter the operation code. For example, V["+",v1,v2] returns the sum of two exponent vectors (in internal form), V["Gcd",v1,v2] computes the greatest common divisor, V["Lcm",v1,v2] computes the least common multiple, etc. - see [And02].

We give below the pseudo-code for defining the exponent vector domain, using the notation conventions presented in section 4.

Algorithm 5.1. – defining the exponent vector domain

```
Contextual_module VectExp(V:Simbol; lv:List)
//Creates the exponent vector V with the base baza lv.
//We assume the base identifiers as lexicographically ordered
//An exponent list {e1, …, en} is represented as a Mathematica
//list or by using the number p1^e1 ...pn^en , where p1, …, pn are the
//first prime n numbers. The latter will be considered
//internal representation within VectExp module.
//Primi = list of primes
  Local variables: n, k : Integer; min, max, en : List;
   // minimal - maximal value and neutral element
  n:=Length(lv); // base dimension
  min:={};  max:={};  en={}; //lists
  For k:=1, n do
   min:= min U Z("Min"); //minimal element in Z domain
   max:= max U Z("Max")); //maximal element in Z domain
   //see coefficient domains - algorithm 5.3
   en:= en U 0;
  End For
  MonoidCom(V,"+",en); //algorithm 4.2.2.3
  V("0"):=en;  V("Max"):=max;  V("Min"):=min;
  ∀ list l∈V, V("ListaInVectorNr",l):= Function ()
//transforms the list l into internal number representation
    Local variabiles: i,p,nr : Integer; nr:=Length(l); p:=1;
    For i:=1,nr do p:=p*Primi[i]^l[i]; End For;
```

```
    Return p;
  End Function
     ∀ nr∈Integer, V("VectorNrInLista",nr):= Function ()
  //transforms the internal number representation into a list
  Locale variables: i, x, d, aux : Integer;  l : List;
   x:=nr;  i:=1;  l={};
   While x>1 do
     d:=Primi[i]; aux:=0;
     While x mod d=0 do
       x:=x div d; /*quotient*/  aux:=aux+1;
     End While;
     If aux≠0 then l:=Adaug(l,aux); End If;
     i:=i+1;
     End While;
     Return l;
  End Function;
     ∀ lists l1, l2 ∈ V, V("+",l1,l2):= Function ()
     //exponent vectors are multiplied by multiplying the
     //internal number representations
     //Alternative method: Mathematica "+" on the two lists
  Return V["VectorNrInLista",
      V["ListaInVectorNr",l1]*V["ListaInVectorNr",l2]]
  End Function;
     ∀ list l ∈ V, V("Pozitiv",l):= Function ()
     //returns True if all list elements are positive
       Local variables: i : Integer; sw : Boolean;
       sw:=True;
       For i:=1, n do
      If l[i]<0 then Return False; End If;
       End For
     End Function;
     ∀ lists l1, l2 ∈ V, V("Gcd",l1,l2):= Function ()
     //Computing GCD for two exponent vectors is reduced to
     //computing GCD for the two internal number representations.
     //In Mathematica, we may also apply built-in GCD function
     //upon each two correspondent numerical pairs from the lists
       Return V["VectorNrInLista",
      Gcd[V["ListaInVectorNr",l1], V["ListaInVectorNr",l2]]];
     End Function;
     ∀ liste l1, l2 ∈ V, V("Lcm",l1,l2):= Function ()
     //Computing LCM for two exponent vectors is reduced to
     //computing LCM for the two internal number representations.
     //In Mathematica, we may also apply built-in LCM function
```

```
//upon each two correspondent numerical pairs from the lists
  Return V["VectorNrInLista",
 Lcm[V["ListaInVectorNr",l1], V["ListaInVectorNr",l2]]];
End Function;
∀ lists l1, l2 ∈ V, V("Rel",l1,l2):= Function ()
//Auxiliary function for determining the relation between
//two exponent vectors. Tests the relation <, =, > between
//l1 and l2 and returns correspondingly -1,0 or 1.
  Locale variables: i, rel : Integer;  rel:=0;  i:=1;
  While i<=n and rel=0 do
 If l1[i]<l2[i] then rel:=-1;
   Else If l1[i]>l2[i] then rel:=1; End If;
 End If;
 i:=i+1;
  End While;
  Return rel;
End Function;
∀ lists l1, l2 ∈ V, V("<",l1,l2):= Function ()
 Return V["Rel", l1, l2] = -1;
End Function;
∀ lists l1, l2 ∈ V, V("=",l1,l2):= Function ()
 Return V["Rel", l1, l2] = 0;
End Function;
∀ lists l1, l2 ∈ V,:= Function ()
 Return V["<", l1, l2] or V["=", l1, l2];
End Function;
// V(">",l1,l2), V("<>",l1,l2), V(">=",l1,l2) are similar
∀ lists l1, l2 ∈ V, V("|",l1,l2):= Function ()
//Tests whether l1 exponent vector divides l2 exponent
//vector, returning correspondingly True or False.
  Local variables: n1, n2 : Integer;  bool : Boolean;
  bool:=n1<=n2;
  For i:=1,Min(n1,n2) do //Min()- Minimal function
 If l1[i]>l2[i] then bool:=False; End If;
  End For;
  Return bool;
End Function;
∀ list l ∈ V, V("Out",l):= Function ()
//returns the external form of l exponent vector by creating
// the internal Mathematica representation of the expression
//and using the implicit Mathematica external conversion
  Local variables:  lr : List;  i : Integer;
  For i:=1,n do
```

```
      Add to lr the list {lv[i],l[i]} with the head "Power"
    End For;
    Add to lr the head "Times";
    Return lr;
  End Function;
  ∀ monomial expression e, V("Inp",e):= Function ()
  //Processes the monomial expression e and returns its list
  //form. The algorithm is dependant of Mathematica internal
  //representation - see [And00],[And02] - vectexp.m package
  Processes e's Mathematica internal representation,
    distinguishing the cases of exponent=0 (missing base), =1
    missing exponent and >1;
  Returns the list of selected exponents;
  End Function;
End Contextual_module
```

5.2. Defining A Multivariate Polynomial Category over Various Coefficient Domains

We created two implementations for operating upon multivariate polynomials, and studied their efficiency, compared to Mathematica built-in facilities.

The *first representation* (**polinom.m** package) views a polynomial as a list of two elements: the exponent vector list, lexicographically ordered, and the corresponding coefficient list. For example, the polynomial 2*x^2*z-5*y (with the base {x,y,z}) will be represented as {{{0,1,0},{2,0,1}}, {-5,2}}.

The *second representation* (**polin.m** package) views a polynomial as a table T which retains in T[0] the exponent vector list, lexicographically ordered, and the coefficients of each exponent vector V (represented as a list) – in T[V]. For example, the polynomial 2*x^2*z-5*y (with the base {x,y,z}) will be represented by a table P with: P[0]={{0,1,0},{2,0,1}}, P[{0,1,0}]=-5, P[{2,0,1}]=2.

In order to simplify the manipulation of the exponent vector list, we provide it with a sentinel containing maximum exponent values (over the appropriate domain).

The polynomial category is an abelian ring parameterized with the coefficient and exponent vector domains (the latter – over a certain variable base); this category will generate, for different parameters, particular polynomial domains. For each of the two implementations, we defined the following operations:

- selecting the current coefficient and exponent vector domains ("`DomCoef`", "`DomVectExp`");
- initializing a polynomial ("`Init`") and testing null polynomials ("`Nul`");
- for a given polynomial, computing the dimension ("`Nr`"), the "leading" monomial – in lexicographical ordering ("`MonomGrMax`"), the "leading" coefficient ("`CoefGrMax`"), the monomial of a certain index ("`Monom`"), the coefficient of a certain index ("`Coef`") and the position of a certain monomial ("`Indice`");

- adding a monomial with a certain coefficient to a given polynomial ("AdaugMonom");
- converting a monomial into a polynomial ("MonomInPol") and copying a polynomial ("Copy");
- for two given polynomials, computing the sum ("+"), product ("*") and subtraction ("-");
- multiplying a polynomial by a number ("&");
- dividing a polynomial by a given monomial ("/") and performing the divisibility test for a polynomial and a monomial ("|");
- conversions between the internal and external forms of a polynomial ("Inp", "Out"). *Observation*. In implementing these functions we supposed that coefficients are elementary, but the algorithm is easily expandable for list type coefficients (for example, matrices).

For example, within the polynomial domain Pol, defined by Polinom[Pol, DCoef, DVect, l], where DCoef is the coefficient domain and DVect is the exponent vector domain with the base l, the construction DVect["|",v,Pol["Monom",i,P]] performs a divisibility test – within DVect exponent vector domain – between two exponent vectors, the second one corresponding to a monomial selected from a polynomial P (by "Monom" operation, within the polynomial domain Pol). DVect["+",o1,o2] is the sum of o1 and o2 in DVect domain, whereas DCoef["+",o1,o2] is a sum in DCoef domain.

We give below the algorithm for defining the exponent vector domain, based on the first representation - **polinom.m** package, using the previously described notation conventions.

Algorithm 5.2. – defining the polynomial category

```
Contextual_module Polinom(Pol,Dcoef,Dvect:Simbol; baza:List)
//defines a multivariate polynomial domain with coefficients
//in DCoef, over the exponent vector domain DVect, with the
//base baza. We use the representation from polinom.m
  Local variables: n : Integer;
  InelCom(Dcoef, "+", "*"); //algorithm 4.2.2.6
  VectExp(Dvect, baza);     //algorithm 5.1
  Pol("DomCoef"):=Function()
Return Dcoef; // coefficient domain
  End Function;
  Pol("DomVectExp"):=Function()
Return DomVectExp; // monomial domain
  End Function;
  Pol("Init"):= Function() //returns the null polynomial
    //with a sentinel in the exponent vector list
Return {{Dvect("Max")},{}}
  End Function;
  ∀ P ∈ Pol, Pol("Nul",P):= Function()  //null test
      Return P[1]={Dvect("Max")}
  End Function;
  ∀ P ∈ Pol, Pol("Nr",P):= Function() //returns the number of
      //monomials in polynomial P
```

```
    Return Length(P[1])-1;
End Function;
∀ P ∈ Pol, i ∈ Integer, Pol("Monom",i,P):= Function()
    //returns the i-th monomial in polynomial P
    If i>Pol("Nr",P)
      then Return {}; else Return P[1][i];
    End If;
End Function;
∀ P ∈ Pol, i ∈ Intreg, Pol("Coef",i,P):= Function()
    //returns the i-th coefficient in polynomial P
    If i>Pol("Nr",P)
then Return 0; else Return P[2][i];
    End If;
End Function;
∀ P ∈ Pol, l ∈ Dvect, Pol("Indice",i,P):= Function()
//returns the index of monomial l in polynomial P
  Returns l's position in P[1];
  //a built-in Mathematica function is applied
End Function;
∀ P ∈ Pol, Pol("MonomGrMax",P):= Function()
    //returns the leading monomial in polynomial P
    Return P[1][Pol("Nr",P)];
End Function;
∀ P ∈ Pol, Pol("CoefGrMax",P):= Function()
    //returns the leading coefficient in polynomial P
    Returns P[2][Pol("Nr",P)];
End Function;
∀ T ∈ Pol, v ∈ Dvect, c ∈ Dcoef
  Pol("AdaugMonom",T,v,c):= Function() //adds to the
//polynomial T the monomial formed by the exponent vector
//v and the coefficient c taking into account the
//lexicographical ordering; if v exponent vector exists, it
//adds the coefficient c to the appropriate existing one
    Local variables: nr, i, k : Integer;  coef : Dcoef;
l, lc : List; l:={}; /*exponent vector list*/
    lc:={}; //coefficient list
    i:=1;  nr:=Pol("Nr",T); // polynomial dimension
    While i<=nr and Dvect("<",Pol("Monom",i,T),v) do
      l:=Adaug(l,Pol("Monom",i,T));
      lc:= Adaug(lc,Pol("Coef",i,T));  i:=i+1;
    End While;
    If Dvect("=",v,Pol("Monom",i,T))
then //existing monomial; the coefficient is summed
```

```
      coef:=Dcoef("+",Pol("Coef",i,T),c);
      If Dcoef("<>",Dcoef["0"],coef) then
        l:=Adaug(l,v);  lc:=Adaug(lc,coef);
      End If;
      i:=i+1;
  else //the monomial is not in T
      If Dcoef("<>",Dcoef["0"],c) then
        l:=Adaug(l,v);  lc:=Adaug(lc,coef);
      End If;
      End If;
      For k:=i, nr do
        l:=Adaug(l,Pol("Monom",k,T));
        lc:= Adaug(lc,Pol("Coef",k,T));
      End For;
      l:= Adaug(l,Dvect("max"));
      Return {l, lc};
  End Function;
  ∀ l ∈ Dvect, c:Dcoef,  Pol("MonomInPol",l,c):= Function()
      //returns the polynomial containg the monomial formed by
//the coefficient c and exponent vector l
      Local variables:  P : Pol;
      P:=Pol("Init");  P:=Pol("AdaugMonom",P,l,c);
      Return P;
  End Function;
  ∀ P ∈ Pol, Pol("Copy",P):= Function() //returns a
    // polynomial - copy of the argument
      Local variables: l, lc : List;  i, nr : Integer;
      l:={}; //exponent vector list
      lc:={}; //coefficient list
      nr:=Pol("Nr",P); // polynomial dimension
For i:=1, nr do
        l:=Adaug(l,Pol("Monom",i,P));
        lc:= Adaug(lc,Pol("Coef",i,P));
      End For;
      l:= Adaug(l,Dvect("max"));
      Return {l,lc};
  End Function;
  ∀ P1, P2 ∈ Pol, Pol("+",P1,P2):= Function()
    //returns the sum polynomial of P1, P2
    Local variables: n1, n2, i, j, k : Integer; v1,v2 : Dvect;
    Rez : Pol;  c1, c2 : Dcoef;
    n1:=Pol("Nr",P1); n2:=Pol("Nr",P2); //dimensions of P1, P2
    i:=1; j:=1;  Rez:=Pol("Init");
```

```
  For k:=1, n1+n2 do
    v1:=Pol("Monom",i,P1); c1:=Pol("Coef",i,P1);
    v2:=Pol("Monom",j,P2); c2:=Pol("Coef",j,P2);
    If not (Dvect("=",v1,Dvect("Max")) and
      (Dvect("=",v2,Dvect("Max"))) then
          If Dvect("=",v1,v2) then
        Rez:=Pol("AdaugMonom",Rez,v1,Dcoef("+",c1,c2));
              i:=i+1; j:=j+1;
              else If Dvect("<",v1,v2) then
                  Rez:=Pol("AdaugMonom",Rez,v1,c1));i:=i+1;
                      else
                  Rez:=Pol("AdaugMonom",Rez,v2,c2));
                  j:=j+1;
                    End If;
          End If;
    End If;
  End For;
  Return Rez;
End Function;
∀ P1, P2 ∈ Pol, Pol("*",P1,P2):= Function()
  //returns the product polynomial of P1, P2
  Local variables: n1, n2, i, j : Integer;  c1, c2 : Dcoef;
    v1, v2 : Dvect;   Rez : Pol;
  n1:=Pol("Nr",P1); n2:=Pol("Nr",P2); //dimensions of P1, P2
  Rez:=Pol("Init");
  For i:=1, n1 do
    v1:=Pol("Monom",i,P1); c1:=Pol("Coef",i,P1);
    For j:=1, n2 do
      v2:=Pol("Monom",j,P2); c2:=Pol("Coef",j,P2);
      Rez:=Pol("AdaugMonom",Rez,
               Dvect("+",v1,v2),Dcoef("*",c1,c2));
    End For;  End For;
  Return Rez;
End Function;
∀ P ∈ Pol, nr ∈ Dcoef, Pol("*",nr,P):= Function()
  //multiplies P by the number n and returns the result
  Local variables: i, dim: Integer; R:Pol; R:=Pol("Copy",P);
  dim:=Pol("Nr",P); // P's dimension
  For i:=1, dim do R[2][i]:= Dcoef("*",R[2][i],nr));
  End For;
  Return R;
Sfârşit Funcţie;
∀ P1, P2 ∈ Pol, Pol("-",P1,P2):= Function()
```

```
    //returns the subtraction polyomial P1-P2
    Local variables:  P : Pol;
    P:=Pol("*",-1,P2);
    Return Pol("+",P1,P);
  End Function;
  ∀ P ∈ Pol, v:Dvect, c: Dcoef, Pol("/",P,v,c):= Function()
  //divides each of P's monomials by the exponent vector v and
  //coefficient c and returns the result
    Local variables: R : Pol; dim, i : Integer;  w, l : Dvect;
    R:=Pol("Init");  dim=Pol("Nr",P);
    For i:=1,dim do
      w=Pol("Monom",i,P);  l:=Dvect("-",w,v),
      R=Pol("AdaugMonom",R,l,Dcoef("/",Pol("Coef",i,P),c));
    End For;
    Return R;
  End Function;
  ∀ P ∈ Pol, v : Dvect, Pol("|",v,P):= Function()
  //tests whether the exponent vector v divides any of P's
  //monomials and returns True or False
    Local variables: i:Integer; divide:Boolean; divide:=False;
    For i:=1, Pol("Nr",P) do
      If Pol("|",v,Pol("Monom",i,P)) then divide:=True;
      End If;
    End For;
    Return divide;
  End Function;
  ∀ P ∈ Pol, Pol("Out",P):= Function () //polynomial display
    Local variables: l : List;  i : Integer;
    For i:=1,n do
     l=Adaug(l,Pol("Coef",i,P)*Dvect("Out",Pol("Monom",i,P)));
    End For;
    Add to l the head "Plus";
    Return l;
  End Function;
  ∀ polynomial expression e,  V("Inp",e):= Function ()
  //transforms an input polynomial into the internal form; the
  //code is rather complex and based on Mathematica internal
  //forms - see [And00], polinom.m package
    Processes Mathematica's internal representation of
        expression e, selecting each exponent vector and
        coefficient from the polynomial sum;
      An exponent vector is processed according to
     Dvect("Out",…) - algorithm 5.1
```

```
    Returns the lists of selected exponent vectors and
      coefficients
  End Function;
End Contextual_module
```

5.3. Defining the Coefficient Domains

With the view to revealing the practical use of the categorical definition for creating various polynomial domains, we experimentally define, pursuing the same parameterization principles, the following coefficient domains, derived from the abelian ring category: the integer domain `Z` (`DomZ` function), the integer mod n domain, for prime n – `Zmod` and the square matrices domain, with symbolic or numerical elements (`Matrice` function). More rigorously, matrices can be defined over a specific coefficient domain, but this aspect is not of interest within the present application. In order to use `Z` and `Zmod` domains for Gröbner bases algorithms, we define them as integrity and Gcd domains. We observe that the extension of the mod n remainder classes' ring with a `Quotient` operator is consistent for prime n but polynomial operations can be performed in `Z` mod n for any natural n.

We give `below` the Mathematica code which defines the above described domains.

```
DomZ[Z_]:=Module[{}, (*defines the Integer domain*)
  InelCom[Z,"+","*","0","1"];(*abelian ring[And02]*)
  Z["+",a_Integer,b_Integer]:=a+b;
  Z["-",a_Integer,b_Integer]:=a-b;
  Z["*",a_Integer,b_Integer]:=a*b;
  Z["Cat",a_Integer,b_Integer]:=Quotient[a,b]; (*the quotient*)
  Z["Mod",a_Integer,b_Integer]:=Mod[a,b]; (*the remainder*)
  Z["GCD",a_Integer,b_Integer]:=GCD[a,b];
  Z["LCM",a_Integer,b_Integer]:=LCM[a,b];
  Z["0"]:=0; (*neutral element *)
  Z["=", a__, b__]:=SameQ[a,b];
  Z["<>", a__, b__]:=UnsameQ[a,b]; ]
  Z["/",a_List,b_Integer]:=a/b;
    (*the elements of a list divided by an integer*)  ]

Zmod[Zm_,n_Integer]:=Module[{n1,n2}, (*the Integer domain mod n*)
  InelCom[Zm,"+","*","0","1"];                (*abelian ring
[And02]*)
  Zm["+",n1_Integer,n2_Integer]:=Mod[n1+n2,n];
  Zm["-",n1_Integer,n2_Integer]:=Mod[n+n1-n2,n];
  Zm["*",n1_Integer,n2_Integer]:=Mod[n1*n2,n];
  Zm["Cat",n1_Integer,n2_Integer]:=Module[{x}, (*quotient*)
    For[x=0,x<=n-1,x++,
      If[Zm["*",n2,x]==n1, Return[x],]];
    Print["Impartire cu 0"];Return[-1]; (*division by 0*)  ];
  Zm["/",n1_Integer,n2_Integer]:=Zm["Cat",n1,n2];
(*Mod[n1/n2,n];*)
  Zm["/",a_List,b_Integer]:=Module[{i,l},    l={};
    For[i=1,i<=Length[a],i++,
```

```
      l=Append[l,Zm["/",a[[i]],b]]];
    Return[l];  ];
  Zm["Mod",n1_Integer,n2_Integer]:=Module[{c},
    c=Zm["Cat",n1,n2];
    If[c!=-1,
      Return[Mod[n1-n2*c,n]],
      Print["Impartire cu 0"];Return[-1]] (*division by 0*)  ];
  Zm["GCD",n1_Integer,n2_Integer]:=Module[{r,a,b},
    r=Zm["Mod",n1,n2]; a=n1; b=n2;
    While[r!=0,
      a=b; b=r; r=Zm["Mod",a,b];   ];
    Return[a];  ];
  Zm["LCM",n1_Integer,n2_Integer]:=
    Zm["Cat",Zm["*",n1,n2],Zm["GCD",n1,n2]];
  Zm["0"]:=0;
  Zm["=", a__, b__]:=SameQ[a,b];
  Zm["<>", a__, b__]:=UnsameQ[a,b];];

Matrice[Mat_,n_Integer]:=Module[{m1,m2},
  (*defines the square matrixes of dimension n*)
  InelCom[Mat,"+","*"];
  Mat["+",m1_List,m2_List]:=m1+m2;
  Mat["*",m1_List,m2_List]:=Dot[m1,m2];
  Mat["Inv",m_List]:=Inverse[m];
  Mat["Transp",m_List]:=Transpose[m];
  Mat["Det",m_List]:=Det[m];
  Mat["0"]:=Module[{i,l,ll}, (*neutral element*)
   For[l={};i=1,i<=n,i++,
     l=Append[l,0]];
   For[ll={};j=1,j<=n,j++,
     ll=Append[ll,l]];
   Return[l];
  ]; ];
```

We studied the efficiency of our implementation versus the built-in one; the latter is obviously more efficient for common operations but it does not allow polynomial operations over the newly implemented domains, i. e. integers mod n and matrices. Moreover, our implementation is *easily extendable* for new coefficient domains by using the same definition of the multivariate polynomial category. Further execution details, referring to run times in Mathematica 3.0 Kernel [Wol92], on a 16MB RAM, 100MHz Pentium, are given in the following table.

It can be noticed that the efficiency of **polinom.m** and **polin.m** implementations is similar; though, for some cases, referring table elements proves to be faster than selecting list elements. Nevertheless, **polin.m**'s representation has certain drawbacks regarding Mathematica parameter transmission: a polynomial is transmitted by the corresponding table symbol, fact that can create inconsistencies when table elements are modified. For this reason, we use **polinom.m** implementation within the Gröbner bases algorithms which are described in the following section.

Polynomial domain	$Z[x,y,z]$						$Z_7[x,y,z]$						${}_2[x,y,z]$, ${}_2 = 2\times2$ (numeric or symbolic) matrix domain			
Operation (P1 "o" P2)	Sum			Product			Sum			Product			Sum		Product	
Number of terms	2	7	10	2	7	10	2	7	10	2	7	10	2	5	2	5
Mathematica Implementation	< .01 s	< .01 s	< .01 s	.06 s	< .01 s	.06 s	–	–	–	–	–	–	–	–	–	–
Implementation 1 – ***polinom.m*** *package*	.11 s	.27 s	.49 s	.05 s	2.2 s	8 s	.11 s	.28 s	.49 s	.11 s	2.3 s	6.8 s	.16 s	.44 s	16 s	1.5 s
Implementation 2 – ***polin.m*** *package*	.16 s	.22 s	.66 s	.05 s	2 s	7.2 s	.22 s	.28 s	.44 s	.16 s	2 s	6.4 s	.11 s	.22 s	.06 s	.22 s

6. Implementing Gröbner Bases Algorithms

We implemented Buchberger's algorithms for computing the Gröbner basis and the reduced Gröbner basis [Buc85] of a polynomial set into Mathematica packages: **groebner.m** and **groebred.m**. The functions which compute the Gröbner bases are parameterized with a polynomial domain, therefore they can be applied for polynomial domains over any consistent coefficient domain that is previously defined. Note that a polynomial domain is created by using the polynomial categorical definition within **polinom.m** package (algorithm 5.2), which is parameterized with a coefficient domain defined in **domcoef.m** package (algorithm 5.3).

Within **groebner.m** package we implemented Buchberger's Gröbner basis algorithm [Buc85] – algorithm 6.3 (`BazaGroebner[...]` function in [And02]). We completely described the algorithmic iterations for computing the normal form of a polynomial modulo a polynomial set – algorithm 6.1 (`FormaNormala[Pol,F,g]` function in [And02], where `Pol` is the current polynomial domain). For computing the S-polynomial of two polynomials, we implemented the formula proposed in [Gru93] – algorithm 6.2 (`SPol[...]` function in [And02]).

We give below the pseudo-code for the above-mentioned algorithms; one can notice the specific functional and parameterized syntax used for expressing operations over various domains (exponent vector, polynomial or coefficient).

Algorithm 6.1. – polynomial normal form

```
Function PolNormal(Pol:Simbol; F : Set; g:Pol) : Boolean
//F - polynomial set; g - polynomial in Pol domain.
//Tests whether g is in normal form modulo F, i.e no
// monomial from g is divisible by the leading monomial
//of any polynomial from F (given as polynomial list).
//Operations are preformed over the polynomial domain Pol
Local variables: norm : Boolean;  i, dim : Integer;
```

```
  norm:=True;  dim:=Length(F):
  For i:=1,dim do
If Pol("|",Pol("MonomGrMax",F[i]),g) //alg. 5.2
        then norm:=False;
      End If;
  End For;
  Return norm;
End Function;

Function FormaNormala(Pol,Dcoef,Dvect:Simbol; F:Set;p:Pol):Pol
//Returns the normal form of p mod F. Operations are performed
//over the polynomial domain Pol(Dcoef,Dvect)
Local variables: i, j, dd : Integer;  monmaxi, x, u : Dvect;
  fi, afi, rez, pp, rr, aux : Pol;   vv : Boolean;
  coefmaxi, cx, alfa, beta, g : Dcoef;
  rez:=Pol("Copy",p);  vv:=PolNormal(Pol,F,rez);
  While not vv
      For i:=1,Length(F) do
        fi:=Pol("Copy",F[i]); monmaxi:=Pol("MonomGrMax",fi);
  coefmaxi:=Pol("CoefGrMax",fi); j:=Pol("Nr",rez);
        x:=Pol("Monom",j,rez);
        While not Pol("Nul",rez) and Dvect(">=",x,monmaxi)
            If Dvect("|",monmaxi,x) then
              pp:=Pol("Copy",rez);  cx:=Pol("Coef",j,rez);
        pp[1]:=Sterge(pp[1],j); //eliminates monomial j
        pp[2]:=Sterge(pp[2],j); u:=Dvect("-",x,monmaxi);
        afi:=Pol("Copy",fi); dd:=Pol("Nr",afi);
        afi[1]:=Sterge(afi[1],dd); //leading monomial
        afi[2]:=Sterge(afi[2],dd);
        alfa:=coefmaxi; beta:=cx;
        If ∃ Dcoef("GCD",…) then//reduce coefficient order
            g:=Dcoef("GCD",alfa,beta);
                  alfa:=Dcoef("/",alfa,g);
                  beta:=Dcoef("/",beta,g);
        End If;
              pp:=Pol("*",alfa,pp);
              aux:=Pol("MonomInPol",u,beta);
              rr:=Pol("*",aux,afi); rez:=Pol("-",pp,rr);
        j:=Pol("Nr",rez)+1;
            End If;
            j:=j-1;  x:=Pol("Monom",j,rez);
        End While;
      End For;
```

```
vv:=PolNormal(Pol,F,rez);
  End While;
  Return rez;
End Function
```

Algorithm 6.2. – SPol(P1,P2)

```
Function SPol(Pol,Dcoef,Dvect:Simbol; P1,P2:Pol) : Pol
//returns SPol(P1,P2), computed in polynomial domain Pol
Local variables: P, AP1, AP2, R1, R2, R, Rez : Pol;
      M1, M2, M : Dvect;  c1, c2, c : Dcoef;
  M1:=Pol("MonomGrMax",P1);  c1:=Pol("CoefGrMax",P1);
  M2:=Pol("MonomGrMax",P2);  c2:=Pol("CoefGrMax",P2);
  M:=Dvect("Lcm",M1,M2);  c:=Dcoef("LCM",c1,c2);
  P:=Pol("MonomInPol",M,1);
  AP1:=Pol("*",c,P1);  AP2:=Pol("*",c,P2);
  R1:=Pol("/",AP1,M1,c1); R2:=Pol("/",AP2,M2,c2);
  R:=Pol("-",R1,R2);  Rez:=Pol("*",P,R);
  Return Rez;
End Function
```

Algorithm 6.3. – Gröbner basis

```
Function BazaGroebner(Pol,DCoef,DVect:Simbol;baza,M:List):List
//returns the Groebner basis of the polynomial set M (given as
//a list), within the polynomial domain Pol
Local variables: i,j,nrpol : Integer; B, G, GE, l: List;
  h,hn,hh,f1,f2 : Pol;
  Polinom(Pol,Dcoef,Dvect,baza);
    //creates the polynomial domain - see 5.2
  G:=M's internal form;  //see [And02]
  B={};  nrpol:=Length(M);
  For i:=1,nrpol-1 do
      For j:=i+1,nrpol do  B:=B ∪ {G[i],G[j]}
  End For; End For;
  While B ≠ {}
      l:=B[1]; f1:=l[1]; f2:=l[2]; B:=B \ {l};
      h=Spol(Pol,DCoef,DVect,f1,f2);
hn=FormaNormala[Pol,DCoef,DVect,G,h];
If not Pol("Nul",hn) then
  For i:=1,Length(G) do B:=B ∪ {G[i],hn}
  End For;
  G:= G ∪ {hn};
End If;
```

```
  End While;
  GE:=G's external form; //see [And02]
  Return GE;
End Function
```

Groebred.m package ([And00]) implements Buchberger's algorithm for computing the reduced Gröbner basis [Buc85]. Applied on a set of three polynomials with 6-7 terms, its run time varies between 40 and 50 seconds, on the same 16MB RAM, 100 MHz Pentium computer.

7. Conclusions and Future Work

The domain / category theory in symbolic computation combines algebraic and programming principles with the view to modeling symbolic computations within various algebraic structures. In this theoretical context, we propose a few definitions for some type theory concepts, by unifying the algebraic and OO points of view.

The categorical and parameterized approach reveals a general method for defining and easily extending new computational domains (in this case, not implemented in a classical SCS): the same categorical definition can be parameterized with any specific domain, once defined. In the mean time, this approach provides appropriate protection to inconsistent operations over the defined domains, since it simulates OO principles.

The extension of Mathematica, a widely used symbolic computation system, with a new type system, based on algebraic categories which can be used for generating various domains, enables the user to perform operations within new working contexts, such as polynomial domains over various coefficient fields.

Our Mathematica implementation of algebraic categories is suitable for efficiently deriving various categories and domains, on the same parameterized principles, and performing generic symbolic computations in these domains. This statement is proved by defining a polynomial category over several coefficient domains (integers, integers mod n, matrices) and using these polynomial domains for computing Gröbner bases and reduced Gröbner bases for polynomial domains over the previously defined coefficient fields, by using the same algorithms and parameterized type definitions.

We intend to improve the syntax of constructing algebraic categories in order to make it more object oriented, possibly, by using Roman Maeder's package for defining classes in Mathematica - classes.m.

8. References

[And97] A. Andreica - A Possibility to Describe an Algebraic Hierarchy, "Babeş-Bolyai" Univ., *Studia Informatica*, vol. II, No. 1, 1997, p. 78-84.

[And98] A. Andreica – Type Systems in Symbolic Computation, "Babeş-Bolyai" Univ., *Research Seminars in Computer Science*, Preprint No. 2, 1998, p. 153-174.

[And00] A. Andreica – *Symbolic Computation and Applications*, Ph. D. Thesis, "Babeş-Bolyai" Univ., Faculty of Mathematics and Computer Science, 2000.

[And02] A. Andreica – Parameterized Types for Categorical Definitions in Mathematica, *Proceedings of Symbolic and Numeric Algorithms for Scientific Computing - SYNASC02*, Timişoara, 9-12 October 2002, p. 8-25

[Buc84] B. Buchberger – A Critical-Pair Completion Algorithm for Finitely Generated Ideals in Rings, Symposium Rekursive Kombinatorik, Münster, May 1983, *Lecture Notes in Computer Science* 171, Springer, 1984, p. 137-161

[Buc85] B. Buchberger – Gröbner Bases: An Algorithmic Method in Polynomial Ideal Theory, in N. K. Bose (ed.) - *Mathematics and Its Applications, Multidimensional Systems Theory*, D. Reidel Publishing Co., 1985, chapter 6.

[Buc91] B. Buchberger – Gröbner Bases in Mathematica, Enthusiasm and Frustration, *Proceedings of IFIP Working Conference on Programming Environments for High-Level Scientific Problem Solving*, 23-27 September 1991, Karlsruhe, p.80-91.

[Buc96] B. Buchberger – Mathematica as a Rewrite Language, *Proceedings of the Fuji Conference on Functional Logic Programming*, Shonan Village, 1-4 November 1996, (T.Ida ed.), Telos Publishing, p.1-13.

[Dav90] J. H. Davenport, B. Trager – Scratchpad's View of Algebra I: Basic Commutative Algebra, *DISCO 1990*, Springer Verlag, 1990

[Dav91] J. H. Davenport, B. Trager, P. Gianni – Scratchpad's View of Algebra II: A Categorical View of Factorization, *Proc. of ISSAC 1991*, ACM Press, 1991

[FrePar94] Militon Frenţiu, Bazil Pârv – *Elaborarea programelor*, Ed. Promedia, 1994

[GruMon93] D. Gruntz, M. Monagan – *Introduction to Gauss*, MapleTech, Birkhäuser, Issue 9, 1993, p.23-35.

[Gru93] D. Gruntz – *Gröbner Bases in Gauss*, MapleTech, Birkhäuser, 9,1993, p.36-46.

[Pur82] I. Purdea – *Tratat de algebră modernă*, vol 2, Ed. Academiei, 1982

[San93] Ph. Santas – A Type System for Computer Algebra, in A. Miola (ed.) - *Design and Implementation of Symbolic Computation Systems (DISCO) 1993*, p.77-91

[San95] Ph. Santas – A Type System for Computer Algebra, in *Journal of Symbolic Computation*, 1995, p.79-109

[San96] Ph. Santas – Conditional Categories and Domains, *DISCO 1996*, p. 112-125

[Wol92] S. Wolfram – *Mathematica*, 1992.

In: New Developments in Computer Science Research
Editor: Susan Shannon, pp. 161-179
ISBN 1-59454-256-2

Chapter 4

Production Experiences and Persistent Leadership in R&D Competition

Shun-Chiao Chang
Department of Economics, Tun Ghai University, Taiwan
Sangin Park
Graduate School of Public Administration, Seoul National University, Korea

Abstract

This paper directs attentions to the effects of production experiences on the R&D competition and innovations for the next generation product when the R&D knowledge is accumulated by production experiences as well as by R&D expenditure. Based on the numerical analyses of unique Nash strategies in the R&D race, we find that the challenger invests more than the incumbent, and the difference between the challenger's and the incumbent's investment rates increases with the marginal production experience (a rate at which production experiences contribute to the R&D knowledge). However, an increase in this difference is dominated by the increase in the marginal production experience itself, and thus the incumbent has a higher probability to win the R&D race at any time point (conditioned on no occurrence of innovations up to that time point) if the marginal production experience is sufficiently large. Moreover, as the marginal production experience gets higher, the rate of the overall R&D knowledge accumulation increases. The rapid innovations and the persistent leadership in CPUs for personal computers and EPROM chips may be better explained by this effects of production experiences on the R&D competition.

For the last three decades, a great deal of attention has been paid to the effects of production experiences on *production costs*. In many important industries such as the semiconductor, the airframe, and the chemical processing industries, the marginal (or average variable) cost of production has been documented to decrease with production experiences (Benkard, 2000; Park, 2003). This phenomenon is, as well known, called learning by doing. Many theoretical studies have been dedicated to analyzing how learning by doing affects firms' optimal behavior such as pricing (Cabral & Riordan, 1994; Fudenburg & Tirole, 1983; Ghemawat & Spence, 1985; Spence, 1981) or collusion (Mookherjee & Ray, 1991) as well as the industry structure (Dasgupta & Stiglitz, 1988). Possible spillover effects of learning by doing have further caught attentions as a source of endogenous growth in the macroeconomic theory (Lucas, 1988; Stokey, 1986, 1988; Young, 1991, 1993).

In this paper, we direct attentions to the effects of production experiences on *the R&D competition and innovations* for the next generation product. In the cases of various semiconductors such as Central Processing Units (CPUs) for personal computers, Dynamic Random Access Memory (DRAM) chips, and Erasable Programmable Read-Only Memory (EPROM) chips, it has been widely recognized that the production experiences can significantly shorten the innovation time especially in the stage of prototype production (Dick, 1994). This paper highlights the R&D investment strategies of an incumbent firm and a challenger when the R&D knowledge, which the probability of succeeding in the innovation depends on, is accumulated by production experiences as well as by R&D expenditure.[1]

The R&D competition between an incumbent firm and challengers has been studied by Gilbert and Newbery (1982), and Reinganum (1983, 1985).[2] Gilbert and Newbery (1982) showed the persistence of monopoly in the R&D race for process innovations when innovations occur *deterministically*. Reinganum (1983), however, pointed out that the persistent leadership in the R&D race is not likely to occur when the process innovation is *uncertain* and sufficiently radical.[3] Furthermore, as shown in Reinganum (1985), the incumbent could soon be overthrown in a series of uncertain product innovations which introduce new-generation products replacing the previous-generation products. In uncertain drastic innovations, the incumbent always invests less than each challenger since the incumbent enjoys the monopoly profit flow from its post-innovation production and thus has less incentives for R&D investments which are likely to shorten the length of the current monopoly period.

Empirically, however, we can observe a persistent leadership in the R&D race for new-generation products in the case of CPUs for personal computers and EPROM chips.[4] Intel has maintained the leadership in the R&D competition since the innovation of the 386 CPU. Intel unveiled its 486 CPU in 1989 and announced the Pentium in 1991 when the Power Computer Assembly (PCA) of the three rival companies (IBM, Motorola and Apple), which matched the 486 CPU in terms of operational power, was introduced. In 1995, Intel introduced the Pentium II, one-and-a-half years ahead of its rivals' (AMD and Cyrix) K6 CPU. Intel's persistent leadership has continued, introducing the Pentium III in 1999. In the market for EPROM chips, Intel also has been the leader in the successive innovations of 8K, 16K, 32K, 64K, 128K, 256K, 512K, and 1M EPROMs (Gruber, 1994; Yu, 1995).

---

[1] Athey and Schmutzler (2001) discussed a general condition in which firms with higher state variables make higher investments in equilibrium if firms are symmetric in identities (or if firms' profit functions are exchangeable). However, the exchangeability assumption in Athey and Schmutzler (2001) cannot be applied to our case because of the asymmetry between the incumbent and the challenger due to the incumbent's current monopoly profits and production experiences.

[2] For the previous studies of the R&D competition, refer to the literature cited in Gilbert and Newbery (1982) and Reinganum (1982, 1983, 1985).

[3] The persistence of monopoly in the R&D race for uncertain process innovations is also possible when the monopolist incumbent has a first-mover advantage to commit himself/herself to an entry-deterring level of investment (Gilbert & Newbery, 1984; Reinganum, 1984), or when the incumbent and the entrant bid to a R&D technology (developed by an independent research lab) in an auction framework (Yi, 1995).

[4] On the other hand, we do not observe persistent leadership in the DRAM case. As discussed in section 2, the persistent leadership is not likely to occur if production experiences do not significantly affect the probability of its success in innovation for the next generation.

In this paper, we will show that *the persistent leadership is likely to occur* even in a series of uncertain drastic product innovations[5] if the incumbent's production experiences from current-generation products (significantly) affect the probability of its success in innovation for the next generation. We will say, "the persistent leadership is likely to occur" if the probability that the incumbent wins the patent race at any time point (conditioned on no occurrence of innovations up to that time point) is greater than that of the challenger.[6] The model of the paper posits the same situation as in Reinganum (1985) except that the R&D knowledge is accumulated by production experiences as well as by R&D expenditure. Hence, in our model, the incumbent firm enjoys production experiences as well as a monopoly profit flow from the post-innovation production, and both the incumbent's and the challenger's investment strategies are simultaneously affected by five factors: the rate at which production experiences contribute to the R&D knowledge (called the incumbent's *marginal production experience* in the paper), the flow of monopoly profits, the rate at which the R&D knowledge contributes to the hazard rate of the innovation process (called the *hazard rate coefficient* in the paper), the expected terminal value of being the incumbent next period, and the expected terminal value of being the challenger next period.

We will prove the existence of the unique Nash equilibrium of an incumbent's and a challenger's (closed-loop) investment strategies in our model but are not able to obtain closed-form solutions for these investment strategies. Hence, we conduct numerical analyses based on the nonlinear first-order differential equations of the dynamic first order conditions. For a given value of the marginal production experience, we can confirm that our numerical analyses reach the same conclusions in Reinganum (1985). Our numerical analyses of unique Nash strategies also indicate that the challenger invests more than the incumbent for any given value of the marginal production experience, and the difference between the challenger's and the incumbent's investment rates increases with the marginal production experience. However, an increase in this difference is dominated by the increase in the marginal production experience itself, and thus the persistent leadership is likely to occur if the marginal production experience is sufficiently large. Moreover, the likelihood of persistent leadership is increasing in the terminal value of being the incumbent next period and the hazard rate coefficient of the innovation process, but decreasing in the terminal value of being the challenger next period and the flow of monopoly profits.

The paper is organized as follows. Section 1 posits a dynamic patent race game and proves the existence of the unique Nash equilibrium strategies of an incumbent firm and a challenger. Section 2 discusses comparative dynamics based on the numerical analyses of these Nash equilibrium strategies. Section 3 concludes the paper.

---

[5] Instead of 'the persistent leadership is likely to occur', we may use the terminology of 'weak increasing dominance' as in Cabral and Riordan (1994) and Athey and Schmutzler (2001).

[6] Sometimes 'persistent leadership' refers to the ex ante (unconditional) probability that the incumbent wins the race. Hence, our term of 'the persistent leadership is likely to occur' is a stronger concept.

1. The Model

1.1. Notations and the Framework

The multistage model developed in the paper highlights the R&D investment strategies of an incumbent firm and a challenger in a series of uncertain innovations for new-generation products when the R&D knowledge is accumulated by production experiences as well as by R&D expenditure. Note that our model builds on Reinganum (1982) instead of Reinganum (1985) since an extension from either one does not lead to analytical proofs of our main results but the extension from Reinganum (1982) assures the existence of the unique equilibrium. We posit a continuous-time framework in which an incumbent (*I*) and a challenger (*C*) engage in R&D competition in each stage. For simplicity, we assume that the incumbent produces and sells one unit per time and only current production experiences are relevant knowledge for the next innovation.[7] We also assume that the incumbent's R&D knowledge accruing from production experiences at time τ is proportional to its cumulative output, say $\theta\tau$, where θ (> 0) is called the *marginal production experience* in the paper. Hence the marginal production experience indicates the rate at which production experiences contribute to the R&D knowledge. The R&D knowledge is also acquired by R&D investments. In each stage, these two firms compete to be the first to introduce the next innovation, investing $u_j(\tau)$, $j = I$ and C, at time τ. Let $X_j(\tau)$ denote firm *j*'s R&D knowledge accruing from R&D investments with $\dot{X}_j(\tau) = u_j(\tau)$, where the dot denotes the time derivative. Hence at time τ, the R&D knowledge of the incumbent and the challenger is $Z_I(\tau) = X_I(\tau) + \theta\tau$ and $Z_C(\tau) = X_C(\tau)$, respectively. We assume that the state of R&D knowledge is common knowledge.

Let τ_j denote the time at which firm *j* succeeds in innovation. We assume that the probability that firm *j* succeeds in innovation at or by time τ is distributed by an exponential distribution such that $\Pr\{\tau_j \le \tau\} = 1 - \exp\{-\lambda Z_j(\tau)\}$ where $\lambda > 0$ and is called the hazard rate coefficient.[8] Let $Z(\tau)$ denote the overall R&D knowledge at time τ, i.e., $Z(\tau) = Z_I(\tau) + Z_C(\tau)$. Then, the instantaneous probability that the incumbent succeeds at time τ but its challenger has not succeeded by time τ is: $\Pr\{\tau_C > \tau, \tau_I < \tau + d\tau\}$ = $\exp\{-\lambda Z(\tau)\}\lambda[u_I(\tau) + \theta]d\tau$. Similarly, the instantaneous probability that the challenger succeeds at time τ but the incumbent has not succeeded by time τ is: $\Pr\{\tau_I > \tau, \tau_C < \tau + d\tau\}$ = $\exp\{-\lambda Z(\tau)\}\lambda u_C(\tau)d\tau$.

---

[7] If all the previous generations' production experiences are the relevant R&D knowledge, the persistence of monopoly will be more likely to occur once a firm establishes itself as a leader in several successive innovations.

[8] The value of the hazard rate coefficient, λ, may depend on the accumulated investment expenditure. For example, as time passes without success, firms may become more pessimistic about the eventual innovation (Choi, 1991; Malueg & Tsutsui, 1997).

In our dynamic game of the patent race, we assume that at each time τ, an incumbent firm and a challenger choose their investment strategies simultaneously to maximize their own expected payoffs. Hence a firm's investment strategy is a closed-loop strategy. The incumbent receives a flow of monopoly profits at the constant rate of R, and each firm has to pay a lump sum fixed cost, say F, at the outset as well as the recurrent flow costs of R&D investments, say $u_j^2/2$. The firms' common discounted rate is γ. We consider a sequence of innovations as in Reinganum (1985). Each stage of the R&D race will end when the next innovation occurs, and the winner and the loser will receive the terminal values. We assume that the present values of these terminal values of being the incumbent and the challenger next period are v^W and v^L, respectively. As argued in Reinganum (1985), we reasonably assume that $v^W \geq v^L$. As discussed in Reinganum (1985), the (present values of these) terminal values represent the values of continuing optimally in the R&D race and may be treated as parameters in each stage when the sequence of innovations is finite due to technological reasons. We also assume that firms abandon their R&D projects if no innovation has occurred by time T. Therefore, at time s, the incumbent's expected payoff function for any strategy pair (u_I, u_C) can be written as follows:

$$V^I(s,u_I,u_C) =$$
$$\int_s^T e^{-\lambda Z(\tau)}\{v^W\lambda(u_I(\tau)+\theta)+v^L\lambda u_C(\tau)+e^{-\gamma\tau}(R-u_I(\tau)^2/2)\}d\tau - F. \quad (1)$$

Similarly, the challenger's expected payoff function is:

$$V^C(s,u_I,u_C) = \int_s^T e^{-\lambda Z(\tau)}\{v^W\lambda u_c(\tau)+v^L\lambda(u_I(\tau)+\theta)-e^{-\gamma\tau}u_C(\tau)^2/2\}d\tau - F. \quad (2)$$

1.2. Nash Equilibrium Strategies

We adopt a Nash equilibrium concept in the sense that each firm maximizes its own expected payoff, taking its rival's strategy as given. Following Reinganum (1982), we will consider only pure (closed-loop) strategies, assuming that each firm's instantaneous investment rate is bounded. For the existence of a unique Nash equilibrium in our differential game, we need the following assumptions on the strategy space. For notational simplicity, let $z = (Z_I, Z_C)$.

ASSUMPTION R: The strategy space for firm j is $\Omega_j = \{u_j(\tau, z) \in [0, K]$ with $K < \infty \mid$ for all $(\tau, z) \in [0, T] \times \Sigma$, $u_j(\tau, z)$ is continuous in (τ, z) and satisfies the Lipschitz condition: $|u_j(\tau,z)-u_j(\tau,\bar{z})| \leq k(\tau)|z-\bar{z}|$ where $k(\tau)$ is a Lipschitz constant such that $k(\tau) = \sup_{(\tau,Z_I,Z_C)}|\partial u_j/\partial Z_j|\}$.

Let $(u_I^*(\tau,z), u_C^*(\tau,z))$ be a Nash equilibrium of the two firms' strategies. Integrating the first term of the payoff functions in (1) and (2) by parts, we can define the value functions for any time $s \in [0, T]$ as follows:

$$\Phi^I(s,z) = V^I(s,u_I^*(\tau,z),u_C^*(\tau,z)) =$$
$$\int_s^T e^{-\lambda Z_C(\tau)}\{v^W(1-e^{-\lambda Z_I(\tau)})+v^L e^{-\lambda Z_I(\tau)}\}\lambda u_C^*(\tau,z)+e^{-\gamma\tau}e^{-\lambda Z(\tau)}(R-u_I^*(\tau,z)^2/2)\}d\tau$$
$$+ v^W(1-e^{-\lambda Z_I(T)})e^{-\lambda Z_C(T)} - F, \tag{3}$$

and

$$\Phi^C(s,z) = V^C(s,u_I^*(\tau,z),u_C^*(\tau,z)) =$$
$$\int_s^T e^{-\lambda Z_I(\tau)}\{v^W(1-e^{-\lambda Z_C(\tau)})+v^L e^{-\lambda Z_C(\tau)}\}\lambda(u_I(\tau,z)+\theta)-e^{-\gamma\tau}e^{-\lambda Z(\tau)}u_C(\tau,z)^2/2\}d\tau$$
$$+ v^W(1-e^{-\lambda Z_C(T)})e^{-\lambda Z_I(T)} - F. \tag{4}$$

As shown in Friedman (1971, Theorem 8.2.2), under Assumption R, both firms' optimal investment strategies satisfy a system of the Bellman equations as follows.

$$\Phi_\tau^I(\tau,z) + \max_{u_I(\tau,Z)\in[0,K]}[\Phi_{Z_I}^I(\tau,Z)u_I(\tau,Z)+\Phi_{Z_C}^I(\tau,Z)u_C^*(\tau,Z)+$$
$$e^{-\lambda Z_C(\tau)}\{v^W(1-e^{-\lambda Z_I(\tau)})+v^L e^{-\lambda Z_I(\tau)}\}\lambda u_C^*(\tau,z)+e^{-\gamma\tau}e^{-\lambda Z(\tau)}(R-u_I(\tau,z)^2/2)] = 0, \tag{5}$$

and

$$\Phi_\tau^C(\tau,z) + \max_{u_C(\tau,Z)\in[0,K]}[\Phi_{Z_C}^C(\tau,Z)u_C(\tau,Z)+\Phi_{Z_I}^C(\tau,Z)u_I^*(\tau,Z)+$$
$$e^{-\lambda Z_I(\tau)}\{v^W(1-e^{-\lambda Z_C(\tau)})+v^L e^{-\lambda Z_C(\tau)}\}\lambda(u_I^*(\tau,z)+\theta)-e^{-\gamma\tau}e^{-\lambda Z(\tau)}u_C(\tau,z)^2/2] = 0, \tag{6}$$

where $\Phi_\tau^j(\tau,z)$ and $\Phi_{Z_i}^j(\tau,z)$ denote the derivative of $\Phi^j(\tau,z)$ with respect to τ and Z_i, respectively. The terminal conditions from the definition of $\Phi^j(\tau,z)$ are given by:

$$\Phi^I(T,z) = v^W\exp\{-\lambda Z_C\} - v^W\exp\{-\lambda Z\} - F, \tag{7}$$

and

$$\Phi^C(T,z) = v^W\exp\{-\lambda Z_I\} - v^W\exp\{-\lambda Z\} - F. \tag{8}$$

Since the left-hand sides of the Bellman equations in (5) and (6) are strictly concave in u_I and u_C, respectively, the necessary condition is also sufficient for maximization. We will focus on the interior solutions of these Bellman equations,[9] which are given by:

---

[9] The boundary solutions include: $u_j^* = 0$ when $\Phi_{Z_j}^j(\tau,z) < 0$, and $u_j^* = K$ when $\Phi_{Z_j}^j(\tau,z) > 0$.

$$u_I^*(\tau, z) = e^{\gamma\tau} e^{\lambda Z} \Phi_{Z_I}^I(\tau, z), \tag{9}$$

and

$$u_C^*(\tau, z) = e^{\gamma\tau} e^{\lambda Z} \Phi_{Z_C}^C(\tau, z). \tag{10}$$

Substituting these solutions in (9) and (10) into the Bellman equations in (5) and (6), combined with the terminal conditions in (7) and (8), suggests a system of solutions in the form:

$$\Phi^I(\tau, z) = a_I(\tau)\exp\{-\lambda Z_C\} + b_I(\tau)\exp\{-\lambda Z\} - F, \tag{11}$$

and

$$\Phi^C(\tau, z) = a_C(\tau)\exp\{-\lambda Z_I\} + b_C(\tau)\exp\{-\lambda Z\} - F. \tag{12}$$

Note that since the two firms are not identical, $b_I(\tau)$ ($a_I(\tau)$) can be different from $b_C(\tau)$ ($a_C(\tau)$).

Using the suggested solutions in (11) and (12), the optimal investment rates in (9) and (10) can be rewritten as: $u_I^*(\tau, z) = -\lambda e^{\gamma\tau} b_I(\tau)$, and $u_C^*(\tau, z) = -\lambda e^{\gamma\tau} b_C(\tau)$. Substituting these results as well as the partial derivatives of the system of solutions in (11) and (12) with respect to Z_I and Z_C into the Bellman equations of (5) and (6) and the terminal conditions of (7) and (8), we obtain the nonlinear differential equations and the boundary conditions as follows:

$$\dot{b}_I(\tau) + \frac{3}{2}\lambda^2 e^{\gamma\tau} b_I(\tau)^2 - \lambda\theta b_I(\tau) + 2\lambda^2 e^{\gamma\tau} b_I(\tau) b_C(\tau) + \lambda^2 e^{\gamma\tau}(v^W - v^L) b_C(\tau) + \mathrm{Re}^{-\gamma\tau} = 0,$$
$$b_I(T) = -v^W, \tag{13}$$

$$\dot{a}_I(\tau) + \lambda^2 e^{\gamma\tau} a_I(\tau) b_C(\tau) - \lambda^2 e^{\gamma\tau} v^W b_C(\tau) = 0,$$
$$a_I(T) = v^W, \tag{14}$$

$$\dot{b}_C(\tau) + \frac{3}{2}\lambda^2 e^{\gamma\tau} b_C(\tau)^2 - \lambda\theta b_C(\tau) + 2\lambda^2 e^{\gamma\tau} b_I(\tau) b_C(\tau) + \lambda^2 e^{\gamma\tau}(v^W - v^L) b_I(\tau)$$
$$- \lambda\theta(v^W - v^L) = 0,$$
$$b_C(T) = -v^W, \tag{15}$$

$$\dot{a}_C(\tau) + \lambda^2 e^{\gamma\tau} a_C(\tau) b_I(\tau) - \lambda^2 e^{\gamma\tau} v^W b_I(\tau) + \lambda\theta v^W - \lambda\theta a_I(\tau) = 0,$$
$$a_C(T) = v^W. \tag{16}$$

As well known, the general solution to the nonhomogenous linear ordinary differential equation in (14) is $a_I(\tau) = v^W$. Consequently, we can obtain the solution to the differential equation in (16) as $a_C(\tau) = v^W$. However, due to the asymmetry between the incumbent and the challenger, we cannot obtain closed-form solutions of $b_I(\tau)$ and $b_C(\tau)$ from the set of first-order nonlinear differential equations in (13) and (15) (Hubbard and West, 1990). Although we cannot obtain analytical solutions of $b_I(\tau)$ and $b_C(\tau)$ and thus closed-form equilibrium investment strategies, we can still prove the existence of the unique Nash equilibrium of our patent race model.

THEOREM**:** The unique Nash equilibrium exits for our R&D competition model.

Proof: We have to prove the incumbent's and the challenger's value functions obtained in equations (11) and (12) with the terminal conditions of equations (7) and (8) are continuously differentiable in z. Once we prove this, then we can apply basically the same proof for the existence of the unique equilibrium in Reinganum (1982). Recall that $u_I^*(\tau,z) = -\lambda e^{\gamma\tau} b_I(\tau)$ and $u_C^*(\tau,z) = -\lambda e^{\gamma\tau} b_C(\tau)$. By definition, $b_I(\tau)$ and $b_C(\tau)$, the solutions to (13) and (15), depend only on time and exogenous variables (or parameters). In addition, as discussed above, $a_I(\tau) = a_C(\tau) = v^W$. Therefore, the incumbent's and the challenger's value functions in equations (11) and (12) with the terminal conditions of equations (7) and (8) are continuously differentiable in z. *Q.E.D.*

2. Comparative Dynamics

As discussed in section 1, we are unable to obtain closed-form solutions of the unique Nash equilibrium investment strategies. However, the first-order differential equations of (13) to (16) indicate that the Nash equilibrium investments of the incumbent and the challenger depend on the marginal production experience (θ), the terminal value of being the incumbent next period (v^W), the terminal value of being the challenger next period (v^L), the flow of monopoly profits (R) and the hazard rate coefficient (λ) as well as on the rival's investment intensities. To analyze how the two firms' optimal investment strategies are affected by these exogenous variables, it is necessary to numerically solve the nonlinear differential equations of (13) and (15). For these numerical analyses, we use the Runge-Kutta-Fehlberg method with the fourth-order and fifth-order Taylor series expansions, which is one of the most popular methods for solving the nonlinear differential equations. Refer to Gerald and Wheatley (1994) for the discussions on the algorithm of this numerical methodology. In the following numerical analyses, we will assume that firms are convinced that the innovation is infeasible if they fail to succeed by $T = 3$.[10] We will also set the producer's discount rate, γ, to be 0.1 and restrict v^W to be greater than v^L. As the baseline case, we will set: $\theta = 1$, $v^W = 250$, $v^L = 30$, $R = 150$, and $\lambda = 0.3$. Since we do not explicitly consider the entry of potential

[10] The variation in the value of T does not affect our numerical results.

challengers in this paper, without loss of generality, we set a lump sum fixed cost, F, equal to 0 in these numerical analyses. We have tried several different combinations of parameter values of (θ, v^W, v^L, R, λ) as alternatives to the baseline case in our numerical analyses and found no exception for any result that follows. In what follows, however, we will report only visually evident cases in each figure.

We begin by confirming that our numerical analyses reach the same conclusions in Reinganum (1985) on how the equilibrium investment strategies of the incumbent and the challenger respond to different values of the three factors: the terminal value of being the incumbent next period (v^W), the terminal value of being the challenger next period (v^L), and the flow of monopoly profits (R). We conduct three numerical experiments, in the absence of production experience ($\theta = 0$), by varying the values of v^W, v^L, and R, respectively (see figures 1 – 3).

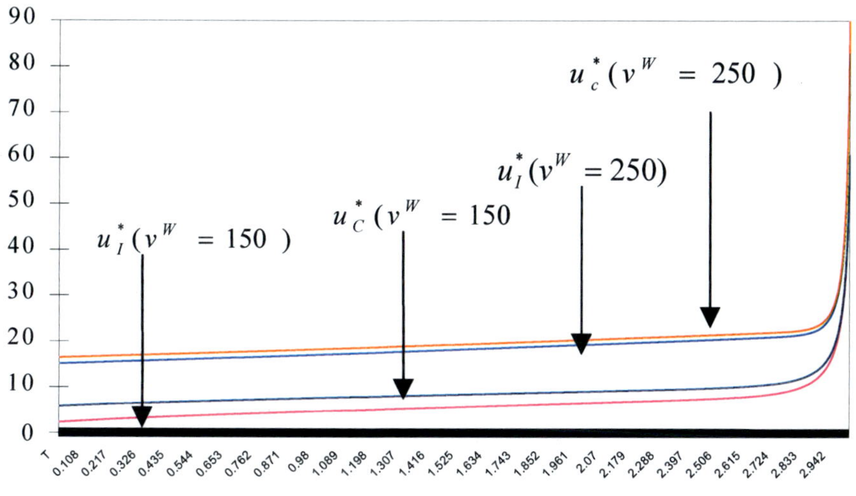

Figure 1. Parameter specifications: v^W = 150 or 250; v^L = 50; R = 150; θ = 0; λ = 0.3; γ = 0.1; T = 3.

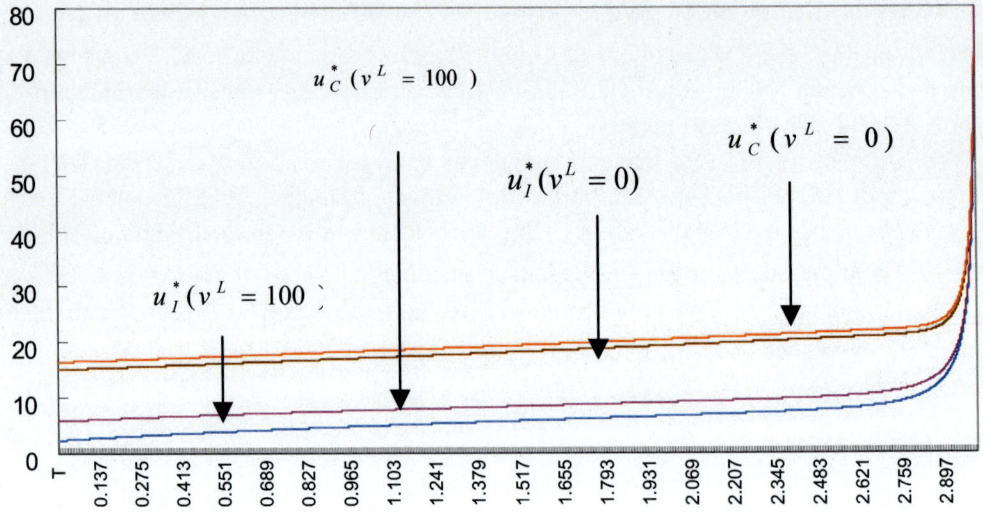

Figure 2. Parameter specifications: $v^W = 200$; $v^L = 0$ or 100; $R = 150$; $\theta = 0$; $\lambda = 0.3$; $\gamma = 0.1$; $T = 3$

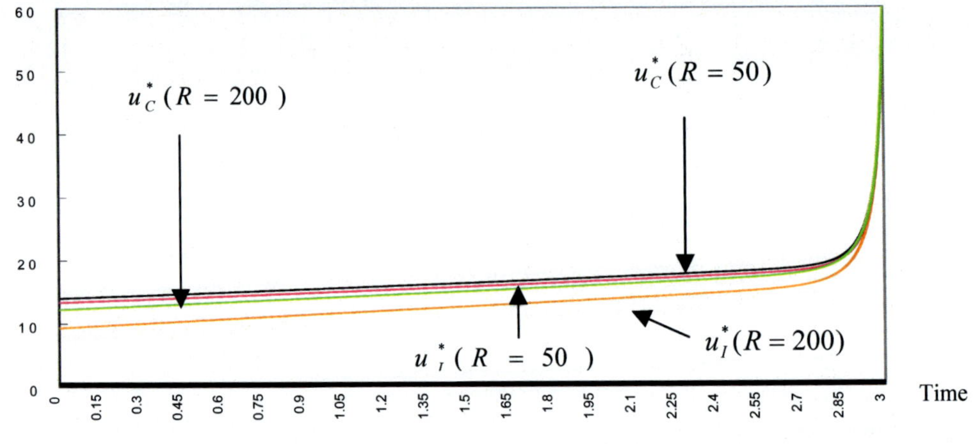

Figure 3. Parameter specifications: $v^W = 150$; $v^L = 30$; $R = 50$ or 200; $\theta = 0$; $\lambda = 0.3$; $\gamma = 0.1$; $T = 3$.

RESULT 1: (i) The challenger invests more than the incumbent. (ii) Both the incumbent's and the challenger's investment rates increase with the value of being the incumbent next period (v^W), but decrease with the value of being the challenger next period (v^L) and the flow of monopoly profits (R).

As discussed in Reinganum (1985), the conclusions in Result 1 are intuitive. Indeed, for any randomly chosen value of the marginal production experiences (θ), we can reach the same conclusions in Result 1.

Our numerical analyses also show that both the incumbent's and the challenger's investment rates increase with the hazard rate coefficient, λ (see figure 4). Since λ

represents the inverse of the expected waiting time of the occurrence of an innovation in our model, a higher value of λ would indicate that both firms are more optimistic about the R&D project and thus lead both firms to invest more in the R&D competition. Note that Reinganum (1982) reached the same conclusion when the identical firms compete in R&D race.[11]

RESULT 2: Both the incumbent's and the challenger's investment rates increase with the hazard rate coefficient (λ).

Furthermore, our numerical analyses enable us to exam how the difference between the challenger's and the incumbent's investment rates responds to the variations of these four factors: v^W , v^L , R, and λ. Figures 5- 8 illustrate our numerical analyses.

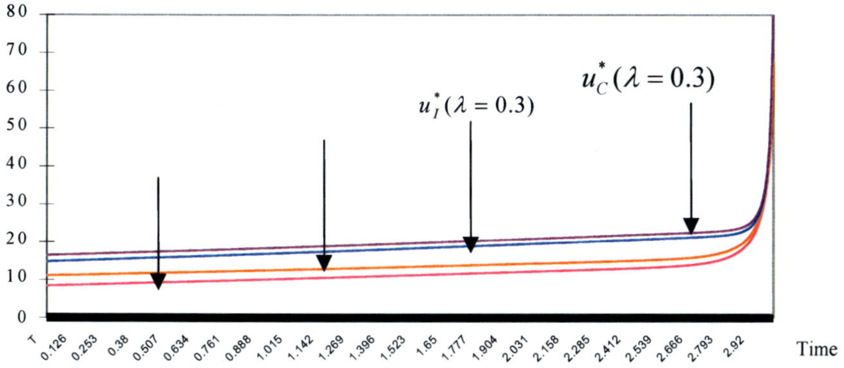

Figure 4. Parameter specifications: v^W = 150; v^L = 30; R = 50 or 200; θ = 0; λ = 0.3; γ = 0.1; T = 3.

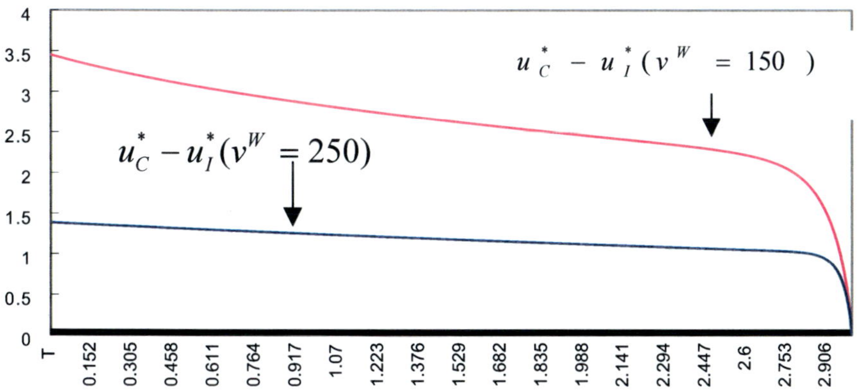

Figure 5. Parameter specifications: v^W = 150, 250; v^L = 50; R = 150; θ = 0; λ = 0.3; γ = 0.1; T = 3.

---

[11] In Reinganum (1982), when the number of firms in the patent race is equal to two and v^W has a positive value, both firms' investment rates always increase with λ.

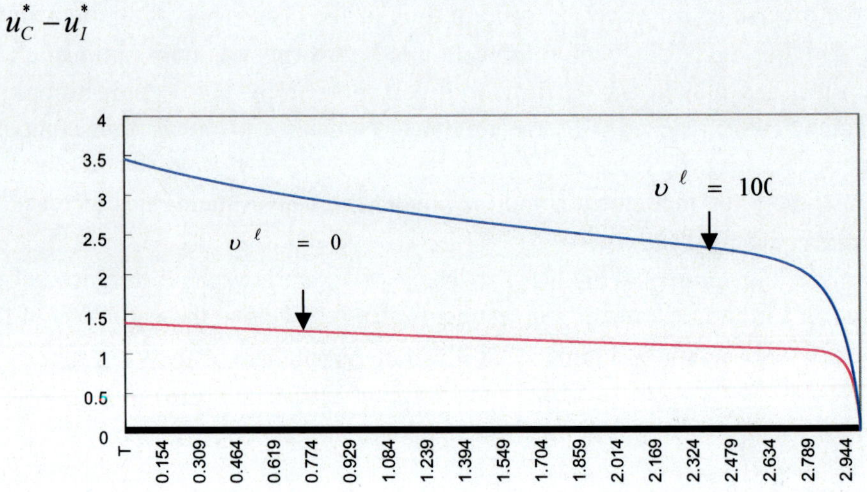

Figure 6. Parameter specifications: $v^W = 200$; $v^L = 0$ or 100; $R = 150$; $\theta = 0$; $\lambda = 0.3$; $\gamma = 0.1$; $T = 3$.

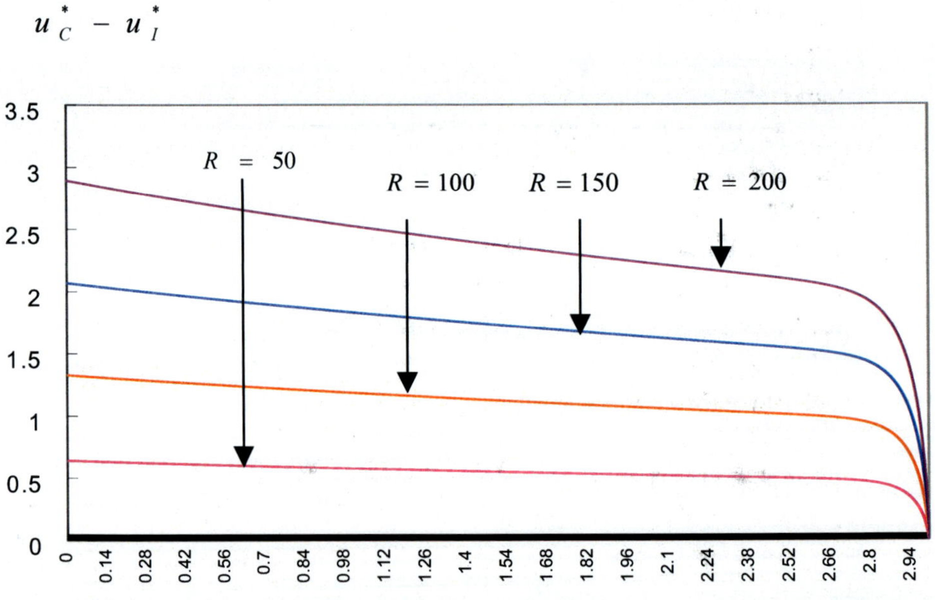

Figure 7. Parameter specifications: $v^W = 150$; $v^L = 30$; $R = 50$, 100, 150, or 200; $\theta = 0$; $\lambda = 0.3$; $\gamma = 0.1$; $T = 3$.

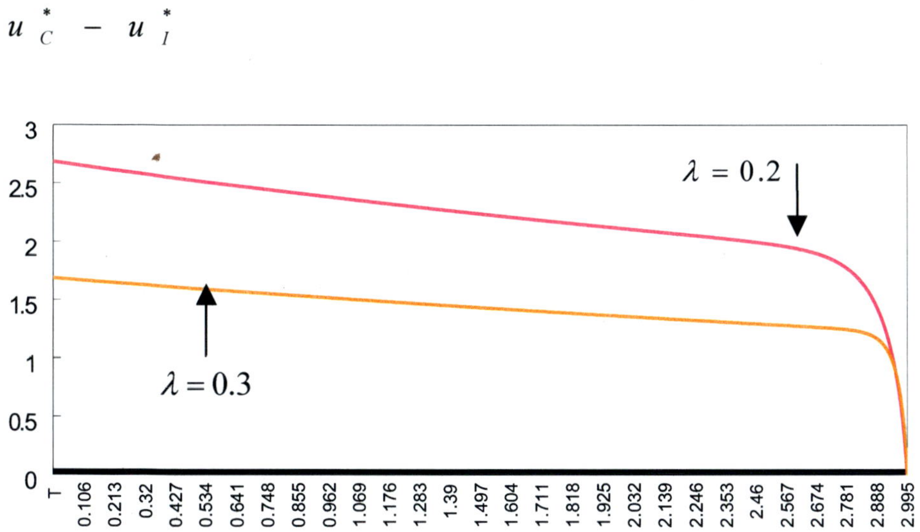

Figure 8. Parameter specifications: $v^W = 250$; $v^L = 100$; $R = 200$; $\theta = 0$; $\lambda = 0.2$ or 0.3; $\gamma = 0.1$; $T = 3$.

RESULT 3: The difference between the challenger's and the incumbent's investment rates decrease with the hazard rate coefficient (λ) and the value of being the incumbent next period (v^W), but increase with the value of being the challenger next period (v^L) and the flow of monopoly profits (R).

The intuition for Result 3 is as follows. As shown in Results 1 and 2, both the incumbent and the challenger will invest more if v^W (or λ) gets higher or v^L (or R) smaller. However, the incumbent has less incentives to enhance his/her R&D investment rate than the challenger since a higher investment rate is likely to shorten the length of the current monopoly period.

We now proceed to examine how the incumbent's marginal production experience affects both the incumbent's and the challenger's R&D investment rates. Figures 9 and 10 illustrate these numerical analyses. Recall that for a given value of the marginal production experience, the incumbent invests less than the challenger, i.e., $u_C^* - u_I^* > 0$.

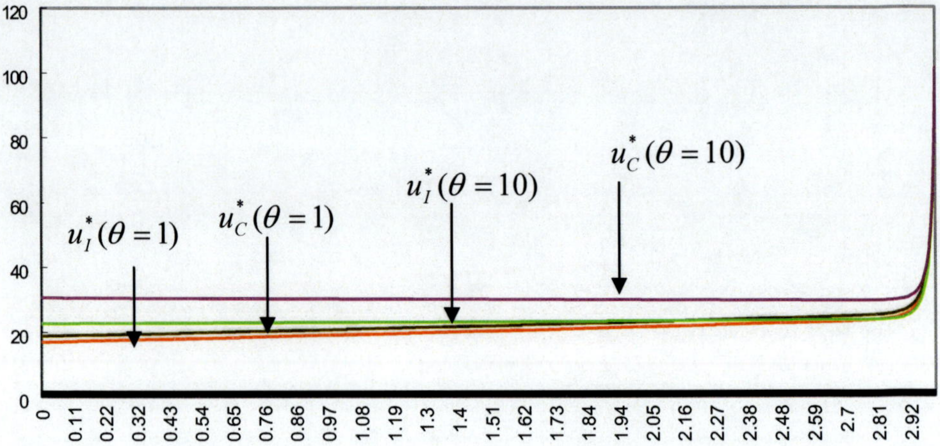

Figure 9. Parameter specifications: $v^W = 250$; $v^L = 30$; $R = 150$; $\theta = 1$ or 10; $\lambda = 0.3$; $\gamma = 0.1$; $T = 3$.

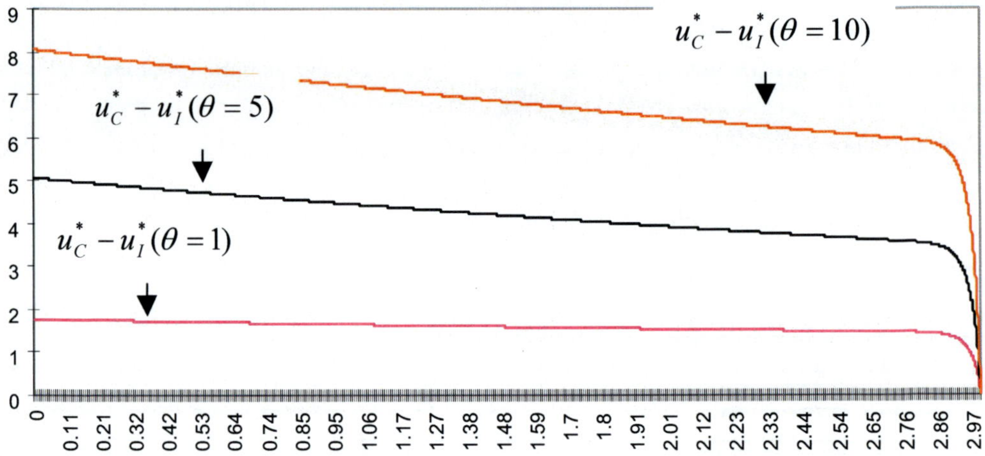

Figure 10. Parameter specifications: $v^W = 250$; $v^L = 30$; $R = 150$; $\theta = 1$, 5 or 10; $\lambda = 0.3$; $\gamma = 0.1$; $T = 3$.

RESULT 4: (i) Both the incumbent's and the challenger's investment rates decrease with the marginal production experience (θ). (ii) The difference between the challenger's and the incumbent's investments increases with the marginal production experience.

The intuition for Result 4 is as follows. If the marginal production experience (θ) gets higher, the incumbent will lower his/her investment rate since a higher θ is more likely to shorten the length of the current monopoly period. Since R&D investment rates are strategically complementary in our model (as well as in Reinganum (1985)), a decreased investment rate of the incumbent due to a higher θ will be met by a decreased investment rate of the challenger. However, this decrease of the challenger's investment rate will be smaller than that of the incumbent's investment rate since the incumbent always has greater incentives to reduce R&D investments which are likely to shorten the length of the current monopoly period.

However, our numerical analyses indicate that the increased difference between the challenger's and the incumbent's the investment rates caused by an increase of the marginal production experience is smaller than the increase of the marginal production experience itself. As shown in figure 10, when θ increases from 1 to 5, $u_C^* - u_I^*$ increases by less than 3.5. Therefore, for a sufficiently large value of θ, we have: $\theta > u_C^* - u_I^*$. For instance, in the example of figure 10, when θ is greater than 5, we have $\theta > u_C^* - u_I^*$. Recall that the instantaneous probability of the incumbent's winning (conditioned on no occurrence of innovations up to that time point) is $e^{-\lambda Z(\tau)}\lambda[u_I(\tau)+\theta]d\tau$ while this instantaneous probability of the challenger's winning is $e^{-\lambda Z(\tau)}\lambda u_C(\tau)d\tau$. Therefore, if the marginal production experience, θ, is sufficiently large, the probability that the incumbent wins over the challenger in the R&D race at any time point (conditioned on no occurrence of innovations up to that time point) will be greater than that of the challenger. In other words, the persistent leadership is likely to occur in the R&D race if $\theta > u_C^* - u_I^*$.

RESULT 5: The likelihood that the incumbent wins over the challenger in the R&D race at any time point (conditioned on no occurrence of innovations up to that time point) is increasing in the marginal production experience, θ. In this sense, the likelihood of the persistent leadership is increasing in the marginal production experience. Moreover, if the marginal production experience is sufficiently large, the persistent leadership is likely to occur in a sense that the (conditional) probability of the incumbent's winning the R&D race at any time point is greater than that of the challenger.

Although the equilibrium R&D investments of both the incumbent and the challenger decrease with the production experiences, the overall R&D knowledge increases with the marginal production experience in our model (see figure 11). In other words, the increase in θ dominates the sum of the decreases in both the challenger's and the incumbent's R&D investment rates.

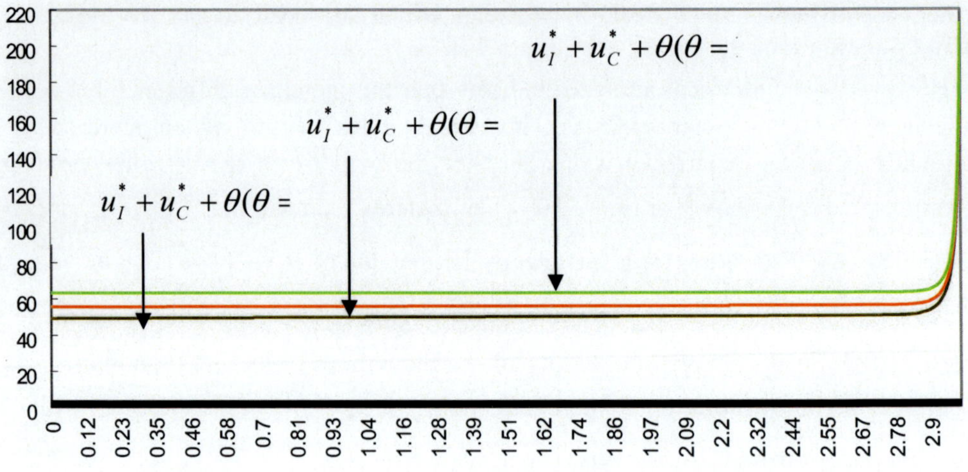

Figure 11. Parameter specifications: $v^W = 250$; $v^L = 30$; $R = 150$; $\theta = 1$, 5 or 10; $\lambda = 0.3$; $\gamma = 0.1$; $T = 3$.

RESULT 6: The rate of the overall R&D knowledge accumulation, $u_C^* + u_I^* + \theta$, increases with the marginal production experiences (θ).

Hence, a greater effect of production experience on the R&D knowledge reduces R&D investments but increases the likelihood of the occurrence of innovations at any time point.

As discussed above (see Result 3), for a given value of the marginal production experience, the difference between the challenger's and the incumbent's investment rates decrease with the hazard rate coefficient (λ) and the value of being the incumbent next period (v^W), but increase with the value of being the challenger next period (v^L) and the flow of monopoly profits (R). Hence, we can infer as follows.

RESULT 7: For a given value of the marginal production experience (θ), the likelihood of persistent leadership is increasing in the hazard rate coefficient (λ) and the value of being the incumbent next period (v^W) but decreasing in the value of being the challenger next period (v^L) and the flow of monopoly profit (R).

3. Conclusion

In this paper, we have analyzed a patent race for new generation products when the R&D knowledge is accumulated by current production experiences as well as by the R&D expenditure. Based on the numerical analyses of unique (closed-loop) Nash strategies of the R&D investments for uncertain product innovations, we have found that the result in Reinganum (1985) can be reversed: the persistent leadership in the R&D race is likely to occur if the marginal production experience (the rate at which production experiences contribute to the R&D knowledge) is sufficiently large. Moreover, the likelihood of persistent leadership is increasing in the hazard rate coefficient of the R&D success and the value of being the incumbent next period, but decreasing in the value of being the challenger next period and the flow of monopoly profits. Although our conclusions are based on numerical analyses, these numerical results are very robust. In various numerical analyses with several different combinations of parameter values of the model, we found no exception for any of our numerical results.

In our model, production experiences are modeled to be a substitute for the R&D expenditures in the R&D knowledge accumulation. If production experiences are considered an example of the incumbent's advantage in Rogerson (1982) and modeled to be a complement for the R&D investments in the R&D knowledge accumulation, the incumbent may have a greater incentive for the R&D investments than the challenger. However, even in the case that production experiences are a substitute for the R&D investments, this paper shows that the persistent leadership is likely to occur if the incumbent's marginal production experience is sufficiently large. When production experiences are a substitute for the R&D investments, an increase of the marginal production experience will reduce the incumbent's investment rate which will be met by a decrease in the challenger's investment rate. This increase of the marginal production experience raises the difference between the challenger's and the incumbent's investment rates since the incumbent always has greater incentives to reduce R&D investments which are likely to shorten the length of the current monopoly period. However, an increase in this difference is dominated by the increase in the marginal production experience itself, and thus the incumbent has a higher probability to win the R&D race at any time point (conditioned on no occurrence of innovations up to that time point) if the marginal production experience is sufficiently large. Moreover, an increase in the marginal production experience dominates the sum of the decreases in both the challenger's and the incumbent's R&D investment rates. Therefore, the rate of the overall R&D knowledge accumulation increases with the marginal production experiences.

The model of this paper can be extended to the case in which there exist one incumbent and n identical challengers in the R&D competition. As proved in Reinganum (1985), the increased number of challengers lead to a larger difference between the challengers' and the incumbent's investment rates. Hence the likelihood of the persistence of monopoly will decrease with more challengers. Other possible extensions of our model may include the consideration of all the previous generations' production experiences as the relevant R&D knowledge. Our model of the representative stage developed in section 1, however, will not be applicable in this extension since all the paths of the two firms' histories will be relevant state variables. Hence, it is not clear whether this extension may lead to a tractable model. Yet, our intuition is that the likelihood of the persistent leadership of the R&D competition may increase in this extension once a firm establishes itself as a leader in successive innovations.

References

Athey, S., & Schmutzler, A. (2001). Investment and market dominance. *RAND Journal of Economics*, 32, 1-26.

Benkard, C. L. (2000). Learning and forgetting: The dynamics of commercial aircraft production. *American Economic Review*, 90, 1134-1154.

Cabral M. B., & Riordan, M. H. (1994). The learning curve, market dominance, and predatory pricing. *Econometrica*, 62, 1115-1140.

Choi, J. P. (1991). Dynamic R&D competition under hazard rate uncertainty. *RADN Journal of Economics*, 22, 596-610.

Dasgupta, P., & Stiglitz, J. (1988). Learning-by-Doing, market structure and trade policies. *Oxford Economic Papers*, 40, 246-226.

Freidman, A. (1971). *Differential game*. New York: John Wiley.

Fudenburg, D., & Tirole, J. (1983). Learning-by-doing and market performance. *Journal of Economics*, 14, 522-530.

Gerald, C.F., & Wheatley, P. O. (1994). *Applied Numerical Analysis*. Addison-Wesley.

Ghemawat, P., & Spence, M. (1985). Learning curve spillovers and market performance. *Quarterly Journal of Economics*, 100, 839-852.

Gilbert, R. J., & Newbery, D. M. G. (1982). Preemptive patenting and the persistence of monopoly. *American Economic Review*, 72, 514-526.

________ (1984). Uncertain innovation and the persistence of monopoly: Comment. *American Economic Review*, 74, 238-242.

Gruber, H. (1994). *Learning and strategic production innovation*. Amsterdam: North-Holland.

Hubbard, J.H., & West, B.H. (1990). *Differential equations: A dynamic system approach*. Springer.

Lucas, R. E., Jr. (1988). On the mechanism of economic development. *Journal of Monetary Economy*, 22, 3-42.

Malueg, D.A., & Tsutsui, S.O. (1997). Dynamic R&D competition with learning. *RAND Journal of Economics*, 28, 751-772.

Mookherjee, D., & Ray, D. (1991). Collusive market structure under learning-by-doing and increasing returns. *Review of Economic Studies*, 58, 993-1009.

Park, S. (2003). An empirical evaluation of the 1986 semiconductor trade arrangement. Retrieved June 30, 2003 from http://ms.cc.sunysb.edu/~sanpark.

Reinganum, J. F. (1982). A dynamic game of R&D: Patent protection and competitive behavior. *Econometrica*, 50, 671-688.

________ (1983). Uncertain innovation and the persistence of monopoly. *American Economic Review*, 73, 741-748.

________ (1984). Uncertain innovation and the persistence of monopoly: Reply. *American Economic Review*, 74, 243-246.

________ (1985). Innovation and industry evolution. *Quarterly Journal of Economics*, 100, 81-99.

Rogerson, W. P. (1982). The social costs of monopoly and regulation: A game theoretic analysis. *Bell Journal of Economics*, 13, 391-401.

Spence, A. (1981). The learning curve and competition. *Bell Journal of Economics*, 12, 49-70.

Stokey, N. L. (1986). The dynamics of industrywide learning. In W. P. Heller, R. M. Starr, & D. A. Starrett (Eds.), *Essays in Honor of Kenneth J. Arrow, Vol. 2, Equilibrium Analysis*. New York: Cambridge University Press.

________ (1988). Learning by doing and the introduction of new goods. *Journal of Political Economy*, 96, 701-717.

Young, A. (1991). Learning by doing and the dynamic effects of international trade. *Quarterly Journal of Economics*, 106, 369-405.

________ (1993). Invention and bounded learning by doing. *Journal of Political Economy*, 101, 443-472.

Yi, S. S. (1995). Uncertain innovation and persistence of monopoly revisited. *Economics Letters*, 49, 319-322.

Yu, A. (1995). *Inside Intel*. Taiwan: Commonwealth.

INDEX

A

B

C

D

E

F

G

H

I

J

L

M

N

P

Q

R

S

T

W